PENGUIN BOOKS

Landlines

Raynor Winn is the bestselling author of *The Salt Path* and *The Wild Silence*. *The Salt Path* won the inaugural RSL Christopher Bland Prize and was shortlisted for the 2018 Costa Biography Award and the Wainwright Golden Beer Book Prize. *The Wild Silence* was shortlisted for the 2021 Wainwright Prize for Nature Writing. She is a regular long-distance walker and writes about nature, homelessness and our relationship to the land. She lives in Cornwall with her husband Moth.

Landlines

RAYNOR WINN

PENGUIN BOOKS

PENGUIN BOOKS

UK | USA | Canada | Ireland | Australia
India | New Zealand | South Africa

Penguin Books is part of the Penguin Random House group of companies
whose addresses can be found at global.penguinrandomhouse.com

First published by Penguin Michael Joseph 2022
Published in Penguin Books 2023

001

Copyright © Raynor Winn, 2022

The moral right of the author has been asserted

Text permissions: p.vii, *A Room with a View*, E. M. Forster, Hodder and Stoughton Limited, 1992; p.5,
'This is the Time to Be Slow' from *Benedictus: A Book of Blessings* by John O'Donohue, published by
Bantam Press, copyright © John O'Donohue 2007. Reprinted by permission of The Random House
Group Limited; p.43, *The Living Mountain*, published as part of *The Grampian Quartet* in 1996 by
Canongate Books Ltd, copyright © Nan Shepherd, 2008; p.171, 'Bogland', *Door into the Dark* by
Seamus Heaney, Faber and Faber, 1969; p.233, 'The Whitsun Weddings' by Philip Larkin, Faber and
Faber, first published in the United Kingdom in 1964; p.263, 'The Lycian Shore' by Freya Stark © Tauris
Parke Paperbacks, Bloomsbury Publishing, 2011; p.291, *A Testament of Hope: The Essential Writings and
Speeches* by Martin Luther King Jr., HarperCollins; New Ed edition, 1991

Every effort has been made to contact copyright holders.
The publishers will be glad to correct any errors or omissions in future editions.

Typeset by Jouve (UK), Milton Keynes
Printed and bound in Great Britain by Clays Ltd, Elcograf S.p.A.

The authorized representative in the EEA is Penguin Random House Ireland,
Morrison Chambers, 32 Nassau Street, Dublin D02 YH68

A CIP catalogue record for this book is available from the British Library

ISBN: 978–1–405–94778–7

www.greenpenguin.co.uk

MIX
Paper from
responsible sources
FSC® C018179

Penguin Random House is committed to a
sustainable future for our business, our readers
and our planet. This book is made from Forest
Stewardship Council® certified paper.

For the Team

The world reveals itself to those who travel on foot.

Werner Herzog

Contents

Prologue

Water falls from the mountain with such force that it creates its own wind, driving noise and vapour upwards, until my clothes hang wet from the spray and I'm deafened by the cascading roar echoing back from the hillside. My boot slips on the damp rock, shifting the weight of the rucksack on my back and I skid towards the chasm below. Grasping a boulder ahead of me I stop my fall, but a landslide of stone hurtles down the near vertical wall of dripping vegetation, disappearing into the depths of the gorge. I cling to the rock and shiver, gripped by electric shocks of fear running through my body. Yet, just for a moment, as I look up, I can see another world: a world of blue sky, where a hooded crow glides silently beneath slow-moving clouds.

I breathe, inhaling the green dampness, and wish for wings. Wings, ropes, anything to give us safe passage out of the Falls of Glomach. It takes an almost physical effort to turn my thoughts away from one of the highest waterfalls in Britain and the depth of the gully it carves through the earth, but as my view follows the narrow path upwards among the boulders, fear for myself is replaced by fear for Moth.

'All right up there?' I call up to him, hoping he can hear me above the roar of the water.

'No. No, I can't do this, I need to go down. You? Are you okay?'

I glance back down towards the water and disaster waiting for the slip of a foot. 'Yeah, I'm fine, coming up to you now.'

I scramble up the rough broken rock, over steps that are so high I'm on my hands and knees by the time I reach Moth. He's pressed sideways against the wall of the gully that rises away from us at an eighty-degree angle, as close as he can get with the rucksack on his back, his feet filling the width of the path that cuts into the fall of the hillside.

'I can't go on.'

I stand up close behind him, nowhere else to go. 'We can't go back.'

Walking the Cape Wrath Trail through the north of Scotland had seemed achievable as we planned the trip in the warmth of a Cornish spring, when the sun was shining and the apple blossom about to break. We'd been almost magnetically drawn to this rare place; a land of remote mountains rich with wildlife, a place of beauty and solitude. We knew it wouldn't be an easy trail to navigate, with no signposts or quick ways out, but that was part of the challenge. The moments of awe and wild drama we'd already witnessed had made every long day and hard-to-find path worthwhile. But now, clinging to the side of this ravine, so immersed in nature that the smell of brackish water lingers on my skin and in my breath, those days of planning in Cornwall feel as though they happened in another life. All I can focus on now is the way out. And Moth, whose life-threatening illness hasn't abated. Despite all my hopes and the miles we've already walked, he's still finding it hard to put his rucksack on, says he's forgotten how to read a map and now has developed a seemingly paralysing sense of vertigo.

'I think I'm going to be sick.' Moth's face is grey as he looks back to me, while still clinging to an outcrop of bilberry.

'No you're not. Don't think about it, just keep your eyes fixed on the path and keep going. You have to keep going.'

I'm weak with relief as the path levels to a rocky plateau and a plunge pool of calm water. Moth drops his rucksack and fear-soaked clothes and jumps in.

'Come in, it's okay now, we're nearly there.'

We're a long way from 'nearly there'; the path winds higher and higher, until it almost disappears into a crevice of rock. I can't see any way out of this. I watch him swimming, his thin white body naked in the dark water, his vertigo soothed by the coolness, and I relax for a moment too, feeling the adrenaline fading away but being replaced by exhaustion. What if we never get out of this? My thoughts wander to visions of us camped by the plunge pool indefinitely, surviving on food parcels left by passing hikers. But as I turn to share the prospect with Moth he's already dressed and lifting his rucksack. We climb away from the pool on a slope of wet slippery grass, so steep that when I reach out my hands they're almost on the earth in front of me. Dragging my post-adrenaline legs upwards, I'm beginning to despair; I've barely enough strength left to get out of this terrifying place. So focused on each step I don't see him pass me, don't see him step up the boulder that's too high for me and I can't climb. I just see his hand reaching down and pulling me up.

The path widens, but only for a moment. From here I can see it becomes steeper, narrower and more exposed, as it winds up to the head of the waterfall and the way out.

'Just don't look down. If we spot a way out of this before the waterfall we'll take it.'

I let go of his hand and follow, my eyes on his feet. In the crevice, water runs down through gentler sloping grass before falling over stones to the base of the waterfall, nearly a hundred metres below. My legs have almost stopped responding and all I want is to sleep, but I follow him through water running over slippery grass. Each step up he takes I follow, his hand always there on the hardest parts. And then, finally, the fading blue sky of a Highland evening. I lie on a boulder warmed by the sun with no roar of water, no falling stones, just the hooded crow circling overhead.

We pitch the tent on flat ground among heather and bog-grass, high on a Scottish hillside, and I collapse inside. The mountains of the remote Highlands stretch out in shades of blue on every side, tall rock crags still picking up the pink and peach of twilight, framing Moth in the glow as he makes tea on the small gas stove, reading the map by its flickering light.

'It's downhill all the way tomorrow, I think it could be an easier day.'

Hope rises in the evening dew and takes flight with a thousand crane flies into the soft air.

PART ONE

Lying Low

This is the time to be slow,
Lie low to the wall,
Until the bitter weather passes.

'This is the Time to Be Slow', John O'Donohue

I

Softly rising in an ebb of grey, the tones of colourless half-light track across the room, from its near-white source to the darkest corners. A mist of light creeping into the morning. I know the colours of the room are there, but they're masked, washed into monochrome. A densely woven blanket of stillness lies heavy and I'm afraid to disturb it. I close my eyes and sink into the silence, blocking the light and the new day.

But there's no sanctuary in the darkness; it still holds the stark, raw realities of the night before and I'm caught in the dawn light, too sad to go back, too afraid to go forward. The light grows, separating the greyness, picking out shapes of muted colour, drawing me into the inevitability of the day. I move slowly through the gathering light, a grey wool jumper scratching my cold skin, but as I silently pull the door further ajar his breathing changes. I stop, motionless, waiting for the horrors of the night to return, but a quiet rhythm of breath resumes and I slip through the door into the morning.

Outside, fog hangs white and wet. I walk away from the house into the trees of the old orchard, which stand in twisted dark relief, their lichen-covered branches dripping with vapour, their shapes fading into whiteness down the hillside until they disappear and become part of the water and air. The stream is running fast through the tall oak and ash at the bottom of the slope, invisible in the thick mist that hugs the valley down to the creek; only the sound of falling water suggests how hard the rain fell in the overnight storm. Our small white dog is somewhere down there too, chasing pheasants that rise out of the undergrowth with a commotion of flapping wings and calls of alarm. He appears from the long grass in the wild corner; his posture says he's happy, his morning a success already. The roe deer must be grazing elsewhere, perhaps in the woods down by the creek, or they would have come crashing out of the trees too. The moment of noise is over. As I walk away from the orchard even the sound of the stream disappears, silence returning to the dense air.

Back in the house Monty crawls on to his dog bed under the table, his long hair matted with fog and twigs. He drifts into an untroubled sleep as the kettle boils and I make tea. The silence in the house is even more impenetrable than in the orchard, but the absolute quietness is calming and I draw it around me as I curl into a chair, the mug of tea warming my hands. Wet January coldness pervades the house. I could light the wood burner but the noise would wake Moth, still sleeping in bed, so instead I turn on a small electric heater and wrap myself in a coat. Maybe it's the warmth beginning to fill the corner of the room, or the soothing effect of hot tea, but as memories of the night before begin to return, I don't fight them away, but let them rise and view them from the distance of morning.

I'd woken from a deep sleep to a sudden sense of disorientation and confusion, in a room in complete darkness. No moon shining through the thin muslin curtains, just the total darkness of deep countryside, where no street lights break the night and only the sound of rain against the window gives a suggestion of what might be happening outside. But the noise that had woken me wasn't coming from outside: it was in the bed next to me. A rasping, hoarse intake of breath, the grasping sound of air fighting to pass through closed airways, the bed shaking with Moth's desperate attempts to breathe. Putting the lights on, I sat him up; his face was a portrait of fear, unable to speak, no words escaping from his closed throat.

'Relax, don't fight, just try to relax.'

Slowly, slowly, the spasm relaxed and his breathing settled.

'Were you drinking, did you choke on the water?'

'No, I just woke up and couldn't breathe . . . I have to get to the bathroom.' He leant on me on the way to the toilet, his left side refusing to take his weight, but as we crossed the narrow landing his legs folded beneath him and he crashed down on to the floorboards, pulling me with him. There was a long pause, neither of us able to speak, too shocked by what was happening.

'This is it, it's here.'

'No, no, it won't happen to you, it's just a night moment, it'll pass.'

'For fuck's sake, Ray, listen to me! I can't keep fighting – won't you just listen to me?'

We both lay in a heap of rug and pee, silently crying with the overwhelming sadness of what was happening. It seemed the illness he had fought for so long was wrapping its powerful arms around him, no longer just hugging him but tightening its grip and beginning to squeeze. How long now until it squeezes so tightly that the Moth I know disappears and the end stages of this horrendous illness leave him lost in the shell of a body that can no longer function?

'Well, at least I don't need to get as far as the bathroom now.' How does he always manage to laugh in the worst of moments?

'Let's not try to stand up. Shall we crawl back to the bedroom?'

Crawling along the landing on all fours and then dragging his six-foot-two frame on to the bed, it was obvious, even in the darkness, that we were in danger of losing our balance on the narrow fence that stands between comedy and tragedy; at any moment we could fall off and slip down the side that holds only despair.

I watched him slowly fall back into a deep sleep; then I switched the lights off and listened to his steady breathing in the darkness. It was real now. The illness that we'd hoped would always be on the doorstep but never come through the door was here: malevolent, dark and very much in the room. It had moved in and taken over, throwing all other life out of the house to make way for itself. A cuckoo in the nest, destroying everything that came before.

The greyness of the early-morning fog lifts into a low sky of dense cloud. Not threatening rain, but leaving no possibility of sun either, just a cold day of January dullness. I potter silently around the house, constantly listening for movement from upstairs, but it doesn't come. Finally, as the morning tips into afternoon, he wakes.

'I'm dizzy and this pain deep in my head . . .' The words are slow, not falling from his mouth in the torrent of rapidly skipping thoughts as they have for most of his sixty years, but being carefully formed and tentatively offered out. Since the days became shorter these long, protracted moments of speech formation have hung between us, undiscussed, unexamined, just silent moments of waiting, of knowing that hanging there in the unformed words and unspoken thoughts lies a world of sadness, suffering and loss that has yet to be discovered.

'I've brought you tea. Do you want to drink it and try to get up? I'm sure you'd feel better if we . . .'

'No. I can't. I can't keep forcing myself.' The grey light of the afternoon slowly recedes back towards the source, shadows forming in its wake, as the steam stops rising and the room echoes with silence.

'I'm going through the motions of living when – we both know it now – what I'm really doing is learning how to die.'

The shadows darken as late-afternoon rain falls down the window. Given enough time you can train your face to hold its shape rather than contort with the emotions that lie behind the façade. Smooth, untroubled muscle and skin that mask a twisted cry of sadness, and self-pity, and fear.

'I'll get some more tea then. This one's gone cold.'

★

Daylight comes again, persistent, inevitable; the morning tracks into another day to be faced. I don't hear him get up and dressed, just see him walking downstairs, unaided.

'I didn't hear you get up – you should have shouted.' Most mornings start with me taking tea upstairs and helping him sit up. A depressing moment that usually takes a second cup of tea to put out of our thoughts.

'I managed; there were so many pillows on the bed I was almost sitting up anyway. I'm going down into the old orchard to carry on pruning.'

'What, after that night and yesterday, why? Well, at least eat something first.'

'I'm not hungry.'

I watch him walk into the trees with a slow uneven gait, the pruning saw in his hand and Monty close on his heels, a tennis ball clamped in his mouth: how most January days have started since we moved to this ancient orchard, where Moth spends so much time during the winter, removing dead, broken and cankered wood from the old gnarled trees, that an almost symbiotic relationship has evolved – the trees needing as much care to stay upright and alive as their carer does. Yet the physical effort required to tend them seems to keep him moving when all expectation has been that he would stop, and keep the trees producing fruit when their productive days appeared to be over. Until now. Now the balance seems to be tipping in favour of the trees.

I make food and a flask of tea and follow the dark trail of his feet through the wet grass to a pile of pruned timber beneath the trees. The sound of the handsaw passing through wood stops as I approach and he painstakingly moves his lean frame out on to the open ground. His appetite for food disappeared months ago, and with it all thoughts of eating. Inevitably muscle loss and weakness quickly followed. I open the sandwich box with the efficiency of a school dinner lady, intolerant of food choices or pickiness. I simply present food to be consumed; all that's missing is the blue cap and apron.

'Cheese and pickle.'

'I'm not really hungry.'

'I know but you need to eat it anyway.'

I hold the plastic box towards him as he removes his gloves. The hand reaching out to take a sandwich shakes with a tremor that's more obvious every time I allow myself to notice. He begins to eat and I throw the ball for Monty.

It shouldn't be this way. This man who has run marathons, climbed mountains, reached for the sun throughout his life shouldn't be taking a sandwich from a box with a hand that shakes the pickle from the cheese. Not the hand that has held mine for forty years of wild entangled life, steady, sure and so entwined that I can no longer tell where my hand ends and his begins. He puts his gloves back on, rises unsteadily to his feet, picks up the saw and the trees envelop him again. But even that shouldn't be happening.

I stay in the orchard, sitting on an upturned log in the wet grass, shrouded in memories that I can't hide from. Memories of a doctor sitting on his desk telling us that Moth had a disease without treatment or cure, a disease that would take the man I'd loved for all of my adult life, slowly but surely shut down his ability to move at will, then take his thoughts and his memories, and would eventually be so powerful that his days would come to a choking, breathless end. Moth doesn't have to say the words as I watch him stumble over cut wood in the long grass. I know he feels he's a long way down the road that has led from that diagnosis, and that he has the final corner in sight. Each breathless spasm of choking on food, or fresh air, takes him a step closer to a point where he will stop trying to fight and just let it be.

But even the difficult, painful life he's living now shouldn't be happening. When the diagnosis of some form of corticobasal degeneration fell into that silent hospital room, it had a heavy, unmoveable permanence. There was only one way that this disease would progress and that was forwards: a slow-moving, unstoppable wildfire of destruction, burning through precious brain cells and destroying all the functions they control.

Moth cuts another branch, lowering it to the ground, then sits on it, exhausted by the effort, ready to give in. I head back to the house to find my gloves and another saw, reluctant to leave him to work alone.

Walking up the hill I can see two herring gulls in the field behind the house. They come to the same field every winter and stay for days, sometimes weeks, often just standing together for hours, pecking occasionally at grubs in the grass, but mainly just watching. They separate and head to different points in the field, but always come back together to continue to watch, seemingly content to just observe the buzzard overhead, or the voles tunnelling through the grass, or us wandering through our lives. Then, as suddenly as they came, they'll be gone. Away to the sea and the coast, drawn out and up by the magnetism of the salt air, the call of the wind and the open horizon. They know nothing of doctors, or diagnoses; they simply follow the air currents, knowing instinctively what they need, and how to fulfil that need, however far that flight might take them.

I search through the shed for the thick leather gloves I use to handle the wood but can't find them. Unlike Moth, who has a place for everything, I'll have abandoned them where they were last used. I find them in the house, dropped behind the log basket near the bookshelf. As I pick them up I tip over a pile of small plastic-covered books on the bottom shelf. Guidebooks to other worlds, to wild places, remote mountains and distant shores. I restack them, one heavier than the rest, filled with dried leaves, scraps of paper, sand and feathers, its pages rippled by water like the beach on an outgoing tide. I hold it for a moment, feeling the weight of it, repositioning the black elastic hairband that keeps it closed. Just for a moment I can hear the sound of the sea against the cliffs and taste salt on my lips. I put it back, take the gloves and head down to the orchard.

Before I reach the trees I see Moth, already walking up towards the house. He stops for a moment to look around for Monty, then as he turns back towards me, he falls. Not tripping or stumbling, but simply falls, like a dead tree in a high wind. The air hangs still, breathless, as the road shortens and the final corner comes into clear sight. I'm running, running to him, but his body hits the ground, his torso rising slightly but falling again. I skid to his side, holding his head, talking to him, shaking him, as Monty drops his ball and licks his arm. I can barely speak for the tightness in my throat, can hardly see through eyes streaming with tears. But as I look up the two herring gulls lift into the grey skies, stretching their powerful wings, letting the wind direct them, and I can almost smell the salt air that calls them.

2

'Hey, you.' His eyes open after what could have been seconds or minutes.

He's looking at me, but I'm not there. There's a vagueness in those blue eyes that I don't recognize. Their gaze has held mine with an unwavering intensity since the first time they looked up and caught my shy, hesitant teenage curiosity across a college canteen. But I don't know this watery vacant stare, or the jerky movements of his pupils as he tries to focus. I'm coming to understand this changing face, with its dark lines and deepening contours, but I thought those eyes would always be mine. Those eyes that know the depths of me and can see my thoughts across a crowded room. I thought they would always hold a memory of the long years we've spent together, that they would always be mine. But these eyes are empty, they see nothing but the fog as it begins to lift from the creek and hang wet in the air.

'What's going on?'

'I don't know; you must have tripped.' Monty picks up his tennis ball and heads to the house. I help Moth unsteadily to his feet and we follow him. The fog becomes denser as we walk slowly up the hill, cloaking the trees in its damp haze and enveloping the cider barn near the road until only the tallest trees remain visible. The road and its corner fade from view and a dank, hanging, impenetrable cloud follows us to the house.

'Shall I call the doctor?'

'What's the point? They'll just say "That's the way it goes" and put another tick in a box.'

'But all the same, there could be some other reason – blood pressure, or something else.'

'No. I'm going to lie down.' He crawls up the stairs on his

hands and knees and I help him on to the bed. I know I'm clutching at straws. Every time this disease takes a new leap forward I desperately search for a simple label to put on it, as do the doctors. But his blood pressure always holds steady and the labels remain unwritten.

I make tea and take it up for him but he's sleeping, so I cover him with a blanket and go back downstairs. The house is cold, the damp fog creeping in, laying a wet slimy sheen across the slate floor of the hallway. I find the firelighters and kindling and light the wood burner, the dry wood bursting quickly into flames as I take small pieces from the log basket and build the fire. There's a sense of something other than the fire that I shouldn't touch, and yet my hand wants to reach out to it. I continue to build the fire, keeping my eyes on the flames, not allowing them to shift focus, but I'm pulled with a magnetism I know I'll succumb to. I close the door of the stove as warmth begins to fill the room and give in, as I knew I would. Reaching down to the bottom shelf of the bookshelf I lift out the bound guidebook and stroke its rippled edge, hearing the sea lapping against a rocky shore. I place it on the table and lift out another: sharp and angular like the landscape it describes. As I open it, the smell of sulphur is lingering and real, the same smell that still fills the sleeping bags and tent we used on our trip to Iceland. I put it next to the South West Coast Path guidebook, my hands hovering over them. Old friends. Worn, well-known pages, containing walks burnt into my memory by time, tides and landscapes trodden. But I'm not just feeling the comfort of adventures past, or places visited, it's something more. Something bright and pressing and urgent. I resist the thought that's sparking to light in a dark corner of my brain, threatening to burst into being, to crackle with the same force as the flames behind the glass door of the wood burner. I put the books back on the shelf, stifling the oxygen, extinguishing the spark. Don't let the thought grow; it's too late now, that time has passed.

★

The vague early light echoes the grey folds and creases of the pillowcase beneath my head. Moth opens his eyes slowly and holds my gaze. As the darkness of sleep clears and his eyes find their focus, I see them as they have always been: a blue prism of the passion and possibilities that lie within him. Is it too late? He drags his painful hand from beneath the covers and cups my face, and as his face crinkles into a half-smile I see him return. The same man who just two short years ago waded through a river of rushing glacial meltwater in the ash fields of the Icelandic highlands, the same energy that took him across hundreds of miles of wild headlands to the most western edge of England and proved that hope was possible when those around him said there was none. The same man – but dare I even suggest that we let the oxygen back in and allow the spark to reignite? Could he ever have the strength to try again?

'I think we should try and go for a bit of a walk this morning, just get moving a bit, what do you think? Do you fancy it?'

'I don't know. I'm scared now, after yesterday. What if I fall again?'

'Well, let's have some breakfast, then maybe just go up the hill to the first bend and back. On the road, not up the field, so there's no uneven ground.'

'Maybe.'

The orchard is on a hillside. A hidden Cornish valley, where a small stream cuts down to a creek of deep mud and shallow water, feeding into a river that at its mouth becomes a deepwater harbour, before finally joining the English Channel and the open sea. To stand at the top of the hill behind the house is to sense the solidity of the ground beneath your feet but at the same time the pull of the far horizon that's hidden only by a bend in the river. There is no walking on level ground: to leave the house is to go up or downhill. To go down is easy, but there will always be a hill to return by. To go uphill first means that you save the easy downhill for the return.

'I'll put the kettle on then.'

The air's heavy with moisture as we start a slow ascent of the short but steep hill. Monty runs on ahead, dropping his ball to watch it roll away downhill before running on without it. Moth walks uphill with an unsteady gait, his feet striking the tarmac with their familiar uneven rhythm, one . . . twoo, one . . . twoo, rather than one-two, one-two. His awkward side-leaning move-ment is more pronounced than it's ever been. I try to keep the focus on anything other than the steepness, seriously doubting we'll manage the hundred metres to the top.

'Looked at the weather forecast earlier, seems this wet wea-ther is going to pass, could be a colder, bright spell coming.' I'm not sure if I'm trying to distract Moth from the climb, or myself from the pain of watching him struggle.

'Really? Doesn't feel like it.'

We stop to rest halfway up, Moth leaning with his hands on his knees and taking deep breaths.

'Shall we go on, or do you want to go back?'

'Let's just get to the corner at the top, but that'll be it, it's all I can do.'

The crows are gathering in greater numbers than I've ever seen on the farm, a large flock in a curved line down the centre of the field, feeding in the grass. There's so little to eat at this time of year, they eagerly wait for the sheep to finish jostling for the food put down by the shepherd, before swooping in to clean up any remnants of the high protein pellets that remain in the grass. Opportunistic survivors, they rarely miss the chance of free food. I'm contemplating returning as a crow in another life as we finally reach the field gate at the top of the steep piece of road, leaning over it to take in the grey view down to the creek.

'Shall we go back down the field?' Through the gate the field drops directly to the garden, Monty's preferred route back, but Moth turns his back to the gate and steps on to the road.

'No, let's head up to the top road, then we'll turn around. It'll be easy downhill on the way back.'

I watch him walk away up the shallower gradient, his pace slow and uneven. I shouldn't even think about allowing that spark to catch light.

We reach the top road. Slightly wider than the tiny narrow lane that leads to the farm, it threads past a scattering of houses and the church before slipping downhill to join another even narrower lane that leads back up to the farm from the opposite direction.

'Let's go back now; this is too far for you already.' I take his hand and turn to go back.

'Just to the church, it's always nice to be on this flat section of road.'

'We could, I suppose, then you could wait at the church and I'll go back for the van to pick you up.'

On the flat top road the views open out towards Dartmoor in the far distance, visible today as a white undulating line on the far horizon. The drizzle and wet air of the warmer west must be landing as snow in the cold air of the high open moorland. Snow will be mounding behind granite outcrops and disguising the tufting grass and heather. I can almost feel my body stretching outwards, longing for the horizon. Covid has kept us confined in this small area of countryside for so long that the closest we've been to wide-open space has been in our imagination. But it's more than the confinement of lockdown, my longing for big skies and open country is always there, a palpable sense of deep need. One that may never be satisfied again, now that Moth's health brings our horizons ever closer.

We lean against the wall that surrounds the graveyard. I keep my back to it – as Moth's condition worsens I can't even think about the permanence of cold earth.

'Are you going to stay here? I'll go back for the van.'

'No, let's keep going around the loop, it's mainly downhill now anyway.'

'But it's too far, you'll do too much then be in bed for days again.' So often when he's over-exerted himself it ends in exhaustion that sees him barely able to walk or function for days.

'I want to keep going.'

We carry on. Past the old riding stables and down the hill, where the land falls steeply to the creek, where the egrets, curlews and herons call across the shallow water. The road undulates out beyond the last of the scattered houses, the farm coming back into view among the green hills, beyond a Georgian manor house at the edge of the mud. A priory once stood here, with a handful of monks who probably planted the first apple trees on the land where the farm stands. They lived their quiet life in the valley, growing vegetables, making cider, hanging out by the river, until the dissolution of the monasteries saw them leave and the priory disappear into the hillside it sprang from. But apple trees still grow here, covering the steep hill that blocks the skyline ahead of us.

'This is why we should have turned back at the church. It's way too steep for you here.'

We stand at the corner, ankle-deep in water, where the stream passes under the road in dry weather but after a storm gushes across the tarmac, forming a ford of brown water and twigs. From here the road climbs between two high hedgerows, a steepness that makes heads pound and breath catch in throats – a sting in the tail of our two-mile circuit.

'Let's go through the gap in the hedge, then back up the orchard.'

I watch Moth step over the broken wire fence without tripping and I pass Monty to him, who runs away into the tufted grass as soon as his feet hit the ground. He reaches his hand out, and for a second I'm taking the last few steps through a freezing Arctic river and he's pulling me up on to the bank of black ash, but that's only a memory now.

We wind our way through the orchard, between gnarled trees and conical piles of pruned wood. When he began pruning these trees three years before, Moth formed the cones of cut timber with the intention of burning them. Some were burnt, but all of those that remained in the spring became nest sites for small birds, filling the air with activity and song. So now only a few are burnt, the rest remain, waiting for the longer days to bring new life to dead wood.

Back at the house I light the fire. Monty sits on the hearth licking his wet feet. Moth sits in the chair next to it, unlacing his boots and hanging his socks to dry. By the time I've made tea and brought it back to the fire, Moth is asleep, his legs stretched out, arms crossed over his middle, bare feet steaming in the heat. I leave the tea and watch him from the other side of the room. He's walked further today than I thought possible, so maybe, just maybe.

I scan my hands along the spines of the plastic-covered books on the bottom shelf of the bookcase, until I find one that's clean, new and unused. I hold it in my hand. A small book, with limited content, but as I crouch by the fire the sparse words represent something vast, limitless, free. I flick through the unread pages. Maybe. Irresponsible, irrational, selfish, unfair: I can find all the reasons not to, but I do it anyway. Quietly, without disturbing him, I place the book next to his mug of tea and then go to the kitchen and begin peeling potatoes.

Maybe, just maybe.

'Don't even think about it.' He's standing in the doorway to the kitchen, the small book in his hand. He puts it carefully on to the worktop and turns to go. 'My feet are really painful. It used to be just the numbness, but now they hurt all the time and worse when I've walked.'

'I hoped you'd be okay, but really I knew that walk was too far for you today.'

'Well, it was you who suggested a walk.'

'Yes, but not that far.'

'I know what you're trying to do, but it's too late. I know it's too late now, I can feel it taking over, like it's not my body any more. I'm heading towards the end and there's no point us pretending otherwise.'

I look away, my throat tightening, my eyes burning but searching for a distraction. I fill the kettle, again. He goes upstairs, lies on the bed and is asleep within seconds. Sleep has drifted into his life like the fog in the trees, wiping out time and space and energy; he visits the waking world for a few hours each day but is always ready to leave, given the opportunity.

His anger and sadness and frustration hang in the room long after he's gone. They leave me with a sense of time freezing, an impenetrable cold stillness that I can't break away from. Staring out of the window at rain blowing in squalls between the house and the zinc barn opposite, I know I need to do something to help him, but there's nothing to be done. Moth's finally accepting the recommendation of the doctor in that first diagnosis: 'Don't tire yourself, and be careful on the stairs.' But that acceptance feels like the edge of a vortex from which there'll be no return.

I go upstairs and watch him sleep. His face on the pillow displays few of his sixty years; it's strange how sleep wipes away time, stress, pain and fear, just leaving the body in an untroubled, smooth state. Other than when he sleeps I've only seen his face look like this a few times in the years since his diagnosis. Moments when he'd looked out to sea as a curtain of rain fell on the far horizon, or stood on the edge of a rocky outcrop with volcanic ash on his boots and a cold wind in his hair. Maybe there's something about a totally relaxed state that allows the symptoms of tension and pain to subside, leaving him in a natural state of comfort.

Back in the kitchen I pick up the guidebook again. The Cape Wrath Trail. Two hundred and thirty miles running from the north-west corner of Scotland south to Fort William. A trail renowned among long-distance walkers as being the toughest, most remote trail in Britain. What am I thinking? I try to put it back on the shelf, but I can't, the flame's already alight and I can't put it out. If we were to walk again, would it give him one more chance? Would one more long trail set him free from the shackles of CBD, at least for a little longer? Would it allow me to keep him for just a little longer?

But this trail? Surely I could look at an easier trail, not an extreme one through the mountains and bogs of the wild Highlands. I thumb through the guidebook, looking at pictures of glens and lochs, and I know the answer. It has to be *this* trail, through the Great Wilderness and into the Rough Bounds of Knoydart. A place he's longed to spend time in but where he has rarely managed to stay more than a week. If any trail will encourage him to try one more time, then it's this one. But it's too hard and too far. I put the book away on the shelf and sit in the old chair in the corner, sending a cloud of Monty's hair rising into the room. I try to resign my thoughts to more walks around the block and to finally accepting his slow demise with grace and empathy. But I can't do it. My head feels heavy, the weight of sadness expanding like a dense pressure. I press my fingers against my eyes, trying to hold the thoughts and the tears inside, hoping to see only blackness. But I don't; all I see is our life together, running like a video reel behind my closed eyes. Moth's face as he turns to look back at me from the gritstone edges of Staffordshire, the sun on his skin, the wind in his hair, on rocky outcrops of high Scottish mountains, on coastal cliffs and glacial ice fields. A face alight with excitement and passion, not just for the wild places, but alive with a passion for life. It has to be Cape Wrath, it's the only trail that will make him lace up his boots and turn his back on that last corner in the road, that will force him to walk away from it, to let it reach him another day.

I'm under the zinc barn filling a wheelbarrow with logs when I hear the gate shut and watch him walk up the hill with Monty. Should I go with him? What if he falls again? I drop the logs and start to follow, then realize he hasn't spoken to me this morning and would surely have said if he wanted me with him. Through all the decades we've spent together we've barely argued – surely now isn't the moment we're going to start? Not now when I'm facing the endless void of life without him. Not now, when all I want is to cling to him tighter than ever before.

I take the logs to the house, a dark anxiety tying knots in my stomach. The Cape Wrath Trail guidebook is back on the table. I didn't put it there. I picture him walking up the hill, angry and saddened, feeling I don't listen to him when he says he can't go on, don't let him rest when he says he can't move, don't accept that one day he'll be gone. My mind runs in circles trying to escape the thought of how uncompassionate I must appear to him. Minutes become an hour and I can't tell if my vision is blurred by rain on the window or the tears that make my eyes sore and my face swollen.

The gate closes and the door opens, Monty rushes in shaking muddy water up the walls from his wet coat and Moth follows behind. I can barely look him in the face.

'Where have you been? I'm sorry, I'm so sorry . . . It's just that I'd do anything to stop this illness, anything to keep you well.'

'I walked round the block. If we're going to do the Cape Wrath Trail I thought I should at least be able to do that without sleeping for three hours afterwards.'

'Of course we can't do it. It's too far and too difficult, it was stupid of me to even think it.'

'It was, but the thought's there now.'

'No, don't say that. I'm not making you do it.'

'Oh, but you are.'

3

Corticobasal degeneration is a rare and progressive neurodegenerative disorder that can cause problems with movement, speech,
cognition and swallowing, as well as a whole raft of other symptoms that the neurologist may see as subsidiary, but for the
patient can be primary: problems with sight and appetite, with
sleeping and thinking. Diagnosing CBD is like trying to catch
an eel in a bath of seaweed. There are no definitive tests that
allow a neurologist to say unequivocally and without a shadow
of a doubt that a patient has CBD, they can only rule out other
possibilities. With its slow movements, stiffness and walking
problems, CBD displays similar symptoms to many other syn-
dromes that are termed Parkinsonism, in that they show some
but not all the symptoms of Parkinson's. It overlaps in part with
Parkinson's disease itself, as well as progressive supranuclear
palsy, Alzheimer's and a number of other conditions.

No one knows the actual cause of CBD, but it's classed as a
tauopathy – a disease that arises when a protein called tau, which
is normally present in the brain, accumulates in an abnormal
way, resulting in the deterioration of brain cells. We were sitting
in a hospital consulting room when Moth received his original
diagnosis, listening to a doctor explain, as carefully as he could,
that it would be impossible to say without question that Moth
had this hideous illness until post mortem. I now know he told
us that because it's only when a scientist has the brain under a
microscope that it's possible to see the shape the tau filaments
take, and from there be able to distinguish the difference between
a CBD filament and that of, say, Alzheimer's or a range of other
tauopathies.

Although Moth suffers many typical CBD traits, his original

diagnosis was only reached after years of medical tests and observations, where other diseases were ruled out; scans that showed what it wasn't, not what it was; courses of drugs that were ineffective so ruling out other conditions they would be effective for; nerve conductivity tests; cognition tests; time and analysis. None of which can tell the neurologist with 100 per cent certainty that the condition he's seeing is CBD. They can only tell him what it isn't, and in doing so narrow the field until the only logical remaining conclusion is that the patient possibly has CBD. Each time a neurologist puts their hand in the bath they think they're lifting out an eel, only to find that, yet again, it's only seaweed. Remove enough seaweed and eventually only an eel will remain, but even then it could be hard to see it in the brown, murky water.

But one test was definitive. Not telling us what species of eel remained in the bath, but unquestionably that there was one there and very much making its presence felt. A DAT scan is used to measure the levels of dopamine receptor cells in the brain. Dopamine is a chemical messenger that transmits signals between nerve cells and muscles. Moth's scan showed that he had a distinct reduction in his receptor cells, which show up as lights on the screen. His lights were undoubtedly going out. There was no way of knowing exactly what breed of eel remained in the bath – we may never know until the plug is pulled and the water drains away – but combined with all his other test results, the strongest possibility is that he has CBD. The process he has gone through is the same experienced by anyone who eventually receives a diagnosis of one of a range of Parkinsonisms that aren't actually Parkinson's disease itself.

Moth's diagnosis categorized him as suffering from a disease without treatment or cure, where the only advice that could be offered was not to get too tired and to be careful on the stairs. But that diagnosis came in the same week that we were evicted from the house we had lived in for twenty years, a week when we became homeless. We couldn't concern ourselves about not getting too tired as we had nowhere to sleep, couldn't be careful on the stairs as we no longer had any. So instead we filled our rucksacks with the basics for survival and began a 630-mile walk along a national trail that has an ascent equivalent to climbing Everest nearly four times. Irrational, irresponsible, maybe, but in that desperate moment our decision to walk offered everything we needed – shelter in the form of our tent and a line on a map to follow. It gave us a route forward, a purpose, a reason to go on into the next day when all other reasons had fallen away.

But something strange happened on that walk, strange and totally unexpected. After two hundred miles of walking over endless headlands, carrying everything we needed to survive on our backs, Moth's health began to improve in ways that should have been impossible. His gait became almost normal, his thoughts cleared, his short-term memory sharpened and movements that had been almost impossible before became easy. This shouldn't have happened. CBD is a one-way street; Moth shouldn't have been able to go back to an earlier time when his body responded to requests, or when he could put up the tent without help, or carry a rucksack without pain, or read a map and actually reach his destination. Once those markers have been passed there should be no going back.

In the years that followed Moth studied for a degree, his life becoming more sedentary, and his health quickly declined. But then we came to live in the orchard, taking up a life that required Moth to be physically active in the outdoors on a daily basis. In the early days of that life his health improved slightly, his memory again becoming clearer, his body stronger, his movements more sure. But then winter came, Covid restrictions and lockdown came, stillness came, and with that an acceleration into a worsening of his symptoms. All leading to that moment when he fell, that moment when I knelt in the grass, shaking him, begging for this not to be the end of it all.

Since walking the coast path doctors, physiotherapists and neurologists have contacted us suggesting reasons why his health improved as it did. Physiotherapy is one of only a few ways in which a patient can be helped with the physical symptoms of CBD, gentle motion to help retain a little movement for as long as possible. So it could be argued that what Moth undertook on that very long walk was an extreme form of physio. Or maybe it was the very low-calorie diet we survived on because we couldn't afford to eat, or the time spent in nature, or any number of other reasons that have yet to be considered. What was without question was the speed with which his health deteriorated when he returned to a more sedentary life, all the old symptoms returning more aggressively than before.

4

Lockdown blankets the country in a sense of inertia, winter days drag into weeks and there's a sense of hibernation in the air. Food is handed over the wall from a delivery truck, dog walkers wave from the other side of the single-track lane. Everyone is suspicious, doubtful, wary, as the Covid death toll rises and we stay close to the trees. Inside the house the guidebook is permanently on the table, emanating a faint light of possibility. In early-morning darkness I read blogs about walkers who have completed the Cape Wrath Trail, stories of hardship, wild weather, vast deep bogs and men who, despite it all, make it through with a resigned look of accomplishment. I glance back through all the many stories – where are the women?

In the evenings we watch a series of blogs filmed by a man who walks the trail in two weeks with his trusty collie dog by his side, or over his shoulders as he wades across rivers at the same time as talking into his activity camera, or curled asleep in the super-lightweight tent, unmoveable, exhausted. I look online for a guidebook to the South Downs Way, in the hope of persuading Moth to look at an easier, shorter walk, and alleviate my growing sense of guilt. But it's too late; he has visions of remote glens in his sights and no matter how hard I try to sell the benefits of a gentler trail, there's no going back. He walks around the block, every day, only sleeping for thirty minutes on his return.

The guidebook describes an unfixed trail, a path without way markers. The pages show a route, but a few pages later offer an alternative, or even suggest making it up if glens are blocked by floods, fires or other natural disasters. We need bigger maps covering a wider area. If we stray away from the guidebook we'll be completely lost in a wilderness of mountain and bog.

The Ordnance Survey maps arrive, a bundle of pink-covered, intricately folded paper. Pages of indecipherable contour lines, bog symbols and little else. No wonder part of this route is called the Great Wilderness: one whole map shows nothing but hills and water. I suddenly realize what a fool I've been. How had I forgotten that it took me three attempts to pass O level Geography, mainly because I couldn't read OS maps?

'It's no good, Moth, you'll need to do the map reading, I'll get us completely lost.' I'm trying to trace the line of the path across the map, which covers the whole table when fully opened, but all I can see is a huge game of snakes and ladders, where landing on a snake will find us neck deep in a bog, or falling off a cliff.

'I don't know if I can. You know how hard I'm finding it to make decisions or work out problems; even to think what I want for dinner feels impossible most days. We'll stick to the guidebook but take the maps.'

'Have you still got a compass?'

'Yes, of course. Don't know if I remember how to use it, though.'

I sit at the table in the evenings, the maps spread out under the laptop, watching the blogs of the man and his collie, comparing his route to that described in the guidebook, then tracing a pencil line of the route across the map. At night I wake from horrifying dreams of trying to read the map on a hillside as torrential rain washes the pencil marks away and the wind rips the map from my hands. As I jump up in bed from yet another nightmare, I've obviously woken Moth too. Even without opening his eyes he knows what's happening.

'You could draw the line on in pen, then it won't wash off.'

'I can't yet, it might be wrong. I've used pencil so I can rub it out and change it.'

'I told a chap in the village what we were doing, he said forget paper maps and downloaded the OS map app on to my phone for me. Didn't have the heart to say: "What happens when I run out of battery?"'

Moth drifts back to sleep, as if he's never really woken, and I stare at a dark ceiling in a whole new world of worry. Having spent days with the maps I can see there'll be multiple days with nowhere to buy food, let alone charge a battery. No battery, probably very little reception and, at our inevitably slow pace, days between civilization. What if something happens to Moth on one of those stretches, what if he falls again, what if . . . ?

I watch a woodpecker flying backwards and forwards to its nest in the sweet chestnut tree, caring for its newly hatched young, keeping them safe while they're too weak to survive alone, and all I feel is guilt. If we're going to leave we should be preparing to go, but Moth's sitting at the table, flicking through the corners of the guidebook.

'It's not too late to stop this. I should never have suggested it.'

'You still don't get it, do you?' He puts the guidebook down and stops fiddling, sure of what he's saying. 'I'd stopped allowing myself to think of trips like this, put those thoughts away, tried to accept that there won't be any more. Then you got this book out.'

'I know, I'm sorry, it was stupid . . .'

'I'm afraid. Afraid of where this illness will go and when. You know that's how I feel, but you also know all the buttons to press and despite that – or because of it, I'm still not sure – you went ahead and you pressed them anyway, when you got this book off the shelf.'

I put my head in my hands, hardly able to look him in the face.

'But it has made me think – there are still so many places I haven't seen. I hate the idea of bucket lists, I've always thought you should do what you can while you can, and live without regrets, then there's no need for bucket lists. But this place . . . this place has always drawn me, eluded me, so let's go.' He gets up from the table, opens the door for Monty to go out, then puts his boots on, tying the laces with slow, meticulous care.

'Anyway, it might be a disaster. I might fall down a gully and die, or spend a week sitting in a café just staring at the view. But at least it won't be something to regret, something we didn't do.'

I watch him step out of the door. Will I ever completely understand this man? 'I think there might be some regret if you fall down a gully and die.'

'Not for me.'

'What are we going to do about the orchards? We could be gone for a month.' If lockdown ends and allows us to travel, we'll be walking during the spring when the orchard needs very little care other than the grass paths cutting, as the time of pruning and hedge laying has passed. But I'm really starting to panic about the dangers of the route and trying everything I can think of to steer Moth towards another, less arduous path. 'And Monty. It's going to be too far for him, his legs are too short, we'll lose him in the bogs. So we can't go. We'll have to go somewhere easier so he can come. What about the Two Moors Way? Much easier and it's on our doorstep.'

'Tom.'

Our son drops in to help in the orchard whenever he can, but a month of grass cutting could be pushing it, even for him. And will he really want a ball-obsessed dog who's wary of people, barks at other dogs and leaves a trail of hair wherever he goes – for a month? This is the way out. No one will want Monty.

'He's coming over later, I'll ask him.'

'Hi, Tom, your mum thinks if I ask you to cut the grass and look after Monty for a month, you'll say no.'

I'm making tea, confident in the thought that Tom will say no and my reckless idea hasn't gained so much momentum that there's no way back.

'Of course, we love Monty, when are you going? Where are you going?'

I pour the tea into the cups, the ever-growing sense of trepidation making me feel slightly nauseous. It seems we're going to walk the Cape Wrath Trail and something that began as just a rash and desperate thought is becoming real.

Moth's feet cause him endless pain and discomfort as a result of minor peripheral nerve damage. He often has his shoes off, complaining that his socks feel wet, or he has a stone in his shoe, when neither are the case. And his old walking boots are worn out. We search for new ones, looking for a pair that will keep his feet comfortable for as long as possible as well as dry in what, according to the collie-owning hiker, could be deep wet boglands for much of the walk. The boots are either too short and will allow water to pour in over the tops, or too heavy, or not waterproof at all. The search seems hopeless.

'I think I've found them.'

I look at the computer screen, at a pair of black ex-army combat boots. Ugly, but lacing up to half-calf and fully lined with a waterproof membrane. Might be just the thing for the bogs described by collie-man, which seem to be getting worse the further north he gets and I'm beginning to suspect might be waist deep by the time he reaches Cape Wrath.

'Okay. You can always return them, I suppose.'

'I'll get you a pair as well, in case you like them.'

'No . . .' He's already pressed 'Pay now'.

'I'll definitely send mine back.'

The boots arrive. Moth's so happy with their foam insoles that he's reluctant to take them off. Success. The pair he bought for me lurk in the corner, waiting to be returned. I've tried them on a couple of times but they're heavy and stiff and I can't imagine walking far in them.

We slip into spring. Lockdown is lifted in England but the border with Scotland remains closed. April comes with harsh frosts, worse than we've seen all winter. The orchards break into

blossom in the warmth of the days, but in the valley the therm-
ometer tips into minus figures every night, freezing the delicate
pink flowers into a brown curl long before any fruit has had
time to set. The harvest will be seriously reduced this year. In
the north of Scotland it's even colder; there are nights when the
remote glens reach minus six. I watch the news constantly, hoping that Scotland holds its ground and the border remains closed
for another month.

The border opens.

Everything's prepared and, no matter how concerned either of
us feel about the prospect, it seems we're actually going. The
rucksacks are propped by the door, ready to go, full of trusted
equipment that withstood the winds of the South West
Coast Path and the arctic blasts of the southern uplands of
Iceland, so will hopefully see us through Scotland in May. An
old three-man Vango tent that weighs too much, but feels like
home. Sleeping bags: chilly in Iceland, too warm in an English
summer, so hopefully perfect for a Scottish spring. A tiny
titanium stove that has never failed, with two canisters of gas.
Waterproof coats from a Swedish company, which seem capable of standing up to any amount of rain, and super-lightweight
waterproof trousers. Stainless-steel mugs with plastic lids but
no handles, a small pan, a rechargeable head torch with a spare
battery just in case. A lighter with an Icelandic puffin on the
outside and matches in a plastic bag. A small toilet bag of
essentials, a notepad and pen, one change of clothes, a thin
down jacket and a phone charger. And a dry sack containing
the guidebook and the pile of pink-covered OS maps, with
most of the route now plotted on in ink, not pencil. Can we
really manage for a month with just this? For a moment I can
hear the slap of the straps against the pack as we stand on granite cliffs at the very western edge of England, blasted by
gale-force winds coming in from the open Atlantic Ocean,

with virtually no food, or money in our pockets. I know these rucksacks already hold everything we need.

'Are we ready?'

'I think so.'

Tom packs the dog basket into the back of his truck, with a month's supply of dog food and a pile of tennis balls, and I hand Monty over with a lump in my throat. I watch them drive away, Monty's wet nose pressed against the window, not knowing what's happening, and with no concept of how long we'll be gone for.

'Don't worry, Monty, we'll be back in a few weeks.' I wave to him as if he's a child.

'We'll see how it goes. It might not even be that long.'

Time, it's an elusive thing. Hours can pass like days, but months can feel like moments. It's all a matter of how you fill it.

5

I sit in the long grass at the wild margin of the garden, sucking up the feeling of a Cornish spring before we leave it behind. There was so little insect life on this over-used farm when we came, but simply changing the way the farm is managed – reducing the use of chemicals and the numbers of grazing animals in the fields – gave nature space to rebuild itself and the pollinators have returned. The air is buzzing with the sound of insects in search of nectar and birds in search of insects. A wren's building a nest in the fake nest put up to attract house martins, and sparrows are nesting in the bird box near the door that last year held a family of nine blue tits. Something catches my eye on a stone wall. A bird I've never seen before, one I only know from books. A wheatear, sharp and alert, with its blue-grey back and black flash across its cheek. He bobs for a while on the stones, picking at the spiders that live there. A late migrant from Africa, he should have been here in March, not hitting our shores in early May. Maybe he's been held up by the late frosts or, like us, closed borders. But we both need to go: the wheatear to find other wheatears before it's too late to breed, us before the weather gets too warm and we hit the Scottish midge season. He had no fear of his journey, he simply knew he had to make it. Our journey has the same magnetic instinctive pull, and although I can't escape the sense of fear and doubt, it feels every bit as essential. I stand up as he takes to the air; it's time for us both to leave.

Travelling during a pandemic, with a person who could have a greater degree of vulnerability to the virus than most, is a nerve-racking process. We've had our first vaccination, but not the second, so decide not to take the train, which would have required too many stops in big, busy railway stations, and load the rucksacks into the van instead. A transportation company will collect it from a village near Cape Wrath, then Tom will come and pick us up from Fort William, if we're still nervous about train journeys by the time we need to return.

In the first week of May we close the gate on the farm, feeling certain we'll be back before midsummer, when the normal cycle of life in the orchard will continue as if we've never been away. We drive up the hill and head north.

After a day of pollution, congestion and roadworks we arrive in deepest Lancashire, an oasis just a few miles west of the M6, where arriving at our destination and pulling into the driveway feels like coming home and all that represents. A house filled with welcome, comfort, warmth and friendship, a place that connects us to adventures past and yet to come. We met Dave and Julie next to an ice cream van on the South West Coast Path, trekked with them through the volcanic Icelandic landscape and explored wet and windy British moorlands in between. Their home is a place to share food and stories, hopes and dreams and, having finally committed to the journey, breathe, if only for a moment. We're wheatears eating spiders in a Cornish garden before the final push north.

'You have looked at the guidebook, like?' Dave: big, northern and always very much to the point.

'Of course, it's not as if we'd head to such a remote corner without doing a bit of homework. Why, what are you saying?' I know Dave well enough to know that he won't bother starting a conversation if he doesn't intend finishing it.

'Well, it's just Moth, he's not as strong as he was a couple of years ago.'

I look over at Moth with the eyes of someone who hasn't seen him for two years and the room begins to darken with the fears I thought I'd left behind. 'I know, you're so right. We shouldn't be doing this, should we?'

'I'm not saying that, but I can see he's not confident about this trip.'

I suddenly feel slightly sick, knowing that he wouldn't have considered this walk if I hadn't encouraged him into it.

'Look, all I'm saying is we live well north of most people you know. If things go wrong, just hole up somewhere for a day or two and I'll come and get you. It's too far for your son to be coming up from Cornwall.'

A closely woven safety net of friendship spreads out beneath me, a simple sincere offer that brushes through the fears, moving them gently aside.

'I don't know if I could put up with you for a month, but I sort of wish you were coming with us.'

'Get yourselves down to the Pennines and I'll come and meet you for a week or two.'

'Jeez, Dave, there's no way we can walk that far. We'll be lucky if we make it to Fort William.'

'Well, just a thought.'

I watch his big frame walk to the kitchen to carry a bowl of vegetables that Julie's prepared. She follows him with glasses and a bottle; she's half his size and twice as tough. I really would feel far more confident if they were coming. Julie pours me a glass.

'He means it, you know. Take him up on it if you need to.' She catches Moth's eye as he looks up and quietly moves the conversation on. 'Anyway, we've got a two-week holiday and no way of filling it.'

'Don't you start, there's absolutely no way we'll make it as far as the Pennines.'

'We'll see.'

We stay for an extra day, regrouping, checking kit, eating spiders before flying on. We walk along the estuary, watching silage being cut in fields along its banks. Small meadows of tall grass being invaded by an army of tractors, trailers, tedders and silage blowers, which ravage a hundred acres of land in ninety minutes. The fields are stripped bare of grass and with it every living thing that existed within them, no time for wildlife to escape or insect life to move on. It feels as though we're witnessing an Armageddon for a huge area of biodiversity. Like so much of the farmland in this country, this isn't privately owned land. It belongs to one of the huge corporations, so the silage isn't stored in the neighbouring farm buildings, but transported for miles to a vast dairy unit beyond Lancaster. For the corporations, biodiversity isn't part of the equation and certainly can't be balanced against the desire for higher and higher profits.

On the mudflats a rare white stork searches for food, driven, like so much of our wildlife, to the very edge of existence. I wonder where all the life that these fields supported has gone. Has it even survived the day? But this is the choice we make every time we shop, like the dairy cows that never see a grass field, or the hens that never see daylight, this vast area of land stripped of insect life in minutes is the true cost of cheap food. No matter how many wild flower seeds we sow in our gardens, it's an equation that can't be balanced.

We head back through fields thick with meadow pipits.

'Planning's been granted for thousands of houses across these fields, due to start building anytime now.' Julie waves her arm across the landscape of hedgerows and woods.

The meadow pipits fill the air, but not for much longer. Their food source has disappeared in an afternoon and their habitat is scheduled to follow. As I watch them fly, it feels as if it might soon be for the last time.

One last evening of home comforts and home-cooked food, the bags packed and repacked and there's no delaying it any longer: we have to go.

'See you on the Pennines.'

'That's not happening.'

'We'll see.'

★

High winds drive torrential rain against the window of the café in Fort William, as the May afternoon becomes dark. The Cape Wrath Trail begins here, or for us, if we make it this far, it will be where it ends. We've stocked up on dried food and spare socks, and now watch rain driving down the high street, bow waves of water forming behind passing cars. We decide to stay the night, so take our time drinking tea in the café. Through the steamy window I can see a backpacker standing in a doorway. He's a small, slight man, his beard neat and combed, his kit new and unused.

'I bet he's about to start the Cape Wrath Trail, heading south to north. I can't imagine starting out in this weather. Soaked on day one.'

'No, me neither.'

'Remind me again why we said we'd do it north to south.' Moth's holding his knife, tapping it gently on the table.

'Because it would be easier to get back from Fort William, either closer for Tom or straight on to the train south.'

'Today it feels as if none of this makes any sense.'

We stare out of the window at the rain and a group of hikers marching up the street. Bedraggled and dripping, covered in mud, feet in plastic carrier bags shoved into boots that are obviously full of water.

'They look like they've just finished.' Is this what Cape Wrath does to people?

'Some sort of youth group, maybe. I bet they're finishing the West Highland Way.'

The extremely popular West Highland Way runs south from here, for about a hundred miles. I watch the group celebrating as they walk up the street. 'Why aren't we doing that instead? Look, they're still laughing at the end.' I don't know why I didn't think of this trail, easier and shorter, but as Moth looks at me with his eyebrows raised and then continues tapping the table, I wish I hadn't asked.

'I'm thinking I might leave my small boots here, maybe at the tourist information, so I can post these big ones back and have my others to travel home in.' He's become quite attached to his huge army boots, but I can see that if we manage to walk all the way back to Fort William we might need a change of boots. I've worn my big boots a few times and they seemed okay, certainly more suited to this weather than small short ones.

'Okay, makes sense, shall we do that?'

'Are you going to use your army ones as well then?'

Moth has a theory that humans are innately intelligent, but fundamentally reluctant to use their knowledge. That we have a huge wealth of understanding of our history that should prevent us repeating the mistakes of the past, if only we drew on it. I've always argued that he's wrong, that no matter how much knowledge we have, each new set of circumstances presents a new problem, so each mistake is new.

'Might as well if you're using yours. I'm sure they'll be fine.'

PART TWO

From the North

To aim for the highest point is not the only
way to climb a mountain.

The Living Mountain, Nan Shepherd

6

Scotland is heavy with history, myth and legend. The glens and hillsides echo with the sound of its past: armies raised and fallen; battles fought, won and lost; hard lives carved among unforgiving mountains; crofters, clearances, heroes and monsters. I wonder how any country can exist in the present under the weight of so much past. Driving alongside Loch Ness, my eyes are drawn more to the water than to the road, searching constantly for a sighting of the mythical monster that's said to lurk in its depths. I don't see her.

The loch finally recedes behind us and we stop for fuel. The petrol station carries as much Nessie memorabilia and trinkets as it does confectionary and petrol cans; it feels like a meeting place of the old and new country. I've found this in almost every store we've stopped at in the north and it makes me feel slightly uncomfortable. As if somehow I'll be approached by a salesman for the old country every time I buy a loaf of bread. But if millions of visitors come here for the history and myth, then why not package that up for them? It leaves everyone satisfied with the outcome. But Inverness tells a different story; it's now home to a quarter of the Highland population, a centre for high-tech medical businesses and manufacturing to support the offshore oil industry. As we skirt the industrial estates of the city, I suspect there's a lot more to today's Scotland than tins of shortbread and Nessie keyrings.

The road turns west, taking us ever closer to the Cape, along the shores of Loch Shin, a single-track road that never seems to end. Eventually the rain stops, hillsides appearing beneath breaking cloud, but the road and the loch go on and on for forty miles, finally reaching the end and the one and only parking spot that doesn't already have a camper van in it. But there is a small car, with a man sleeping under a blanket on the front seat. We park the van and boil a kettle to make tea.

Fish bones litter the loch-side. Otters. I've seen the tracks and traces left by otters all over the country, sat in wait for them, been to otter sanctuaries, even the zoo, but I've never seen an otter. I don't see one now, so sit on a boulder and watch the changing skies. The passing showers are lessening, leaving occasional curtains of light rain. Late-evening sun paints a line of gold, from the hillside behind us to the darkness of the far horizon, broken clouds picking up the light in a scattering of pale streaks, reflecting back on to the dark surface of the water. Through the wash of light, a rainbow stretches into its full arc from one side of the loch to the other, a brushstroke of wild colour, vivid against the dark mountains beyond. So much more than tartan sporrans and plastic Highland cows.

The man in the parked car gets out and stretches into the morning light, as I'm doing the same. It feels slightly awkward, but I start a conversation anyway.

'Hi. That can't have been a very comfy night for you.'

'No, so cramped in there.'

'Are you just passing through?'

'No, I work in the fish-processing plant away up there.' He nods towards the west. 'Wife kicked me out two months ago, there's nowhere else to go, no houses round here, so I'm in my car every night. Where you heading?'

'Cape Wrath. We're going to walk the trail.'

'You know it's closed, don't you? Military are up there, fucking hundreds of them, you canna go up there.'

The further north we go, even under brightening skies, the darker the landscape becomes. Hillsides of heather as dry as if they've been in a wildfire, but there's been no burning. Moth runs his hands through a plant and it breaks, lifeless and brittle.

'This is so strange. What's going on? I've walked through

moorlands of winter heather all my life and it's never felt like this. I've never seen it so black. And it's May. This feels dead, but it can't be surely, not this much, not thousands of acres like this.' The black hillsides stretch in every direction, a wild, dark, alien landscape. And a noise, like a deep booming distant storm.

'What's that noise?'

'If that man was right, it could be the military. I checked online for the firing times before we left, it said they would finish firing at the beginning of May.'

How had he thought of that? I knew the Cape was military land but it hadn't crossed my mind to see if they were firing. 'I've got no mobile reception to check it. Shall we go into the village and ask around for another opinion?'

Kinlochbervie is a tiny village, but the most northerly port on the west coast of Scotland, where life is dominated by the coming and going of fish. Fish from the village's small fishing fleet and bigger ships from other shores are processed and packed, then sent by road through Britain and into Europe. We get out of the van near the factory, into air thick with the smell of fish, and head into a small café. As we walk inside it's imme-diately obvious outsiders aren't welcome.

'You canna come in here – we don't have incomers in the café. Get out now. There's a bench outside. I'll come to you.'

Outside the café there's a cold chill in the air and the hills of dead heather seem to be closing in. Two large black motorbikes are parked on the road and for a moment all I can think of is our daughter, Rowan, and her huge motorbike that terrifies me every time I think of her riding it. She'll be on her way to the farm this week to take her turn with Monty, and suddenly all I want to do is abandon this wild, impossible trip and go back to Cornwall to spend time with my family. We came to the café for beans on toast, and to ask about the military manoeuvres, but now, sitting on the bench next to the bin, it's not why we're at the café but the sanity of this whole trip that's the real question. It hangs, unspoken, on the cool fish-laden breeze.

'Right, what can I get you?' The woman who sent us outside has come to take our order.

'We were going to have beans on toast, but now we're on the bench maybe a bacon sandwich and a mug of tea? And why can't we sit inside – you've got lots of people in there, the motorcyclists and those others?'

The woman looks at Moth as if he's a child who needs something really simple explaining to them. 'The bikers live up the road, they're local. We can't have outsiders coming in the café. We've managed to stay clear of Covid, so we're not going to let it in now, after spending all this time locked up. Most of the shops and cafés and nearly all of the hotels around here are still closed; you're lucky we're open at all.'

I picture the size of the bag of dried food we bought in Fort William and order two extra sandwiches to go. 'Someone told us Cape Wrath is closed for military operations, is that right?'

'Aye, closed 'til June at least. You canna go up there.'

I can feel a rising sense of panic. We only have a few days before the van is collected; if we're going to change our plan it has to be very soon. 'Are there any campsites around here that are open?' I can see Moth slumping. It's becoming harder for him to deal with a change of plan, as if his thoughts can't change once a decision's been made. I know without asking that his brain is telling him the only option now is to return to Cornwall.

'No, they're all closed. There's Sheigra though, you could go there.'

'Sheigra?'

'Aye, not really a campsite, but you can park your van there for a fiver. It's got an honesty box.'

We eat the food in silence, an awkward atmosphere descending that has nothing to do with fish. I know what he's thinking. He knows I know.

★

We drive through the scattering of houses, past a closed hotel and out towards the edge of the village. Dark clouds obscure any views, other than the rocky moorland bordering the single-track road. Out beyond the village, we follow a line of coastal hills, until a sudden dip reveals a flat sandy field leading down to the sea. Sheigra. We pass the honesty box, unsure if we'll stay, and bump over the grass towards the shore. A few camper vans scatter the hillocky area of grass-covered sand dunes; beyond that the sea washes into a small bay of pink stone and white sand. We park as close to the sea as we dare and walk down to the beach. At the sea's edge an oystercatcher flies low between the headlands, over incoming water that slowly wets the dry sand. I sit on the stony foreshore drinking tea I've brought from the van and as the sea laps higher over the white sand I feel my body relax like chocolate on a hot day. I'm back at the very edge of the land and a calm sense of belonging creeps in with the tide. Moth walks across the beach, scuffing his feet in the dusty sand, leaving footprints where it's wet.

'So we can't even go to Cape Wrath.' He sits on the rocks next to me.

'Does it matter? It's a shame not to go to the Cape, but even if we start from here we'll only be missing about twelve miles.' He's looking out to sea with his hands deep in his pockets. He doesn't have to say it; too many sudden changes of plan and his CBD brain can't keep up, it's rushing to what appears to be its only option: retreat to safety, go back to Cornwall and forget this trip was ever considered. 'Shall we go to the van and eat that cold bacon sandwich, then go up on to the headland?'

We eat the food sitting in dune grass that's scattered with tiny white shells, some kind of sea creature thrown in on a high tide. I fill my pockets with the empty shells as we climb on to the headland, over grass kept razor-short by high winds, but carpeted with tiny yellow potentilla and grass-short Alpine flowers. A final scramble over pink rock and this wild, alien corner of Scotland opens ahead of us. White scudding clouds throw shadows across moorlands stretching south towards the mountains of Sutherland. To the north, a coastline of rocky cliffs shines pink in the early-evening sun, curving away towards the unobtainable Cape Wrath. And to the west, the Atlantic Ocean, dark silver-blue reaching all the way to Newfoundland.

We're sitting with our backs to a huge cairn of piled rock, looking out towards the Isle of Lewis on the far horizon, when two people suddenly appear beside us. Baggy stretch trousers, ripped wool jumpers, a rope and climbing shoes hanging from their rucksacks: they're rock climbers heading to the cliffs as the evening sun hits the west-facing rock creating the best time of day to climb, when the hand and footholds have the greatest grip.

'Hi. You heading down to the slabs?' Moth's voice is quiet, flat, none of its usual effervescence.

'Yeah, it's just the perfect time of day.' The woman, in her forties with curly greying hair falling from under a woolly hat, looks at Moth and then out to sea. 'When the sun catches the gneiss, picking up all this colour and you're hanging from a rope among the sea birds, with the sound of the waves below, it's addictive.'

I know the feeling she describes: most weekends of our early twenties were spent hanging on ropes in the Peak District. No sea birds there though, mainly just crows. I don't bother to tell her, but just ask about the climbs.

'There are some great climbs here: Dulce Dancing, Flotsam, Critical Froth. Anyway, why are you here?'

I don't give Moth a chance to reply with whatever negative fears are filling his head and jump in before he can speak. 'We're going to walk the Cape Wrath Trail. Well, not all of it now, the Cape's closed off.'

'Oh yeah, the military. Well, start from here. Why are you doing that anyway? It's a tough one – don't think I could do it.'

I catch Moth's eye and can see he doesn't know what to say. But somehow, here in this wild place, there's no need to pretend. I open my mouth and I can only tell her the truth.

'Moth's ill. We walked a long trail once before and it helped, so we're really hoping that can happen again. We're hoping we haven't left it too late.' In the corner of my eye I glimpse Moth looking out to sea with a slight shake of his head.

The woman hesitates for a moment, the wind blowing her curly hair and flapping the end of the rope against her rucksack.

'We do the same thing every time we hang on a rope. We hope. Hope we'll get to the top, hope the protection will hold, hope this will be the perfect climb. Hope. It's powerful; it can change things. But you've got to put yourself in the way of it, let yourself feel it. Let the power of it lift you up. That's what you're doing: putting yourself in the way of hope. Do that and anything can happen. Start from here! Who needs the Cape? It's stunning here.'

'Not really the Cape Wrath Trail then though, is it?' I can hear the doubts crowding into Moth's words.

'Who cares? Make it your own, make it the Sheigra Trail. Any walk that starts here can only be magnificent.' They head away over the edge of the cliff, but I can hear her shouting as she goes: 'The Sheigra Trail, make it the Sheigra Trail . . .'

'The Sheigra Trail?'

'I don't know. It all feels wrong now. I don't know if I can do it.'

We watch the sea change colour as the sun begins to dip, shouts of 'climbing' rising over the cliff edge.

The rock turns pinker in the fading light, apparently formed from a mix of Torridonian sandstone and Lewisian gneiss which are, according to an information board I read in a car park, some of the oldest rocks in Britain, the base-layer of our existence. The north-west Highlands are formed of a tangle of rock and time that has been the focus of geologists for generations. So much so that it's now a UNESCO Geopark, of the same global geological importance as the volcano fields of south Peru, or Shilin, the Stone Forest in China. Just how important it is was first understood in the early twentieth century, when geologists fell into a frenzy over the discovery of the Moine Thrust Belt, on the north coast at Loch Eriboll. They realized what they were seeing was a jumble of geo-time, where older Moine rock thrust east over levels of much younger rock: a reversed overlap that finally substantiated their theory of tectonic plates. The Moine Thrust Belt runs south through the Highlands towards the sea and the Isle of Skye, a moving swathe of geo-time beneath our feet. We just need to step on to this ancient conveyor belt of sandstone and gneiss and ride it south.

In the vast open landscape to the south, the enormity of what we're facing rises towards us in a tsunami of miles and steps without end. How can we possibly cross 230 miles of some of the most rugged and remote country in the UK on foot? This overwhelming landscape seems almost too vast to contemplate.

'Maybe we can find somewhere to park the van and just walk to Ullapool, then we could get back here somehow, pick up the van and call it quits.' I'm almost resigned to this trip being a failure, and sure now that Moth wants nothing more than to return to the orchard. He says nothing, just looks out to sea.

Birds come and go from a pink rock just offshore. Terns, black-backed gulls and herring gulls. Then suddenly something leaves the cliffs beneath us, gliding across the sea, leaving a black shadow over the sea-bird-covered rock, something dark, with a flash of white, something much bigger than any of the other birds. It turns, flying back to the cliff face. We scramble to find the monocular. It's a white-tailed eagle, a big dark bird with a huge wingspan and defined white tail. These sea eagles disappeared from Britain, hunted into extinction, until they were successfully reintroduced from Norway in the 1970s, but there are still only around 150 pairs in the country. It stays perched on the cliff, a beautiful life form whose very existence here is precarious, and yet he has no fear, no doubt, his focus is only on survival, on existence in the best form that can take. Moth holds the monocular to his eye, watching for a long time, finally lowering it after the eagle has lifted into the sky, spread its wide dark wings and flown south over the sea.

'The van collection's still booked for Durness, so we need to change that, but if we're going to do this then we really ought to set off.'

'Okay, if you're sure.'

'No, but we should do it anyway, just set off and see how it goes.'

We head down to the van that sits on the short sandy grass, surrounded by sharp little birds with white rumps and black cheeks. Wheatears. They've made it north to their summer home. A journey of danger and exhaustion, but one they had to make.

I end the call and put the phone back in my pocket.

'They say they can't collect the van from here until June; the nearest spot they'll collect from now is Lochinver. I don't even know where Lochinver is. It's certainly not on the Cape Wrath Trail, that's for sure.'

'It's on the west coast, near that mountain called Suilven.'

We'd seen Suilven once, from a distance, when we'd hitch-hiked in the Highlands in our early twenties. We'd always intended to go back to see it up close, but never did.

'Oh, I remember, but what do we do with the van between now and then? And it's way off the trail.' I look across the campsite, at the handful of scattered camper vans and a flock of sheep making their way down from the hillside to the shelter of the bay. 'We could leave it here, I suppose, move it as far back from the sea as we can and put the money for a week in the honesty box, walk to Lochinver, then come back and pick it up. At least that way the trail will start from Sheigra rather than even further south in Lochinver.'

'We'll need to make up a trail diversion. It's a good job we've got the OS maps.'

The wheatears collect on the dunes, picking among the white shells.

'The Sheigra Trail?'

'So it seems.'

The rucksacks stand propped together, back-to-back, supporting one another, as I lace up the black army boots. I close the van door. Closing the door on safety and a way out, on easy access to food and water and security, on warm shelter and news of the outside world, on dry socks, cosy blankets, a comfortable bed and pillows. I'm more afraid than excited. My eyes are drawn once more to the horizon, to the waves that seem to lift and stretch its line. I don't want to walk a step further, I want to stay here, with the familiar sense of being held by the coastline, bound by an invisible thread floating on the salt air. Moth locks the van, puts the key in a zipped pocket and we face away from the waves, towards the dark interior. I know what he's thinking – this trail is far more remote and difficult than he feels capable of; he wouldn't be here if I hadn't put the idea in his head. And he knows I know.

The Sheigra Trail

Sheigra to Fort William

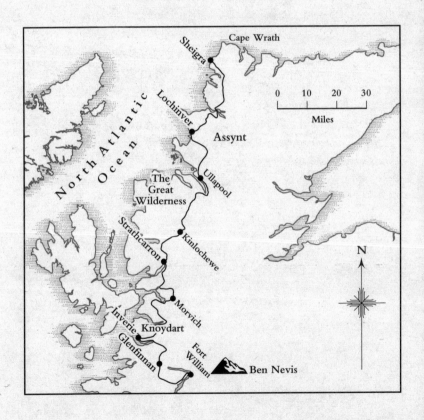

7

'You canna come in — stay at the door. What do you want? I'll bring it to you.'

The shopkeeper leans across the threshold, hands us a bag of food, and we leave the tiny scattered fragment of civilization behind. We follow the stream from the lay-by at Rhiconich. For a while the landscape is something we understand, ordinary moorland and well-known vegetation, but as we turn away from the stream the views spread out over a vast unknown land. I'm strangely comforted by the excessive weight of the rucksack on my back, stuffed full with food. In this empty landscape it could be days before we can buy more.

Black heather stretches on for miles, snapping and brittle as we brush past it, and ahead, in the far distance, Arkle. I remember seeing this mountain on a stamp, made from a painting by Prince Charles, but I think he must have been looking at a different mountain. What lies ahead of us looks nothing like the stamp. A black fin of rock rises up from the ground, a giant wedge of darkness that could still be forming, breaking through the crust below to loom threateningly over the boggy, rocky landscape. According to geology websites it's formed of glittering quartz over Lewisian gneiss, but there's nothing glittering here. Maybe it's the dark gathering skies that hang over the black mountain, or the thousands of acres of dead or dying heather, but this landscape feels intimidating, threatening even, and I'm slightly afraid. Moth looks back at me and I know he feels the same. We want to go back to the van.

There's a river ahead, lined by a few low-growing shrubs and stunted, twisted rowan trees. There's no way over without wading, so we walk along the bank looking for a shallow point.

Suddenly, like a jack-in-a-box when you haven't seen the box, a man appears from behind the shrubs, making my chest pound with the surprise of seeing him in this desolate, empty landscape. Dressed from head to foot in tweed, a long jacket and plus-fours, ending at his knees above long woollen socks and leather boots, he looks every bit the stereotypical English country gentleman, the ideal sold by catalogues of 'country' clothing aimed at foreign markets. But when he opens his mouth, he's as Scottish as the mountains.

'Good day to you. Are you here for the fishing?'

'No, we're just walking.'

'Walking out here, why? You must be mad!'

'Why are you here?'

'The fishing, of course. Grand fishing here. I've been up at the lochan on the side of Foinne Bhein since first light, just a couple of miles away on the hill.' He nods to the north. It looks like miles of tortuous rocks, bogs and pools of water, yet he seems totally unfazed by the distance or the landscape. I'm beginning to wonder if we've just encountered a slightly delusional tourist practising a too-strong Scottish accent, when I notice his fishing equipment by the river.

'What have you caught today?'

'Nothing. But the fishing's grand here. Aye, it's grand. Well, away with your walking. Don't know why anyone would want to be walking here.'

I look across the miles of dead heather towards the lochan in the hills. Obviously that's not walking, that's just fishing.

We ford the river with our boots over our shoulders, through water as cold as the glacial meltwaters of Iceland. It isn't too deep, or fast running, but Moth's tense and picks his way across with extreme care. I pass him my pole so he can steady himself with two. In this dark oppressive landscape, knee-deep in icy water, I'm finding it hard to fight a rising sense of foreboding. Watching Moth crawl up the riverbank on his hands and knees I'm more afraid than I've ever been in the wild. If I hadn't put the idea on the table we'd still be safely in Cornwall. There'd be no hope of Moth's health improving, but at least he wouldn't be in any danger. I put my boots back on, hoping that we don't find ourselves in the deep bogs described by collie-man, fearing how Moth will cope if we do. But as I do so, I catch sight of my feet. Already pink, and rubbed on my big toes and heels. I should have known. When will I ever learn?

Wet bog and black heather go on and on. Apparently, this type of landscape is known as 'knock and lochan', a low-lying, glacially formed topography that's eroded along the lines of the weakest rocks, where the knocks are low hillocks of rock smoothed by passing ice and the lochans are the small lakes that are scattered between. A landscape that covers a lot of the north-western corner of Scotland and through the Hebridean islands, it forms most obviously over zones of Lewisian gneiss. Comforting, to some small extent, to know, as we put the tent up on a flat patch of damp bog, just above a lochan but on the leeward side of a knock, that the rock beneath our feet hasn't visibly moved for millennia. Although not comforting enough, as the bog water forms pools in the porch of the tent and feels like a waterbed to lie on. I sit in the tent and unlace the army boots with a sense of dread, knowing without looking that the knocks aren't the only thing to have eroded in this desperate landscape.

I daren't take my socks off, so instead unroll one of the new airbeds that we invested in. Not too heavy, but much thicker and more supportive than our old ones, bought in the hope that they would provide Moth with a full night's sleep. Unlike the self-inflating mats we've used before, these inflate by applying pressure with both hands on an intake valve built into one side of the mat, then pumping as if you're administering first aid to someone who's just had a cardiac arrest. These worked perfectly when I inflated them on the floorboards in Cornwall, but now I'm pressing the valve and nothing's happening. Moth takes the gas stove and sits on a knock to make tea. He doesn't usually use the stove as it's too fiddly for his unresponsive fingers, and too risky – he might incorrectly attach the titanium head to the gas and then ignite something that could turn into a flame thrower.

'Leave the tea. I'll do it in a minute.'

I put the valve on my foot, then begin to press, holding my foot rigid against the force of the pressure from my hands. Sweating, down to a T-shirt in the cold wind, my head feeling as if it's going to explode, my left foot cramped and sending shooting pains up my shin . . . only a hundred presses later and the mat is inflated. It is impressively thick and supportive, but I'm on the point of needing resuscitation myself and can't possibly inflate the second one yet. I force my feet back into the boots before crawling out to take huge gulps of air. But as I try to walk to the knock where Moth's sitting I can hardly put my feet to the ground. They're balls of hot pain. I know what I've done, but I'm too embarrassed by my own stupidity to say anything to Moth, so sit on the rock and make the tea. How many hundreds of miles do I have to walk before I finally learn that well-fitted boots are more important on a walk than anything else?

'How are your feet? Are the boots okay?' I try to sound calm, casual even.

'They're great, probably the most comfortable boots I've ever worn.'

For a moment I envy his lack of feeling in his feet. 'Maybe you should just take them off and check.'

'I will, when I get in the tent. How are yours?'

I search for words to describe the pain I'm feeling, but there are none. 'Bit sore, but you know me and boots, always a bit sore for a day or two. I'm sure they'll be fine.' We drink the tea, shivering in the wind while the water boils to heat up some dried rice and peas.

'Do you want me to blow up the other mat?'

I imagine Moth trying to contort his six-foot-two-inch frame in the tent in order to inflate the mat. It's great that he offered, but he'd have found it tricky when he was a bendy thirty-year-old, and virtually impossible now. 'It's okay, it shouldn't take too long now I've got the hang of it.'

I fall back into the tent, hold my breath and take the boots off, then twist myself into position ready for the next one hundred pumps. Finally, the second mat's inflated and together they fill the whole of the bottom of the tent, very comfy, and thick enough to level out all the bumps and sharp bits. Moth gets in and removes his boots and socks, revealing perfectly normal, undamaged feet. We eat the rice.

'Are you going to check your feet then? You can't keep putting it off, I can see the way you're walking.'

I peel my socks off and it's worse than I feared. A one-inch blister sits in a smooth bubble on my left big toe, the ball of the same foot is red and swollen and my right heel is unbearable to touch. 'Shit.'

'Oh fuck, how have you done that on the first day?'

'I'm such an idiot, I should have known better than bring boots I've hardly worn.'

'Well, look on the bright side: at least your feet are dry. They'd have been soaking in your others. Do you want to go back?'

'No, I don't want to backtrack over the horrid ground we've covered today. I'll patch them up with blister plasters, they'll be fine.'

Of course I want to go back, but I fear that if we get back into the van so soon it won't be just Moth who wants to return to Cornwall. Instead, Moth takes a needle from the sewing kit, sterilizes it in a mug of tea and pops the blister as we watch rain blow in, turning the dark landscape black.

The sun rises in a watery glow as I make blister plaster bootees in an attempt to save what's left of my feet. It takes two whole boxes of plasters. I thought bringing four boxes was over cautious, but it won't be anywhere near enough. I'm not the only one suffering. Moth's feet are painful, his shoulders and back are stiff from carrying the weight of his rucksack over such difficult ground and, as we head away from the protection of our knock, he's finding it hard to walk in a straight line. Following him feels like driving a car with the wheels out of alignment: he needs to steer to the right to stay out of the hedge on the left. We stop for a moment and Moth spreads the map on a rock. Very soon we'll hit a road that follows Loch Stack down to Loch More and the idea of walking a couple of miles on tarmac instead of bog is irresistible. We turn left up the road, leaving the carefully plotted line on the map, heading into previously unconsidered territory that will lead us towards Lochinver. The relief is instant. The scraping pain in my feet reduces to a burning heat and Moth can hold a straight line by following the verge. It doesn't last; very soon we're crossing a boggy hillside, but thankfully distracted by views towards the monstrous black giant of Quinag that fills the skyline. We've only crossed a few miles, but it's already late afternoon as we reach a windy loch-side and check the map.

'There's a hotel over there at Kylesku, maybe we can sit inside for a while, have a cup of tea and work out how to get to Lochinver.'

Moth doesn't answer; he's asleep with his head propped on his hand. I can already see there's no sign of life outside the hotel and, like most of this corner of Scotland, it's probably closed. The wind rises from the west, blowing up the small sea loch and whistling through a chunky metal bridge – a huge Meccano-like construction, totally alien in this remote wilderness landscape. Shivering in the cold wind, I fish in the rucksack for the down jacket. I'm wrapping it around Moth's shoulders while eating a biscuit, when a snorting noise behind me makes me leap in fright. A large black pig is poking its nose through a wire fence, obviously keen on a biscuit too. Reluctant to get my hand too close to the mouth full of teeth, I throw her a biscuit through the fence, then instantly regret it. What if Lochinver's closed too – who knows where we'll find any more food? A wave of panic blows up the loch. What if we get to Lochinver and we can't get provisions, what if we can't get a lift or a taxi back to pick up the van? We certainly don't have enough food to last while we walk back to Sheigra on what would then be a tortuous, circular, very hungry route. Undoubtedly if that were to happen, we would just give up and go back to Cornwall, writing off this whole trip as a disaster. The pig snorts really loudly, waking Moth up. I put the duvet jacket away and we walk on, across the noisy bridge towards the hotel, which is inevitably closed.

A cold blast of wind shakes the tent, waking us to a grey view north and low cloud obscuring the summit of Quinag. There are only two viable ways to Lochinver from our camp behind a boulder on the northern side of the mountain: either follow the small, winding coastal road for many miles as it weaves up and down and in and out, or follow a path south across the lower slopes of the mountain until we hit the main road heading west. Going overland in a direct line will be impossible, it's a landscape of more lochans than knocks. We follow the steep narrow road up to the shoulder of Quinag until we find the path heading south. High on the hillside the views to the west are wide and endless. Or would be if the cloud hadn't now dropped so low that we walk through fog, with no smell of the sea or views of the Summer Isles. We barely speak, too focused on not losing the faint, tenuous path, with the threatening black monster rising invisibly to one side and the impassable bogland to the other. It's early evening by the time we reach the road; we've only crossed a few miles but Moth's exhausted from the concentration and desperate to close his eyes and sleep. Instead we walk west up the road, hoping that a car might stop, but no vehicles pass.

'We must have some reception on this side of the hill, shall we check the internet and see if we can find a taxi?' I'm hoping we can get a taxi into town and find somewhere to sleep; if not we need a flat patch for the tent very soon, or he'll be asleep standing up.

'Yeah, I'm done.'

I check, but there's still no reception.

We hear a car coming out of the mist, going in the opposite direction. Neither of us have our thumb out, but it pulls to a stop anyway.

'What you doing up here in the fog? I could have run you over!' A man with a grey beard and a woollen hat that nearly covers his eyes leans out of the window.

'Heading down into Lochinver. Thanks for stopping, but we're going the other way.'

'What you going there for? Everything's closed, except one B & B and the shop for an hour in the morning.'

'It's a long story.' Moth seems too tired to bother with an explanation.

'Well, get in out of the rain and tell me it.'

'What about Covid?'

'Fuck that, just get in anyway.'

We get into the battered red estate car, loading our sodden rucksacks into the boot among cardboard boxes, waterproof coats and plastic toys. Moth starts to explain about the van being at Sheigra, so needing a taxi, as the man starts the car and begins to drive east, away from Lochinver.

'No, no, sorry, we can't go this way, we need to go to Lochinver to get a taxi back north to pick up the van.' But he doesn't stop driving and we're already heading past where we joined the road, in completely the wrong direction. What have we done? We're in a car with a complete stranger taking us away from where we need to be. What if he's a madman, or a serial killer? Have we just been abducted? I try to think what else was in the boot, had I seen anything that could be used as a weapon, or could we just jump out while the car's moving? I decide against it, Moth has a vest but that doesn't make him Bruce Willis. Far more practically, he just shouts instead.

'NO, STOP.' The car screeches to a stop.

'What, what's happening?' The man turns around flustered.

'I don't know where you're going but we need to go to Lochinver to get a taxi.'

'I thought you said you wanted to go to Sheigra.'

'We do, but we'll have to get a taxi from Lochinver to get there.'

'You won't get a taxi, they're not running – well, they are, but only for locals.'

What have we done? We're in a remote corner of the country, miles away from a van that we need to have collected in two days and no way of getting back to pick it up. I'm fifty-eight but beginning to think I had more sense when I was eighteen. Now we're in a car that has taken us miles in the opposite direction.

'Aye, no way you'll get a taxi.'

'So where were you taking us?'

'Kylesku. I'm going to see a man about a pig.'

'But we've just walked from there.'

'Aye, you would have.'

'Then why have you picked us up? This makes no sense!'

'It was raining. I'll take you up to Sheigra, but I need to see the man about the pig first. So can we go now?'

'But it's miles out of your way.'

'Aye, it is, but there's nothing else to be done.' He starts the car and we drive back into Kylesku, the engine rattling so loudly it's impossible to try to speak. Moth shrugs his shoulders, settles into the seat and closes his eyes.

The van still sits exactly where we left it, by the fence in the corner of the campsite. We shove petrol money and a torrent of thanks into David's hand and as quickly as he appeared, he's gone. A rare and gentle man, prepared to make a sixty-mile round trip for complete strangers. We unlock the van, pull the bed out, and Moth is asleep within seconds. The clouds begin to break and although it's nearly midnight it's still light enough to see sheep on the shoreline and waves catching the moonlight out at sea. The Highland semi-darkness eventually fades into night, but the scene remains: a painting in blue shadows.

8

Lochinver sits on the west coast, at the head of a small sea loch, in the shadow of the Assynt mountains. Built on a history and tradition of fishing and the movement of fish, now it spreads quietly along the loch-side, with hardly any movement on the streets, or in the sea, other than large red deer that sleep on doorsteps and promenade along the seafront. We drive around until we find the one B & B that David mentioned and hope that it's open, as Moth needs a proper night's sleep, somewhere to take a moment and decide what happens next. If we let the van go tomorrow we're committed, or stranded, depending how you look at it. And we need food, enough to take us through to Ullapool, the biggest town in the Highlands, but a few days' walking away from here.

The couple who own the B & B welcome us in; of course they have a room, 'There's no one around right now.' They show us to a huge room with views across the harbour.

'There aren't any boats in. Do they just come on the high tide?' It's a harbour renowned for fish, yet I can't see a single fishing boat.

'No, we don't get the trawlers in like we used to. Not so long ago the Klondyke boats used to come in and fish would go all over Europe from here. They built a harbour extension to support them, then they stopped coming. The British fishing's gone now, it's all processed out at sea on the factory ships and the harbour's empty. So much money spent, and it's come to nothing. We're really glad of the Spanish and French boats coming in now, at least they keep the harbour open.'

We sit on a bench watching deer grazing on the football pitch, neither of us wanting to bring up the subject that sits between

us, unspoken. Not really an elephant in the room, more something the size of a factory ship in the harbour. Eventually I have
to break the silence.

'How are you feeling about it all now? It's not too late to can-
cel the van collection; we'd have to pay something, but I'd rather
that than you trying to carry on just because it's all arranged,
when really you're sure you can't.'

'We could just stay in the van, work our way south, do day
walks along the way.' Moth stands by the wire netting, clearly
deep in thought about what he's saying, running his fingers
across the mesh as the deer graze their way closer.

'We could.' I've feared it would come to this, even before we
left Cornwall. The chance of him pulling out because it's such a
tough trail has been possible since the first moment he agreed to
walk. If that's the only reason. 'Are you thinking this trail is too
hard, that carrying on will be too hard?' I hold my breath,
unsure whether to say it, but it comes out of my mouth anyway.
'Or maybe you think it's too difficult to even try, maybe what
you really want is just to give up, just give in and go back to sit
on the sofa and wait for this thing to overtake you.'

He gives me a sharp look through narrowed eyes, shaking his
head as he sits back on the bench and looks over the empty harbour to squalls of rain out at sea. 'You always knew it was too
hard.'

'But *you* know why we decided to try.'

'I didn't decide anything, you know how hard I find making
decisions now.' His hands slowly move around each other as he
gently massages his numb left hand with his shaky right. 'That's
why I think we should carry on, let the van go tomorrow
because when it's gone there are no more decisions to make,
we're just walking.' He stops rubbing his left hand and reaches
out and holds mine. 'No matter how much you force me to keep
going, you know as well as I do that this illness has gone too far
now. So let's make the most of it while we're here. I think we
both know I'll never be here again.'

The squall moves closer to shore as we sit in silence, tears dripping from my chin. He's wrong; he has to be wrong. I can't allow myself to think that this is the last time we'll be together in this wild empty landscape. But he's wrong about something else too. If we carry on there'll be endless decisions to make, from trivial to life-threatening, and I can't make them alone.

The couple from the B & B make us a plate of sandwiches while we empty the van of everything we might need and secure everything else for the journey back to Cornwall. Tomorrow, it will be just us and our rucksacks.

Roberto ties the van to his trailer, takes photos of it looking suitably secured, then jumps into his four-by-four to tow it away. He lives his life on the roads, crossing the country from north to south, east to west, on a daily basis, sleeping in hotels, service stations and lay-bys. Not an easy life, not one that many people would choose, but one that's allowed his family to live comfortably even though they rarely see him.

'Okay, I'm off, but I still think you're mad. Why would you send your van home and say you're going to walk? You make no sense.'

As the van disappears around the corner I want to run after it. I feel as if I've just jumped off a life-raft in a stormy sea because I fancied a swim. He's right: it makes no sense.

We head into the foothills of Assynt and the world turns to gold. Every hillside is covered in a golden glow. In the first real sunlight we've seen since we left Sheigra the green gorse bushes, usually barely noticeable in the green landscape, have burst into flower, filling the air with the smell of coconut and bathing the path in their reflected golden light. But behind the glowing hills of gorse, a rounded dome of dark rock fills the skyline. Suilven. A pillar of Torridonian sandstone and Lewisian gneiss, set in a landscape eroded away by glaciers, and recently made famous by a film about an old lady who defies the call of the care home and escapes to Scotland to climb this mountain. I try to forget the part of the film where she nearly dies in a storm as she crosses the very bit of landscape we're heading into.

'Did you hear that?' Moth has stopped and is listening intently. I listen but I can only hear the wind.

'I can't hear a thing.'

'Quiet and just listen, don't tell me you can't hear that.'

'What?'

'I'm sure it's a cuckoo.'

I haven't heard a cuckoo in England for years and I can't hear one now. They were a common summer visitor when I was a child, but are now a protected species on the Birds of Conservation Concern Red List and a priority species on the UK Biodiversity Action Plan, so the likelihood of him actually hearing one is slight. Although not impossible here in Scotland. Tracked birds have shown that most English cuckoos migrate back to Africa south-west via Spain, where droughts are drastically reducing their food supplies, meaning many of the birds don't make it. But Scottish and Welsh birds tend to head south-east through Italy, where there are much better feeding conditions, meaning more birds safely make it home for the winter. No one really knows why their routes differ, or what winds direct their fate. I listen hard, hoping to hear what he can hear, but I can't, all I can hear is laughter.

Groups of young people begin to pass us, twos and threes, then larger groups. Every time we ask them where they're heading we get the same reply: 'Suilven.' Eventually, after possibly thirty people have passed, we have to ask why so many of them are heading up the incredibly steep side of Suilven in the late afternoon, when there's hardly enough room on the narrow top for them all to collect.

'We're just going up for the night.'

'Is it some kind of celebration?'

'Na, there's just nothing much else to do in Lochinver on a Wednesday night.'

I try to imagine some of the young people I've met in so many rural areas and the trouble that boredom leads them into. It makes me wonder: if they had a notoriously difficult to climb, 730-metre-high mountain, just seven miles from their doorstep, would they head for the summit on a Wednesday night, or continue trashing the bus shelter for entertainment?

The tent looks very small on the stony shore of Loch na Gainimh, totally overshadowed by the sheer-sided immensity of Suilven rising on the opposite side of the loch. The temperature drops rapidly as the sun sets, sending shafts of bright yellow light across the northern side of the mountain, highlighting the gully that allows access up the side of this seemingly unclimbable pillar of rock. I watch Moth, bent over a stream that feeds the loch, filling the water bottles with water so clear that only its movement makes it visible, and just for a moment, as the lights of the party on the summit begin to glow, I have a sense that maybe the remote isolated beauty of this place might just be enough to draw Moth forward, maybe we might actually be able to find our way through this remote landscape and wherever that journey leads. Then I take my boots off, pull the socks away from the glue of the plasters and feel the skin lifting from my toes and I'm not so sure.

The rights exercised by the group of young people to access the mountain and spend the night wild camping on its summit, the same rights that are allowing us to sleep at its base, are enshrined in Scotland's Land Reform Act of 2003. This gives everyone the statutory right to pass over the land, to remain and then leave the land, for recreational or educational purposes, allowing for the 'furthering' of that person's 'understanding' of their 'natural or cultural heritage'. There's no encouragement to further our understanding of our natural heritage in England – rather the opposite. To do the same thing in England would make this group of young people guilty of trespass under civil law, effectively making wild camping against the law in England. But there's a great deal of fear among the rambling community that this civil liability could soon become a criminal liability. We left Cornwall at a time when the Police, Crime, Sentencing and Courts Bill was passing through parliament, a bill which will criminalize trespass in England and Wales. If the bill becomes law and trespass is criminalized then the wording 'unauthorized encampments' will allow wild camping to fall under the Act of Parliament and become illegal. Overnight an ancient way of using the land will be lost. Only time will tell how this plays out, but at a moment when the need to reconnect people to nature is one of the greatest challenges we face, England is actually moving in the opposite direction. How are we to teach our children, not just about the beauty of the land they inhabit, or of the need to preserve the wildlife and habitats they share it with, but of its existential importance for our own future existence, if they can't access it? How can any of us understand that we're just a small part of a vast, living, breathing ecosystem if the closest we come to that is the local park? As the night fades into darkness and the lights on the mountain become brighter, I think about the young people on the summit, safe in a landscape where they belong, and how they compare to the youths in the bus shelter, acting as they choose in a land they believe belongs to them.

The zip on the tent door won't move; it's frozen closed. I rub my hands together to make them as warm as I can, then run my fingers up and down the zip until it finally shifts and the flap folds open as if it's made of wood. Outside, the tent is covered in ice and the warm air of yesterday has been swept away by a cold blast straight from the Arctic. Billowing, pink-lit clouds are dropping snow in showers to the west and we're shivering as we wait for the ice to melt so we can pack the tent away. But my feet aren't cold in my boots, they're balls of burning hot pain and I daren't move, afraid that every step will rip off more skin. With the tent packed away, standing still isn't an option in this freezing air, so we begin to walk east, following a winding path between drumlins through the wide glacial valley between Suilven and Canisp, another giant of rock to the north of the path. Something catches my eye on a ridgeline among the foothills. Silhouetted across the top of the hill, like native Americans in a 1950s western, is a herd of deer. Individual against the skyline, motionless, watching our slow movement through their territory. We walk on as the snow begins to fall, always observed, never alone, accompanied by the long-repeated call of a bird I don't know.

The mountains turn from mile-long pillars of rock to sharp fins as they recede behind us, their bulk disappearing with the changing perspective. The snow begins to settle, soft but quickly becoming two inches deep and obscuring the path. Moth hunches behind a boulder, out of the wind, a crust of snow forming over his hat and rucksack as we share a packet of crackers.

'Can you walk any further today, maybe get a little closer to the road? It's a wild spot to be in if this snow really begins to fall.' Moth looks tired and ready to sleep and I really don't want to ask him to keep going, but as the snow gets deeper the features in the landscape are blurring. We've already wandered off the path and I can't see the way back to it.

'Didn't we hitch-hike down that road once? It was fairly quiet, if I remember it right, so if this is real snow and not just May-afternoon snow, then maybe we could follow it into Ullapool, rather than go through the hills.'

How can he remember a walk from nearly forty years ago, but can't remember where he put the cheese to go with the crackers?

The landscape is white and doesn't seem to correspond with the features on the map; we're about to stop and find the compass when we almost bump into a high deer fence. It must be quite a new fence, as hoof prints run alongside it in both directions, where the deer have tried to find a way through but are blocked from their normal route up the hillside. We follow their hoof prints downhill, towards a loch near the road.

It's probably human nature to hold a happy memory of a place and think it will always be the same: the same idyllic view, the same quiet country road. But in reality that quiet road, where once the only traffic was an occasional tourist, the odd tractor and the post bus, has actually turned into the NC500 and is nose-to-tail with coaches, camper vans and drivers who treat it like a speedway. Snow or no snow, it's too dangerous to follow the road. A few hundred metres ahead we can see a sign, so spy on it through the monocular. It's a tea room, and it's open. A place to dry off, check the map and make a plan. Hugging the fence at the roadside we walk towards it as quickly as we can. But when we're twenty metres away a girl walks down the trackway from the tea room towards the sign.

'She's going to take the sign in.' We try to hurry to beat her to it, but my feet can't run; with each step it feels as if they're being shredded. We reach the sign at the same time as her.

'Please don't close, we just need somewhere out of the snow for half an hour while we work out where we're going. And maybe a mug of tea.'

'Well, just for a minute, but no food, only tea.'

We follow her up a gravel track to the tiny Elphin Tearooms, dumping the rucksacks by the door where they begin to steam. An older lady brings us two mugs of tea.

'What you old dudes doing out there in the snow?' She's obviously Australian, and probably an older dude than us.

'Heading to Ullapool. We walked down this road years ago so thought we'd do that, but it's changed a bit.'

'Some old guys at the Highlands Initiative thought it was a good idea to relabel the roads – you know, make them a route, a destination. Thought it would bring some money, be good for tourism. Well, it did that all right, but jeez, it turned the road into a motorway and changed the Highlands completely.'

'I'm sure lots of people have a better standard of living now,

but it's sad, it was always the remoteness that made the Highlands such a special place to visit.'

'Yep, a lot better standard of living, especially for those who
knew it was coming and bought up hotels on the route.'

'Oh.'

'Yeah, "oh". Meantime little villages along the route, well,
they're ruined by coachloads of visitors and, worse still, the
camper vans. They're all hired, which means the drivers don't
know how to drive them. So many crashes now. Anyway, do
you want food?'

'The waitress said it was too late.'

'I'm an Aussie in the Highlands, it's never too late for food.'

We spread the map on the table and start to plot a new route,
but push it aside to make way for a pile of ham and cheese
toasties.

'So, how are you gonna get to Ullapool? You can't walk
down that road, you'll die.'

'We were just looking at the map: we could go east and rejoin
the Cape Wrath Trail in Glen Oykel, but we need to go to
Ullapool for supplies, so that's taking us out of our way. I think
we might stay west of the road and skirt the edge of Coigach,
pick up a few paths going south towards the River Runie and
the coast.' Moth's finger traces the pencil line we've just drawn
on the map.

'You can't do that, it's just boglands down there and in the
snow you won't see them coming. Nope, you're gonna eat that
toastie and I'm gonna get you into Ullapool.'

'How?'

'My mate's a taxi driver; he'll come out and get you.'

'But that feels like cheating.'

How can he think anything is cheating? We're not even on
the trail now.

'Fuck cheating, she's walking nowhere, look at her feet.'

I have my boots off, trying to unpeel the plasters from the
blood and mud-soaked socks.

'Shit, Ray, why didn't you say they were that bad.' Moth immediately has his glasses on looking at my feet.

'It's trivial compared to what you put up with every day. And it's my own fault for bringing these stupid boots, my fault we're here at all.'

'Don't give me that crap.' He turns to shout after the woman as she heads to the telephone: 'Thanks a lot, we'll definitely take the taxi.' He puts my sock back on. 'Don't do that, don't hide things because they don't feel as important as me fucking dying. How the hell have you been walking with those? They must be agony.'

'They are.'

We get into Gordon's taxi, leaving the saviours of the Elphin Tearooms behind. He has all the windows open 'to blow the Covid out'. I'm not sure how it works for viruses but it certainly blows the shower curtain he has hanging between the front and rear seats as a protective screen. Gordon's a native of Ullapool, his whole life has been spent in this small town on the edge of a sea loch. He tells us he used to run a guest house for the Klondyke fishermen, 'but they don't come any more', so he drives his taxi instead. As we head down to the coast we dip below the snow-line and back into weather that's just a very cold May in the north of Scotland. Without asking, Gordon takes us to his friend's guest house.

'It's okay, we'll go to the campsite.'

'No you won't, they're only taking the big camper vans that have their own toilets and water – it's the Covid, they're not taking tents or anyone who needs to share facilities.'

'Does your friend have any vacancies?'

'Aye, I've already booked you in, he's expecting you.'

Suddenly, unexpectedly, life feels normal. I know how the people of the far north felt about strangers; the pandemic has made the most welcoming people wary of outsiders – we'd been the same in Cornwall, staying behind the wall, reluctant to speak to anyone we didn't know. But to suddenly be greeted by the openness we so often take for granted comes as a warm reminder of normal life, like arriving unannounced at a friend's house to find a slice of cake waiting for you and the kettle already on the boil.

I sit in the porch and unlace the boots, holding my breath and distracting myself by watching a man walking up and down the car park opposite playing the bagpipes, then pull them off quickly as the hot pain spreads to my ankles.

'Aye, he's the world champion of pipe players, but you get a lot of those in the Highlands. How long are you staying for?'

Moth answers before I have a chance.

'Three nights if we can.'

The owner shows us to a small room at the back. It could be a cupboard and I'd be grateful, but this is cupboard luxury, with two big single beds and a shower.

'Why did you say three nights? We'll never get to Fort William if we keep stopping.' I don't know why I bother saying it, it doesn't really matter. This already feels as if it's the end of a very unsuccessful trail. Moth has had enough, as really I always knew he would, and my feet are shredded. I try to comfort myself with the thought that Mallory made two attempts to climb Everest, and died on the second, so for our feeble attempt to walk the Cape Wrath Trail to end with us in Ullapool but still alive isn't that bad.

'Well, your feet are going to take a few days to heal before we can carry on. I'm going to catch the owner before he disappears and ask for a bowl and some salt.' I watch him walk out of the door, exhausted, the same leaning gait, but more positive than he's been for a while. Confident that I'll be able to buy more blister plasters in town, I peel off the ripped, blood-streaked old ones, taking layers of skin with them. My feet are raw and I've completely lost the feeling in my big toe.

Moth puts a handful of salt in a bowl of water and watches as I put my feet in. For a second the warmth is soothing, but then the salt finds the open wounds and I have to bite my hand to stop myself screaming.

'Good, keep them in there for a bit, I'll put the kettle on.'

When the Scottish civil engineer, Thomas Telford, designed the herring port at Ullapool, his thoughts were probably focused on the technical details of the steel structure and the depth of water in Loch Broom. He probably didn't consider that over three hundred years later, a large village would have grown around his construction, or that the main use for the port wouldn't be for the landing of herring, but for the landing of tourists and freight going to and from Stornaway in the Hebrides. Maybe it's the dark backdrop of hills and mountains, or the reflection of miles of yellow gorse, or just the angle of the sun, but there's a luminous quality to Loch Broom; something about the way the light seems to spark into fragments as it catches the sea reminds me of St Ives in Cornwall. And like St Ives, Ullapool's becoming a centre for artists: painters, ironworkers and weavers, all attracted to this remote northern outpost by the light in the summer and the isolation in the winter. I understand the draw of this place, after only a few days I'm feeling a sense that part of me might never leave. We sit on the stony shore of the loch eating chips and watching for otters. Apparently there are many otters here, but not today. Unlike the seagulls, they've probably seen the rows of huge camper vans on the campsite just back from the shore, weighed up the value of eating scraps against the intrusion of cameras and noise and chosen to move to a quieter spot down the loch to focus on the fish.

'There's that noise again. I could swear it's a cuckoo.'

I listen as intently as I can, but all I can hear is the call of the oystercatchers skimming low over the water and the horn of the ferry as it pulls out of the harbour. 'I can't hear anything. I think you're imagining it.'

'I'm not. I definitely heard something. Anyway, let's go to the outdoor shop and find you some different boots, you can't carry on in those.'

My feet are freezing in the plastic sandals I brought for river crossings, but far less painful now they're out of the boots. 'Not sure if they'll be any better in yet another pair of new boots.'

'Well, let's see anyway.'

The tiny cramped outdoor shop holds every piece of outdoor gear you can imagine, for hikers, climbers and everyone in between. But no boots in my size.

'It's a popular size, that's why we haven't got any.'

'Surely that's why you would have them.'

'No, they've all sold out and we can't get any more.' I feel as if the man serving me is speaking a foreign language. Why can't the shop get any more stock in their most popular size? 'It's because they're coming through Europe. Brexit means all our stock is held up in the ports and it can't get through. It's hard enough to get stock this far north anyway without all this extra hassle. We didn't even vote for Brexit but we're the ones suffering for it.'

I buy all the blister plasters they have and two pairs of new, glue-free socks, and hope that my feet heal quickly.

Back on the loch-side we sit on a picnic bench and share a cake we bought from the deli. Moth raises the cake to his mouth, the tremor in his hand as obvious as ever. Maybe this walk was always going to be impossible; he's exhausted, his shoulders are aching more than normal from the weight of his rucksack, the numbness in his feet turns to pain within a few miles of beginning to walk each day, meaning we either stop shortly after getting started or he just tries to tolerate it, and I feel nothing but guilt as I watch him struggle. Just a few days into this trail and we've already used all the painkillers I'd brought with me, thinking they'd be enough to last until we reached Fort William. It makes no sense to go on. We should probably admit defeat and get on the bus.

'I'm so sorry for almost forcing you to come here. You were

right, the time for walks like this has probably passed. You've accepted what's happening to you, maybe I need to find a way to accept it too and stop fooling myself that there's a way back, that I can keep you when you've already let go.'

Moth puts my half of the cake back in the bag and pushes it across the table towards me. 'Yes, you forced me. Not physically, but definitely mentally, in that way you have of making me think things I haven't thought of. But then I look at this – the loch, the incredible landscape we've walked through already – and I know you were right.'

'But it's too hard, and you're suffering, and I feel so guilty.'

'Yeah, so you should. Just eat the cake, then we'll buy our dried rations and head south tomorrow. Next stop Kinlochewe.'

We buy dried food to last a few days, empty the rucksacks of everything we can live without – spare clothes, a heavy penknife, spare batteries, sunglasses, spare notebooks, anything to lighten the packs and literally take the weight off our feet – and post them back to Cornwall. We're ready. Ready to cross the edge of the Great Wilderness.

9

We leave the guest house on Sunday morning, in search of Gordon who's going to take us to where the Cape Wrath Trail overlaps the treacherous NC500, but he's not there. Instead we see a man in the middle of the road, hoovering. He's in his late twenties with a big woollen hat and the electric cable of the hoover slung over his shoulder, hoovering as if he's cleaning his mum's living-room carpet.

'Hi. Um, you're hoovering the road.'

'Aye, I am.' He continues to do so.

'Why? Surely it'll just get dirty again?'

'That's Saturday night in Ullapool for you.' I realize he's outside a pub. 'I'm hoovering broken glass. There's a lot of wildlife around here – lots of deer are down right now, they'll cut their feet, so I canna leave it.' He pulls his hat down and carries on hoovering.

Gordon pulls up and we get into his taxi, on the back seat behind the shower curtain.

'Are there always a lot of deer in the village?'

'Aye, some, but a lot more than normal this year. They're hungry.'

'Isn't there any grass on the mountains?' I find it hard to imagine that in this vast open landscape there isn't enough grass for a few deer to eat, it's not as if we've even seen any sheep on the hills, so no livestock for the deer to share the grazing with.

'No, it's late coming this year. We had a really dry spell in the winter, a drought even, then harsh late frosts, now the snow. They're starving, just waiting for the grass to come – we all are, then they'll stop eating our fucking gardens.'

'We saw thousands of acres of heather further north that seemed as if it was dead. Do you think it is?'

'I've heard that, we'll just have to see if it comes back later in the summer, but it's not looking good. The weather's been getting stranger year after year, and it drives the deer down. Then everyone hates the deer. But it's not their fault; we'd do the same if we were starving.'

Gordon drops us off in a lay-by, does a U-turn in the road and speeds away north. This is it; we're truly turning inland. A daunting, almost claustrophobic realization settles over us that we might not see the sea again for weeks. After spending months living on the headlands of the South West Coast Path, then the following years within minutes of the sea, it's become an integral part of our lives, constant and necessary. But we turn away, climbing upwards under gathering clouds, past a herd of Highland cows grazing among trees at the base of An Teallac, an angry-looking mountain pointing black crenelated summits into the sky. Two young men yomp past, stopping only momentarily to ask where we're heading.

'Kinlochewe.'

They seem strangely pleased by our answer. 'So you're not going to Sheneval then?'

'No, hadn't planned to.'

'Good, good.' And they're gone, yomping into the distance. I'm sure they could make it to Kinlochewe in a day, rather than the three we've allocated. Sheneval is one of many bothies along this route, deserted houses and huts that have been utilized as shelters for walkers, probably the most famous as it has a greater recorded history than most – it was even used for an overnight stay by Prince Charles when he was a young man. But we've chosen to stay away from the bothies. The idea of sharing a hot damp enclosed environment with a bunch of sweaty strangers during a pandemic isn't too appealing.

Instead we eat more crackers on the edge of the Strathnasheallag Forest, looking south-west into the Fisherfield Forest. This is the most remote, inaccessible corner of Britain, where thousands of acres of mountain and bog have no road access, other than a few stalkers' trails, and virtually no trees. Lots of areas of mountain and moorland in Scotland are called forests, but there's hardly a tree to be seen. Six thousand years ago much of Scotland was covered in forests of birch, rowan, oak and pine, until humans began farming, clearing and burning patches of woodland. Despite that, much of the forest remained, until three thousand years ago and a climactic shift to cooler, wetter weather – a bad time for trees but great for peat expansion. By the time the Romans left, at least half of the Highland forests had disappeared. The Normans brought the word forest, but it didn't mean woodland as it does now; in their time it meant hunting grounds. And that's what the Highlands have remained. The expansion of the deer herds came soon after, hundreds of them nibbling off young trees, then the burning of the grouse moors, felling for war, industry and building, until we reached the point we're at now, where only 1 per cent of the old forest remains. Looking around, I can see the effects of deforestation have been absolute; the only trees here are in small patches of scrubby young birch and rowan.

Dark clouds are building in the east, bringing curtains of rain west, but we stay dry. All the rain seems to be funnelling down the valley ahead. The more we watch, the more it appears as if the valley holds some giant water magnet, sucking every drop from the sky.

'Glad we're not going down there.' I get the map out and try to read it as it flaps in the rising wind. Moth can't seem to locate where we are, but I can faintly see the pencil marks I hesitantly drew on when we were safely in Cornwall, ones I didn't trace over with ink. 'Oh, that's exactly where we're going.'

We're trying to refold the map in the wind when another couple appear.

'Where are you heading?'

'Kinlochewe. What about you?'

'Sheneval, just for the night, then back to Ullapool.' They head away down the Sheneval track and we follow the rain into the valley towards Loch an Nid. By the time we reach the valley bottom torrential rain is falling and immediately we're faced with a river to cross. We consider camping near a small group of flimsy trees, until the rain passes, but as we get closer we can see the flat land is all taken by a group of mountain bikers and their tents, so walk up and down the river looking for a shallow place to cross instead. More bikers ford the river, the water as high as their wheels, shouting through the rain as they pass.

'Where are you heading?'

'Kinlochewe. You?'

'Sheneval. Get beyond Nid this afternoon if you can, the rivers are rising.'

We need to cross this river, then another one at the other end of Loch an Nid, about three miles away, before we reach higher ground. It's late afternoon, but we should have plenty of time.

'What do you think?' Moth's pacing up and down the riverbank looking for a crossing place while the river rises by a foot as we hesitate.

'There's nowhere safe to camp here and Sheneval's going to be crammed, so shall we just go for it? We should be able to do three miles before the rivers are too high?'

Rain pours down, cascading from the mountainsides, as the hills become waterfalls. We wade across, thigh deep through powerful water, squelch across bogland in our plastic sandals and shelter behind a ruined wall to put our boots back on. I try to hold wet blister plasters in place with wet socks and we carry on through rain that pounds our faces in powerful jets.

Standing under an overhanging boulder on a narrow stony track, I watch Moth walk towards me. Even through the rain I can see he's exhausted, but we can't camp here, surrounded by waterfalls, we have no choice but to keep going. I wait for him to pass and follow behind, the consultant's words loud in my ears: 'Don't tire yourself, and be careful on the stairs.'

The valley narrows to a carved glacial U, with a river running with increasing fury through the bottom, as the path winds its way through the boulders of the rising moraine. The sky darkens and the afternoon turns into evening. Moth's finding it harder and harder to pick his way through the rocky landscape and our pace has slowed to a crawl.

'I don't know if I can go much further. Think we'll have to find somewhere to put the tent.' Moth is standing upright with his eyes closed, as if he could sleep where he stands. But there's nowhere to put the tent here, nothing but water, bog and stone.

'But where, I can't see anywhere? Maybe there'll be somewhere at the other end of the loch. I just hope that river hasn't risen too high.'

'Don't think I'll get that far.'

We stumble on, through rain that now seems to be driving horizontally up the valley from behind us. There are two figures ahead; as we get closer we see they're more mountain bikers.

'Hi. This seems a really popular valley for people on bikes. What's it all about? I can't imagine dragging a heavy bike through this difficult terrain.' Moth's trying to make conversation but I can see he barely has the strength to speak.

'It's the miles you can cover without ever seeing a road, you can just get lost out here.' The taller one's covered in mud from head to foot, water pouring from his clothes. 'We've come over from Strathcarron today, heading to Ullapool. It's been an incredible ride.'

'Wow, that's such a long way.'

'We'd have been there by now if you hadn't left the rubbish bag behind.' The smaller of the two wipes the mud from his face; he sounds annoyed but I can tell he's only joking. 'He left the bag with all today's rubbish in it where we had lunch, had to go back two miles to pick it up.'

For a moment I'm reminded of lockdown headlines in the newspapers of people heading into the countryside and leaving mountains of rubbish behind, and try to equate the two thought patterns.

'Doesn't matter, it's been a good day.' The tall one drinks

some water, then fixes the bottle back on to the bike frame. 'We've got to go if we're going to get to Ullapool tonight.'

'Watch out for the river at the end of the valley, it's rising.'

'Same the other end.'

We head away in our opposite directions, enveloped in the rain and out of sight within seconds.

We're almost at the loch when I turn to see Moth take a faltering step and catch his boot on a rock. The fall is instant. He's vertical, then his face is skidding through the water on the stony path, with no time between. The weight of his tall frame and the rucksack on his back force him to skim forwards, causing a plume of water to rise around his head like a jet-ski on a summer sea. He lies in the water, confused by the suddenness of the fall, but as I help him back on to his knees blood is running from his forehead, diluted into pink rain by the time it drips from his chin. He can't stand. For long minutes he's too confused and the blood continues to trickle down. Eventually I help him back to his feet.

We find a spot for the tent just a hundred metres away. Too close to the waterfall that drops from the loch and too near the river, but we have no choice. We climb inside, leaving the wet things to drip in the porch. Moth gets into his sleeping bag and I clean the cut on his head, holding the skin together with a stick-on suture. I'm not a first aider, definitely not the person you'd hope to be with if you had a heart attack, but I hold a finger in front of his face because I've seen it done by rugby medics to test for concussion. He thinks there are three. Perhaps that's a good sign – at least he can't see five. I try to Google for how to test for concussion, but there's no signal. I think I know the symptoms would be dizziness, lack of balance and nausea, but that's a fairly normal state of being for Moth, so quite an inconclusive test. He swallows some ibuprofen, maybe not the most effective treatment for concussion, while I boil water to heat up a packet of dried noodles; comforting familiarity to soothe our jangled nerves.

He takes more painkillers for a growing headache and we try to sleep. The sound of water is overwhelming: rain beating against the flysheet, water thundering down the waterfall, the deafening noise of the river cascading by. The chance of being washed away is more than a fear – it's a palpable reality.

In the early light the sound of water is lost beneath the roar of the wind, increasing in speed as it drives into the narrowest part of the valley. Bending and distorting the flexible poles of the tent, leaving us to ride out the storm in a strange elliptical nylon bubble. Eventually the need to pee forces us out of the tent, but as Moth unzips the door flap, he sits back suddenly, shushing me with his finger to his mouth.

'What? What is it?'

'Deer.'

We kneel together in the doorway, holding just a tiny section of the door flap open. Outside the tent are nine hinds and in the lee of a huge boulder a large stag standing separate to the herd. Older stags are rarely with the hinds outside of the breeding season, so to see him here with the hinds at the end of May isn't normal. We creep out of the tent as quietly as we can, but with the ferocity of the storm it's doubtful even the deer can hear us. They see us, but don't move, just continue to stand together, heads down with their backs to the wind. For a brief moment I look around, squinting my eyes as the rain lashes my face. I can see why the deer are here. They've risked being so close to humans because there's nowhere else to go. The boggy mountainside to the east is pouring with water, one giant waterfall funnelling rain in channels towards the river. Our small level platform is the only dry piece of ground in a turbulent maelstrom of water. They must have come down to escape the storm and then become trapped in the valley by the rising river, a boiling cascade of spume, fed by the angry, explosive waterfall from Loch an Nid above. On the opposite side of the river the mountain to the west rises in vast black slabs of rock, water racing in waves over their sheer smooth surface. In a dark niche in the rock, there's a shape, something big and black, some kind of creature, hiding.

'Get back in the tent, you're going to be soaked.'

I scramble back in, leaving everything dripping again in the porch. Moth's forehead is swollen, with a large blue bruise beginning to form in his hairline.

'How are you feeling?'

'Dizzy, pounding headache and I've got to say, a bit scared.'

Oh fuck, what if he's got a serious concussion, or even a fractured skull? We have no phone signal and, in this storm, no way out to find help.

'Do you think you've seriously hurt yourself?'

'I don't know. That wasn't what I meant though. If this water keeps rising, then we're really going to be in the shit.'

The rain continues to thunder on the flysheet, making my head rattle as if I'm inside a drum, while Moth slips in and out of sleep. I think we're already in the shit.

It's early evening when the drumroll of rain eases to an occasional patter, the wind lessens slightly and we venture out of the tent. The clouds are breaking, allowing bright shafts of evening sun across the mountainside. Then suddenly, as if the clouds were never there, the brightness intensifies and the valley becomes a cavern of crystal light. Every water droplet captures the low sun and reflects it back in myriad colours of infinite brilliance. We're speechless in the face of the beauty of this moment, I want to capture it, and hold it, and keep it forever, but my phone's in the tent and as the deer start to move apart I don't want to frighten them away. Over by the boulder the old stag shakes himself, like a dog fresh from the river, sending droplets of water flying into a rainbow of light around his body. I hold my breath as the brightness grows, until the whole valley becomes a shimmering world of light. Then, as suddenly as they left, the clouds return, the shadows darken. In the cleft in the rock, the dark creature shakes its sodden bedraggled feathers and emerges into the evening, a golden eagle spreading its huge wings, lifting into the sky and riding the wind south over the loch.

As the night becomes darker the sound of rain on the flysheet lessens, but it's still raining. If it doesn't stop soon we'll be as wet as the bog ground we're camped on and the mountainside waterfalls we lie beneath; we will become the rain. As I try to think of other things, a vision of the crystal-lit valley slips back into my thoughts and with it a picture of those other lights as they flickered faintly across the picture of Moth's DAT scan. Every night in the tent I lie awake for hours, listening to Moth's steady breathing in the darkness, eaten by the gnawing sense of guilt. I encouraged him to put himself in the way of danger and hardship, and now we're on the edge of the Great Wilderness, trapped by the rain, the river and probably concussion, rather than safe in our bed in Cornwall, and for what? For the hope that next time he has a DAT scan it will show that through this difficult physical endeavour he's in some way relit the receptors in his brain and the lights will be there on the screen to prove it. All this for a false hope I know is impossible. In the darkness of the tent I realize that's all this walk is – a hope, a need, a prayer for the dance of light to resume.

10

As I open my eyes I know something is missing. For a moment I'm completely disorientated, but then I realize it's noise: I can't hear anything; it's completely silent. In the faint early light the hinds stand, nose around in the wet bog-grass, then slowly make their way towards the hillside. The stag's nowhere to be seen. The mountain waterfalls have slowed, but the river still crashes by. Even if Moth feels well enough to carry on, it will be impossible to cross here.

The suture is holding and his headache has lessened, so we pack the tent and move further upstream, in the hope that the river is lower on the side where it feeds into the loch. We reach the river. At one point the water seems only thigh deep, but when we test it with a walking pole it's above waist height and flowing so fast we wouldn't be able to keep our feet. We find a flat patch, put the tent back up and wait.

The daylight hours crawl slowly by; hours of watching one small solitary bird moving up and down the riverbank, the eagle gliding by on the wind, the deer high up on the mountain, clouds collecting then dispersing, the water, still powerful and deep. As the day drags by it begins to feel like a very familiar way of living. There's a lot of similarity between the mindset of a long-distance walker and the one needed to survive a lockdown. A walker needs to be able to adapt to the changing weather and landscape, to be content spending long days with no one but the person they're walking with, and they need endurance: the ability to just keep going however long it takes, to keep taking the next step knowing the end will eventually come. It's a mindset that also comes in really handy when you run out of rations, be it food or toilet roll, and the supermarket shelves are empty. The long-distance walker's thoughts will always jump over the hurdle, by finding that forgotten packet of dried noodles at the bottom of a rucksack, or a supply of dock leaves from the hedgerow – use them when they're fresh, they're fairly ineffective as a toilet roll alternative when they dry out. After an hour of plotting the route over the bealach and out of the valley by counting boulders up the side of the hill, I pass Moth a single biscuit. Another long-distance walker skill: rationing your supplies. But the biggest skill, probably something that passes even beyond lockdown, is holding on to the knowledge that however tough it gets – whether it's blisters, mild concussion, or the boredom of one more mile down a path that never ends – you will get through it and, in some as yet undiscovered way, you'll be better for it.

Cuckoos. I might be going slightly deaf, but even I can hear them now. Cuckoos everywhere, in every bent and twisted scrap of windblown tree they can find. The resilient navigational experts that turned north-east instead of north-west. Noisy, unrepentant Celtic cuckoos.

Morning comes again. The wind still roars over the bealach, howling around the dark, oppressive mountains that close in on every side, but the water level has dropped. We wade across without boots or trousers, our packs pulled tight to our bodies, but it's hard to keep our footing in the strong pull of the cold water and I'm caught by hesitation in a deep central pool, my hair flying and blurring my vision in the high wind.

'Don't think about it, just keep going.' Moth's ahead of me, both poles steadying him across. I do as he says, leaping to the next boulder and wading out of the river, falling on to the bank like a landed fish.

We're drying ourselves and putting boots back on when two men appear, hover for a moment on the opposite bank, then stride across fully dressed in boots and trousers. They step out of the river, dripping, drop their packs, take out sandwiches and eat them as if they haven't eaten for months. The younger one tells us they've walked five miles this morning already, from their car to here.

'Where are you heading?'

'We're going to do these three Munros. It's a big day, but worth it.' I look around at the mountains that tower above us, all Munros, named after Sir Hugh Munro who made the first list of Scottish mountains over three thousand feet.

'Shame you're so wet now.'

'Well, if you want to cover any distance there's no point messing about taking your boots off.' They put their packs back on and stride away along their epic route, their egos squelching inside their wet boots.

We pick our way slowly up through bog, rock and heather over the Bealach na Croise, counting the boulders we spotted the day before, each footstep sending small yellow and green frogs jumping in all directions. The higher we go the more frogs appear, until we cross over the rim of the bealach and head down the other side through a near biblical plague of frogs. After taking an entire day to cross just four miles, the sky clears as we reach the iconic Lochan Fada, shimmering in the fading light beneath the immense heights of Slioch. From our campsite at the head of the loch the colours of a late May sunset reflect from the water and the wet hillsides, until fading into a grey-blue sky that never quite becomes dark. The view is more powerful than painkillers for wiping away muscle pains and headaches, more effective than blister plasters for soothing torn feet. We sit on the rocks of the shoreline until we feel as if we're part of the rhythm of the water moving in the wind and the call of the birds crossing the loch.

Away from the loch the morning air begins to warm and the sky remains clear, as if Loch an Nid is retaining its magnetic pull on the rain, leaving the surrounding glens dry. A downhill day, through miles of reforestation of birch and rowan down to a river, but all I can think of is my feet. They're on fire; I want to lose these boots and never ever find them. Turning a corner we meet the first Cape Wrath Trail hikers we've come across. Two ex-soldiers heading north, or so they say.

'Are those boots Corcoran's? How are you finding them?' Definitely ex-army if he recognizes my boots. Moth's immediately impressed.

'They are, they're great, most comfortable boots I've got, and completely waterproof.'

He's right, I haven't had wet feet, but most days I'd have given anything for no blisters, however wet my feet were. 'They're the worst boots I've ever had, my feet are in pieces.'

'Aye, well, they're great boots, so you've probably got the wrong size, probably too big.'

They head away, but within minutes are replaced by a group of three more men heading north on the trail. All geologists.

'If you've come down from the north, you must have noticed the incredible rock formations of Torridonian sandstone.'

'We have. Is it that that makes the rocks pink or is it the gneiss?' I don't know enough about rocks to have the answer, so they seem like the obvious people to ask. They look at each and start laughing

'Did you hear that, she said *gneess*.'

'Is there something wrong with that?' They're spluttering with laughter, a group of middle-aged schoolboys, laughing at someone who isn't in their club.

'You pronounce it *nice* not *gneess*.' They walk away, still laughing about their joke. I carry on downhill repeating *gneess*, *gneess*, *gneess* under my breath, still unsure which rock is pink.

The shop in Kinlochewe arrives like an oasis. I drop my rucksack, collapse on to the bench outside and immediately take the boots off. I'm peeling away glued socks and desiccated blister plasters, allowing my red raw feet to dry in the sun, when a young man with a rucksack that's obviously going a distance sits down opposite. There's a sort of studied casualness about him; curly hair beneath a black beanie, walking tights and shorts, but something else, something very familiar. He's the man we saw sheltering from the rain in Fort William, who we thought was just about to start the Cape Wrath Trail going north. It seems he was.

'Yeah, that would have been me. I'm from Ireland, but I've lived in Glasgow for quite a while now. Thought it was time to explore this country. I've never been this far north. I'm feeling something for this landscape, something really powerful – you must know what I mean.'

It's something more than just the casual familiarity of a remembered face, it's in the way Ian speaks of the land, with a sense of searching. But what's he searching for? A spirituality, or something deeper, a connection? He reminds me of someone, but I can't place it.

Moth puts some things back in his rucksack and sits up, and it's there. I'm seeing a young man I've always known, someone with a passion for life and a curiosity that keeps him searching, even when all those around him have given up. 'I get that – I've always felt that here. As if there's something beyond the views. I've always been able to find my answers here, when everywhere else they're out of reach.'

'That's it, that's it.' The young man sits back as if satisfied by the thought of a conclusion. Moth takes a drink of water and puts the lid back on the bottle with a deliberate turn of his wrist and they sit looking up at the mountains in contented silence.

The hot showers of the campsite have loosened the blistered skin from my feet, so we sit on a picnic bench as Moth contemplates minor surgery. He's holding the flapping skin with the tweezers, while snipping at it with a tiny pair of scissors. And I let him, marvelling at the steadiness of his hand despite the pain that makes me want to pull away. Could I hope, dare I hope?

'Bet you need a cup of tea after that?'

'I really do. I'll put some water on.'

Sometimes in life you don't know how much you rely on something until it's taken away. You don't realize how much you depend on the roof over your head until you lose it, or the money in your pocket until you don't have it – or a cup of tea until the stove breaks and you can't boil any water.

'What do you mean? It can't be broken.'

'Well, look at it yourself.' I hand Moth the stove, hoping I'm wrong and it does still work.

'Oh, you're not wrong.' The switching mechanism in the tiny titanium stove has broken, and it's too small, too fiddly to be mended. I try not to panic, but I can feel it rising. We're miles from anywhere that's likely to stock another one; I look through the guidebook at the route ahead, but can't see anywhere big enough to have an outdoor shop. Moth tries the tiny shop and the petrol station in hope, but it's false: inevitably they don't have one.

'We could try to manage with just cold food and water for the rest of the walk.'

'But we won't, you know how much we rely on a hot cup of tea, we can get by with that, even when we run out of food.'

A man, who has obviously been listening to our conversation, steps out of a camper van parked next to us.

'I'll get you a cup of tea. Jean, put the kettle on.'

Geoff has a lot of time on his hands. He used to be a HGV driver but has just given the job up and is taking a holiday while he decides what to do next.

'Think I'm going to retire early – I can't spend any more days of my life just sitting around in the port, waiting for paperwork. I didn't vote for Scottish independence. Same with Brexit, didn't vote for that either, but I got it anyway. Now I've given up my job because of it. Sick of governments trying to get into people's heads, making them think these things were their idea in the first place, when most people don't give a toss and just want to get on with their lives. Aye, got all the time on my hands now.'

★

It's 2 a.m., but it's still light, everything's bathed in an orange glow from the campsite floodlights and we can't sleep. My phone suddenly lights up with reception for the first time in days. Among the emails and messages I realize we now have an internet connection.

'We could order a stove online and get it delivered to somewhere along the way.'

'Where, though? I don't think there are any shops for days.' Moth's propped up against his rucksack but his eyes are closed.

'Maybe a hotel.'

A few moments of searching and we find a hotel just a few days' walk away.

'Can we carry enough cold food rations for three days? They'll be so heavy.' He still has his eyes closed, but seems to be listening.

'It's that, or we order the stove to be delivered here and sit it out on the campsite over the bank holiday weekend.'

We order two stoves – a spare just in case – to be delivered to the hotel.

'I hope it's open, I'll call them in the morning so they look out for the parcel. Not sure when it'll get there, though, with it being the bank holiday.'

Our packs are loaded with pies, Jaffa cakes and bananas and we're about to leave, daunted by the prospect of at least three days without a stove, when Ian walks over from his tent.

'I've made you a list of places not to miss. Stay low as you head out of the village, don't go high through the felled trees, that was my mistake, the path below looked stunning. And go to Inverie, I won't tell you about it, but you'll know why when you get there.'

Looking back at him as we leave the campsite, his thin freckled legs beneath his too-big shorts, with a beard that seems to have grown overnight, it's as if he has a light around him, a strange pale glow. But it could just be the sunlight, when my eyes are so accustomed to the rain.

II

To walk out of Kinlochewe on a bank holiday weekend, along a link road to the NC500, is to take your life in your hands. Cars, vans, trucks, motorbikes and cyclists. Cars overtaking vans. Motorcyclists racing against each other. Van drivers fighting with cyclists. We should have ignored Ian's advice and taken the high path. But ahead, as the valley opens out, a mountain is rising, snow-capped and vast, and on its flanks another reforestation project. The Beinn Eighe Nature Reserve is a large area of tree planting that's beginning to mature, threaded through with lines of yellow gorse. A sign says it's funded by the EU, 'Scotland and the EU making it work together'. I wonder if Scotland will be making it work alone, now the EU funding has ceased, but I'm beginning to think it will find a way.

We take a path off the road into Glen Coulin and instantly every life-threatening minute in the traffic was worth it. High mountains rise into a clear blue sky. Following the river into the glen, surrounded by lush greenness on every side, feels like we're entering another country. Eagles trace a line across the hillside and then turn to dip over a silver loch ahead of us; this is too breathtaking to walk past, so we lie on the grass in the sun watching ducks on the loch, a line of ducklings in tow. Suddenly they begin to paddle hastily away, noisily sounding an alarm. It seems you can spend your whole life looking for something you never see, but the moment you give up on the search and turn the other way, the thing you long for will appear, as if it was always there, just slightly out of view. A large black shape leaps from the water on to the shore of a small island in the loch, before drying itself on the short grass, like Monty rubbing himself on the carpet after a bath. A huge dark otter. Moments stretch into minutes as he rubs himself against the bark of the trees, before crossing the island and silently disappearing beneath the surface of the water.

At the end of the glen we wade across a shallow river and camp in a stand of Scots Pine. Late evening, it's warm and still as we watch the sun dip behind the mountains through the perfectly straight trunks of the trees. That's when the first one bites. The Scottish midge, the beast of the Highlands, is a tiny flying insect with a minute wingspan of no more than three millimetres. Innocent little creatures you would think, but when the females gather together in clouds of thousands they are a biting, blood-sucking plague of almost unbearable proportions. They're an insect of the northern side of the northern hemisphere, whose favourite habitat is wet boglands. Flying from late spring to early autumn, they're mainly out at dawn and dusk, turning breakfasts and sunsets into an arm-flailing dance of avoidance. In Britain they used to be confined to just the north-west of Scotland, but rumour has it they're spreading. Over the past few years they've become such an issue in Scotland that midge reports follow the TV weather forecast. It used to be the case that their numbers decreased in icy winters, but now the winters are warmer and the seemingly indestructible miniature vampires just wait through the cooler months for their moment to re-emerge in the spring. The only thing that will save you from a midge swarm is wind – they're too tiny to fly in anything more than a light breeze – and apparently a citron-scented moisturizer sold by a company that used to deliver to the door, a favourite with rough and tough soldiers, so we're told. We came armed with a bottle of this, but in the frost and snow at the beginning of our walk it froze solid and although it's now defrosted it seems to have congealed and won't leave the bottle. We cut the top off the bottle and smear it on anyway, but it doesn't work so we get into the tent, trying to avoid letting any midges in with us. But inevitably hundreds follow, so we spend an hour squashing them against the fabric of the inner tent.

★

Two more days of no tea, but lots of conifer plantations, traffic and cuckoos finally leads us to a scattered village and the hotel we're heading for. It feels like an outpost – a lost, half-forgotten collection of people and houses in a remote glen, and the hotel seems closed. We're considering putting the tent up by a shed nearby when we hear voices behind the building. A group of people are gathered around picnic benches outside the hotel; it's mid-morning but they're all drinking. They see us walk up and put the rucksacks down, but they don't speak, they just watch, until Moth asks if the hotel's open.

'Aye, it is, but no it's not.'

'Okay, I'll just go in and see if there's anyone around then.'

'There isn't.'

'Right, so it's open but not open?'

'Aye, that's right.' Three men sit at a bench, nodding. One in shorts and a sweatshirt, another dressed in green hunting clothes, the third – a large bald man – wearing a kilt with pockets and big black boots. They all look as if they could have been drinking for days.

'Och, what are you doing, man? Are you messing with my customers again?' A small woman with purple hair, bright red lipstick and a tartan dress steps out of the hotel. 'You would never think he owns the place, the way he frightens off the guests.' She flicks the man in the kilt around the head as she passes on her way to our table. 'Ignore him. His friend here came up from the south yesterday and they had quite a party last night, so they're all feeling pretty sorry for themselves. They're just having a hair of the dog this morning. How can I help you?'

'We called on Friday about a parcel that would be delivered here: has it arrived? And a pot of tea would be great.'

'Ooh, a pot of tea, that's very southern.' The man in the kilt is quite a joker. I almost wish we hadn't ordered the tea, but I take a deep breath and just laugh along with the joke.

'Yes, I have it, I'll go and get it.' The woman goes back into the pub and I feel my shoulders drop with relief. I don't want to spend days here waiting for the parcel to arrive. She puts it down on the table and they all watch us.

'Well, open it then, we've all been waiting to see what could be so important that you'd have it sent here.'

I open the box and take out the two small stoves, excited by the thought of the hot food they represent.

'Stoves?' The man in the kilt has come over to the table to look at them.

'Yeah. Ours broke days ago. Think it's been three days since we had anything hot. That's why we ordered the tea instead of a beer.'

'Well, what are you doing out here in need of a stove anyway?'

'We're walking the Cape Wrath Trail, down to Fort William. Well, sort of, we seem to be winding our way on and off it at the moment.'

'It's lunchtime – I'll make you some food. I'm cooking a chicken schnitzel today. Will that do?'

I have no idea what a chicken schnitzel is, but I'll take anything that isn't Jaffa cakes.

A huge plate of food arrives. A thin slice of battered chicken, a pile of chips and a spoonful of pickled beetroot, but it's steaming hot and looks like the best food I've ever seen.

'So why are you old guys trying to walk the trail, over these mountains, with all this weight on your backs?' He lifts up Moth's pack to test the weight, and drops it quickly. 'Are you mad or something?'

Moth pauses with his schnitzel halfway to his mouth. I say nothing, but watch the momentary change in his face, a moment of considering his reply.

'We just thought we'd go for a walk, see a bit more of this amazing place you live in.'

'Aye, well, it's not bad, except for the fucking deer.' It's the first time the hunter has spoken and he obviously hates the deer.

'Always on the roads, causing accidents. That's why I keep putting them in the freezer, for road safety reasons. Aye, we all have full freezers round here.'

'Och, man, be quiet. You take no notice of him. Anyway, that's changing the subject. I can see the way she looked at you: there's more to it than that; you're not just going for a walk.' The bald man stands by the door, his hands in his kilt pockets. I can suddenly see there's more to him than a day drinker who's made a business out of his favourite pastime, much more. Something about the way he stands, the way he won't let it go until he has the answer he wants. 'You're not just on a holiday, are you?' He *really* won't let it go.

Moth finishes his food and pushes the plate aside. I eat the pickled beetroot he's left on the side of his plate. They're all sitting on the benches opposite. They've stopped drinking and are waiting for an answer. Moth's inevitably going to tell them; faced with a straightforward question he will always tell the truth. He'd certainly never make it into the SAS – if Ant Middleton asked him where he came from, he'd write down the address.

'A few years ago I was told I had an incurable disease, so I went for a long walk and felt a lot better and didn't die. Then this last winter the symptoms came back thick and fast. I know I'm getting closer to the end now, but Ray's dragged me out for one last walk in the hope that it has the same effect as it did the first time. It won't though, the disease has gone too far.'

'I knew it. I've seen that look before, men in combat when I was in the army, men who are struggling to get back to base.' *So* much more to this man than beer and a strange kilt. 'Irene, get this man a beer, he's drunk too much fucking tea. And your wife's right, you never ever stop until you can't take another step.'

Morning slips into afternoon in a heated conversation about Highland politics and venison recipes. It seems we're passing through Scotland in a time of change – in the way people think about the country they live in and about their borders, literal and figurative. Again and again, the most unexpected people in the most unexpected places are starting conversations about politics. Our kilted friend is like so many others we've spoken to, all expressing a feeling that the agendas of governments and media don't correspond with theirs. They also tell us the village shop closed long ago, meaning we don't have enough food to get us to Morvich, the next place on the path with a shop. But after three beers in the warming sun, it doesn't really seem to matter.

'My mate's on his way with his fiddle, bit of live music tonight and carry on the party. You should stay, camp over by the shed.'

The idea of staying with these strange, big-hearted people is really tempting, in a place where if we stay too long, we may never leave.

'Thanks, we'd love to, but we need to keep going. It's like you said, don't stop until you have to.'

Moth goes into the pub to make the most of a flushing toilet. While he's gone the tartan-clad couple pile food on to the table: sandwiches and multi-packs of chocolate bars and nuts. The bald man pushes two bottles of beer into my hand.

'Put these in your bag, they're for the big man later, don't tell him 'til tonight. What he's doing, being out here, it's a big thing. I might be loud, and drunk, but I know courage when I see it.'

Such generosity from a haven at the edge of nowhere. I wipe the tears from my eyes as we pick up our rucksacks and walk away.

12

There's a silence over Loch Carron despite the main road that runs alongside it; the water is flat, like undisturbed treacle in a warm bowl. We follow it west until we reach the gardens of Attadale House. A sign on the gate says it closes in half an hour, but a woman in the ticket booth says we can stay for as long as we like. A global nomad who's had her wings clipped by Covid, she tells us she's hanging out in the Highlands until she's free again.

'I love it here; it's so welcoming. People look out from here, not in.'

We share an ice cream with the woman, before wandering around the gardens until twilight, then heading away to wild camp.

I scramble out of the tent at one in the morning, moving aside the empty beer bottles to get out of the flap. In the Highland half-light I can see a group of young stags grazing near the river; they look up for a moment before turning and walking slowly away. I'm beginning to envy them their freedom, their easy use of the land on which they're born. They roam through the mountains as they choose, restricted only by the occasional deer fence, sharing the hills with no one other than a handful of walkers, not even sheep. The Highlands are beginning to lose their wildness to gravel roads giving access to the hydro-electric plants being built throughout the big estates, roads that are also giving easy access to stalkers. But beyond those roads, high on the mountainsides, the deer are free to roam, free to live in their natural state. And yet in Britain, it's only here in the wild High-lands where we allow ourselves that same freedom. Further south we're confined, our use of the land restricted by paths, laws and ownership. I walk into the day, wondering if there isn't another way of looking at this land on which we live. A way that gives humans some of the same freedoms enjoyed by the deer.

After a steep climb up a hillside devastated by the harvesting of commercial forestry, where the path constantly disappears among the tangled branches of felled trees, we sit on a pile of brash, confused and almost lost. I've always relied on Moth's skills with a map and compass, but he can't see the route over the bealach to the next valley through the maze of tiny paths on the map that don't correlate with the confusion of tree trunks on the ground, and he refuses to take the compass out of his pack. He doesn't need to say, I know he can't see the connection between the spinning dial, the map and the landscape in the way he used to. It's as if he's lost an entire language, a way of understanding and describing the land as a whole picture.

We're hot, sweaty and dusty as we reach the summit and stand in a cooling wind from the south. The view from the hillside leaves us speechless. Mountains fold into the horizon in every direction, a blue river catches the sun, creating a ribbon of light threading through the valley below us. Glen Ling, a lost, hidden paradise, where swallows swoop for flies across a wide shallow river and stony shore: there couldn't be a greater contrast to the heat and disruption of the morning. We strip off our stinking, dusty clothes and sit in the river eating the last of the chocolate biscuits the tartan-clad hoteliers gave us. We don't want to leave, so spend the rest of the day lying in the river in our clothes until they're washed clean, then sitting on the bank until they're dry, before putting the tent up to hide from the midges as they rise into the cool evening air.

A flat tarmac road curves on for miles through another immaculate Highland estate. Through woodlands thick with yellow azalea – *Rhododendrum luteum* – the rich scent filling the air, through birch thickets carpeted with wild garlic, to what appears on the map to be an easy walk uphill via a narrow valley to the Falls of Glomach. The waterfall takes the river from the high ground, down through a steep gorge and away on a calm quiet course towards the sea. We sit down to drink water among the tight coils of newly emerged bracken, but as I hand Moth the bottle I can see tiredness etched in the lines around his eyes.

'We could camp here tonight, what do you think? There's flat ground, lots of water and the views down the valley are amazing.'

'Good idea, but it's only a mile and a half or so up through the gorge. Let's do it now, better than starting the day with a stiff climb tomorrow – you know how you hate doing a steep uphill first thing in the morning. Then we can camp after the Falls.'

'Aren't you tired?'

'I am, but we'll be at the top with the tent up and the tea on within an hour or so.'

Crossing the gentle slopes towards the gorge we stop on a bridge. The fall of the river is steeper here, making the water jump and bubble over water-worn rocks, droplets of wet light filling the air. The path follows a sharper gradient upwards over more broken ground, but it's easily crossed as it turns away from the valley and rises into the narrowing ravine. We continue upwards, confident that it won't be too difficult; after all, one of the cyclists at Loch an Nid told us he'd descended the Falls path with his bike and 'it was a piece of cake', so to go up on foot won't be that hard. But then, as Moth begins to hesitate, I have a fleeting memory of something collie-man said on his blog. He was walking north, but didn't he say something about this being quite a precarious path, and actually quite dangerous? How did we forget that?

There are moments in life when it's possibly better not to know what's coming. Like when you go on the first holiday with a boyfriend and your tent gets blown away in a storm and your dream trip turns into sharing the night in a plastic bag on the side of a mountain; or you plan a June wedding then it snows all day; or you're evicted from the home you've spent twenty years building, just a few weeks after it's finished. Moth somehow summons the will and the strength to continue up into the gorge, which becomes ever steeper, ever narrower, along a tiny track clinging to a near vertical slope. It's good not to know, as you scramble over boulders gripping at vegetation for handholds, that your partner's vertigo will return abruptly, almost paralysing him with fear. But sometimes those are the moments that can change the course of your life and lead to outcomes you could never have imagined as you shivered in that plastic bag, or filtered the wedding photos for the ones where you're not under an umbrella, or became homeless and found yourself sleeping wild on windswept headlands. Those are the moments we look back to and say: That's it, that's the moment when everything changed. They're the moments which turn desperate, annoying or desolate experiences into an understanding that the person you share the plastic bag with is the one, that you have the ability to laugh at anything, and that even having lost most of your material possessions you can survive on love, hope and a packet of dried noodles.

But knowing this is of no help at all as I stand on a tiny rock platform, my body consumed by fear that feels like an electric shock, trapped in a seemingly inescapable ravine where we are obviously going to die. But then the moment happens, the moment where emotions change from fear to hope, from panic to certainty, from thinking all is lost to discovering you're found. As Moth's hand reaches down and lifts me over a rock, it's as if a hand of hope is reaching down from the clouds. It grips mine with a certainty I haven't felt since the last time it helped me out of the glacial meltwaters of an Icelandic river. A grip that's firm enough to hold at least a chance, a faint kindling of hope, a possibility that this walk might be more than grasping at straws in the face of an inevitable encroaching disease. But there's no time to think of that. In this moment all we can think of is survival, of finding the way out of danger to the safety of the mountain top.

Looking out of the tent flaps at Moth, I try to calibrate what just happened, to make some sense of how the man frozen by vertigo became the man who helped me out of the Falls. I can't; it makes no sense. But, as I watch him put on his glasses and pick up the map, I see the answer – this moment has been coming for days, I just haven't *seen* it. If I hadn't been so focused on the pain in my feet and the guilt in my head, I wouldn't have just glanced at him putting the top back on a water bottle, I'd have noticed him doing it. Rather than being jealous of him wearing the same boots as me and his feet not being scarred by them, I'd have marvelled at him tying his bootlaces a little quicker. And when I was struggling to read the map, I'd have listened to the voice of the man reading it over my shoulder, making tentative suggestions about changes in direction. He's holding the map the right way up, looking at the right sections of the folded paper, he can see that we've made it to the highest point on the path above the Falls and tomorrow it will be downhill all the way to Morvich. He folds the map and puts it away, unconscious of what's happening. I don't point it out, for fear that merely saying it out loud will make this tenuous change disappear.

The night sky becomes pink as the wind picks up, blowing the midges away. But then some other insect comes out of the spongy wet bog-grass, an insect I don't know, a small, translucent insect with long legs like a small crane fly, even though it's the wrong time of year for crane flies. Thousands of the mysterious creatures take flight, their tiny transparent wings picking up the colours of the sunset, turning the sky into a moving fog of light.

13

We head downhill into Morvich, with its promise of a campsite, hot showers and food, passing numerous individual men toiling their way up. A few speak, but most of them just nod as they pass with serious faces and focused, yomping strides. It seems every Cape Wrath Trail hiker is heading north, always men, mostly talking about time taken, miles crossed and midge repellent. Other than the ephemeral Ian in Kinlochewe, not one of them has mentioned the countless number of cuckoos, the deer calling in the night, or the absolute mind-blowing beauty of this place. And where are the women?

Morvich campsite sits in a wooded valley full of thrushes and yet more cuckoos. I delicately take my boots off and peel worn-out, curled-up blister plasters from my feet. I look in the rucksack for more but there are only two left. Swallowing down a rising sense of panic, I head to the camp shop in the hope that they stock them. The campsite's run by ageing hippies who live behind the campsite fence in a truck painted with 'peace and love'; they're incredibly welcoming, but all they have are ice creams and noodles, not a single plaster, but they say there's a shop up the road that will have everything we could possibly need.

They were right, the shop has everything you could possibly need if you want to decorate your hippie truck while eating pasties, but absolutely no plasters.

'Watch out for the seagulls out there, they'll take your pasties.' The old lady in the shop closes the till and goes back to counting incense sticks, while we eat the pasties on plastic chairs outside, more likely to be run over by a truck speeding around the head of Loch Duich than we are to lose our pasties to a seagull.

A taxi pulls up and a man in a kilt runs in, then out again with a pint of milk. Moth gets up before he drives away.

'Do you know where there's a chemist, somewhere that might stock plasters?'

The taxi driver, who on closer inspection is the image of an iconic Scotsman from a 1930s film, with a long ginger beard, wearing a kilt and tweed jacket with long woollen socks and a sporran, doesn't hesitate. 'Aye, that'll be the chemist in Kyle of Lochalsh. Get in: I'm going there now.' We get in the taxi without a thought of how we'll return from the town that's fifteen miles away. It speeds away down the side of the loch, roaring around the bends, throwing us from side to side in the car.

'Are you in a hurry?' I'm clinging to the door handle.

'Aye, I'm a driver for a wedding and I'm late. What else do you think I'd be doing dressed like this?'

'I just thought maybe that was the way you liked to dress? You look great.'

'Aye, I do, but I'm not a pastiche you know, I'm a Viking.'

Moth and I exchange a look as we swerve to the right.

'I saw that – I have a mirror, you know! I'm not mad, if that's what you think. I am a Viking. I run re-enactments, and classes on Viking life, as well as being a location scout for Hollywood.'

'And drive the taxi.'

'Aye, in between.' We screech to a halt outside the chemist and he's gone before the door shuts, or we have a chance to pay him. In this strange mid-pandemic world, this seems to be an approach people are being forced into. Employment has become so precarious that many are taking numbers of small jobs, in the hope that the income they provide adds up to one whole salary. Suddenly, this new world of shortages and insecure wages feels very fragile, even if you're a taxi-driving location scout who's a Viking at the weekend.

We buy all the blister plasters in the pharmacy and a pile of dried food from the supermarket, then catch the bus back to Morvich. When we get back to the site there are three women putting their tent up. They have a robust, sturdy look, like women in their mid-forties who've played hockey every Saturday since they left school. I'm amazed by the sight of other women, finally, and have to speak to them.

'Hi, are you doing the Cape Wrath Trail?'

They're all squatted around the tent, but the youngest of the three stands up to answer. 'We are, heading north. Are you?'

'Yes, going south. I had to say hello, you're the first women I've seen doing it.'

'You're the first *we've* seen. It's all men – we've been talking about it all day: where are the women?'

I leave them to cook their food, wondering what it is about this trail that attracts men, but so few women.

We sit at the edge of Loch Duich as the light begins to fade, watching three deer cross the road and walk down the stony shoreline until they're knee-deep in the water. They're quiet, unhurried, unconcerned about our closeness, just standing knee-deep in the cool water eating seaweed left by the ebbing tide, as night falls across the mountains.

Shaken by our experience in the Falls of Glomach, the next stage of the walk seems daunting: a long, steep, exposed climb over the Forcan Ridge, where the guidebook says 'some boulders provide handholds', as if that makes it okay. But there seems no other way, so we're about to leave the road and take the trail up to the ridge when a familiar car screeches to a halt on an awkward bend in the road. It's the taxi-driving Viking, shouting out of the car window.

'Where you going?'

'South, over the Forcan Ridge.'

'What the fuck! What you going over there for? It's all very well coming down from the other direction, but you don't want to be going up it. Get in, there's a much better way over the mountains to Kinloch Hourn. Aye, much better than the ridge.'

Moth doesn't need to be asked twice: he gets straight into the car. We turn away from Loch Duich, from what would have been an incredible view if we'd been walking north, and head west into the mountains towards Glenelg.

'Aye, it's just as far as going over the ridge, maybe a bit further, we're just taking a sideways ride out of Morvich, so not as if you're missing out on anything. Anyway, this isn't like the ridge, it's really remote, you won't see anyone else for days, I promise you.'

He drops us off in a lay-by on a remote hillside.

'Aye, remote for sure. Well, away with you then, just follow the pylons, you'll be fine. And look out for the gold miners, they're panning down the end of the glen and they're a bit odd.'

And he's gone, down the hill taking the tight turns at breakneck speed.

'Panning for gold? Do you think you should have asked him where he was taking us before you got in?'

'I really didn't want to go over that ridge.'

We climb over fences through a midge-ridden farm, where the beasts seem able to fly despite the wind, eventually finding ourselves at the Suardalan Bothy. We make tea and listen to cuckoos in a rowan tree in full bloom, white flowers against a dark, threatening sky. We're tempted to stay, but it's early June now and there's a sense of days slipping away from us and still so many miles to go to Fort William.

Past locked-up Portakabins, abandoned tractors and a man panning for gold in the river, we walk south, following a line of pylons along the western edge of the Glensheil Forest. Another ghost forest, where high mountains funnel a cold wind through a glen that never seems to end. This is the most remote place we've passed through. Little moves in the wild empty landscape except the wind, howling through giant silver pylons that stand out in sharp relief against a purple, storm-laden sky.

We head relentlessly downhill. Despite the carpet of small pink orchids and the tiny yellow potentilla that seems to cover the Highlands, there's an eeriness about this place. Maybe it's the emptiness, maybe it's the sound of the wind in the pylons, but I'm uncomfortable here and keep checking over my shoulder with a sense of not being alone. A bend in the river reveals a collection of stone ruins and a large square patch of grassland that stands out among the rocky slopes surrounding it. Centuries have passed, but this was once a homestead. A place where crops were cultivated, families raised and lives endured. The inhabitants are gone now, driven out by poverty, hunger and Highland clearances, but the echo of their lives remains.

Darkness is falling and the midges are out in their millions. I have my boots off and stand ankle-deep in the river, my feet soothed by the ice-cold water, with a midge net over my head, waiting for water to boil on the stove that's balancing on a flat rock on the riverbank. Moth's straddling two rocks further upstream, bent over collecting water in a bottle. I can barely see him in the falling light and the fog of midges, but I hear him shout.

'What the fuck?' The water bottle flies out of his hand and he stumbles into the water. By the time I've picked my way across the rocks towards him with bare feet, he's already standing.

'What's the matter, what . . . Have you hurt yourself?'

'Didn't you see her? Shit, she made me jump. I just looked up and she was standing in the river. Where's she gone? You must have seen her pass.'

'No one passed. I'd have seen them; the path's right next to where I was standing.'

'It was a woman with black hair, standing in the river . . .'

I look around in the gloom, but there's no one here.

'Did you hit your head when you slipped over?'

'No, I didn't, but I did see her. I don't know how you didn't.'

We get into the tent and Moth zips it quickly, guarding us against the midges. Maybe the concussion from Loch an Nid hasn't really gone away, maybe he did hit his head again when he stumbled, or maybe he really did see a woman. Either way, I pull my sleeping bag over my head and vow not to get out of the tent until I can see without the headtorch.

In the light of morning, I look back at the ruined homestead from the ridgeline above, before it slips out of sight. A deserted spot that once offered a home and livelihood to a family who lived and strived there, until they were uprooted by whatever fate befell them. Ruins like this are scattered throughout the remote Highland glens, like confetti after a wedding – for one brief, brilliant moment they encapsulated hope, love and possibility, but now are no more than faded memories littering the glen bottoms. I know only too well the aching sense of loss and fear that family might have felt as they left their home for the last time, probably to head into an unknown future. I'm about to turn away, to shrug off the cold hand of connection that's making the hairs rise on my arms, when my eye catches a movement, and for a fleeting moment I think I see someone by the river.

Miles of open moorland and mountainside spread out before us as we pass beneath the Forcan Ridge rising to the east, then down a long, steep, rocky path through old coniferous woods to Kinloch Hourn, at the head of Loch Hourn. This is Knoydart, one of the most remote peninsulas in Britain, and we're about to head into its vast wilderness, known as the Rough Bounds. It's an inaccessible tract of land with a history of Vikings, Gaels, kings and armies, a place of bogs, mountains and historically moving boundaries, where the only way in or out is by boat, or on foot.

An old boat pulls up to the rocky edge of the loch and an elderly couple get out. They're laying out a picnic on a stone as we pass them.

'You look as if you've a long way to go – would you like some cake?' The old lady offers two pieces of fruit cake on a china plate, a moment of strange civility in this wild, rugged landscape and we can't refuse.

'We'd love some cake.' Moth has his rucksack off and is sitting down before I've even formulated a reply, and is deep in conversation by the time I've joined them. They tell us they've lived in these hills for half a lifetime, the husband working as a stalker, tracking the deer herds across the mountainsides in search of the perfect place for the hunters (who pay for the privilege) to take a shot at a stag. He has a deep understanding and real affection for the deer and the mountainsides on which they roam. I sit and listen, watching the movements of this small wiry man, and for a moment I could be on the farm where I grew up, listening to my dad talk with passion and knowledge about the cattle we bred there. For a moment, the stalker's soft Scottish accent transforms into my dad's voice and I can almost touch someone who's been gone for decades. Just for a moment, until the wife offers more cake and the stalker tells us more of their life in the mountains, of farming and sheep.

'But we've hardly seen any sheep in the Highlands, maybe a few on the lowlands and the coast, but not one in the hills. I remember them being here when we were young, so where have they gone?'

'Aye, that's true they were here, but they're gone now. There aren't enough people for the gathering now, certainly not enough that would want to take part. You can't keep sheep if you can't get them down off the hills. Aye, most of the people who worked the land have gone; it's mainly the deer and the visitors now.'

'Do you think you'll always be here, even without the sheep?'

'Oh no, we don't live in Knoydart any more. I've retired now and the house we lived in, well, it was a tied house you see, so when I retired we had to leave.' I see a shadow of sadness pass over the stalker. 'No, we're miles from here now, just come back occasionally when the weather's right.' I watch the look they share; they don't need to say what they're thinking. Separated from the land they love and have devoted a lifetime to, a great weight of sadness seems to hang between them. Connection to the land doesn't come from ownership; it's not something you buy. It comes from time spent immersed in the smell of the earth, the feel of the rocks beneath your feet. It's a physical feeling, an understanding that comes without thought or contemplation. But the loss of it has the power of a bereavement.

I find it hard to shake off the sense of their sadness as we follow the path west by Loch Hourn, along a shoreline thick with midges, where we duck and weave between boulders, scrubby trees and undergrowth, until the rain begins to fall with an immediacy and fury that's painful on our skin. We throw the tent up and jump inside. The evening drags on as the rain thunders down, we make tea, repeatedly, I pick seven ticks out of Moth's scalp with the tweezers and we squash midges against the tent walls until it's dark.

14

Barrisdale Bay can only be reached on foot or by sea. That's possibly why it's one of the most stunning beaches anywhere. A sandy bay of crushed oyster shells, backed by high mountains, opens out to the blueness of Loch Hourn beyond. We seem to have left the Torridonian sandstone behind and moved into quartz-strewn hillsides reflecting blue light back from sky and water. The tide is right out when we sit on a flat boulder. We've already been on this trail for over three weeks, but it feels like days. We're slipping into trail life, that other place where the boundaries of time begin to fade. The only marker of the days passing seems to be the bracken. It was barely unfurled when we camped by the River Ling; it's now eight inches high, but still has weeks of growth before it reaches maturity. I stroke my hand through some unknown flowers of blue harebell-like petals on a long stem, emerging from a star-shaped succulent leaf, and our plans become like light on water, fluid, windblown. We abandon our idea to walk the many miles inland to Sourlies Bothy, giving ourselves at least a chance of getting to Fort William before the rations run out completely, and hand ourselves over to fate and wherever that leads. We'll go without food rather than leave this rock; the wild power of the place has us transfixed.

Two walkers appear as black dots, but quickly grow into rapidly moving hikers. They stop momentarily as they pass to answer Moth's inevitable question.

'Hi, are you on the Cape Wrath Trail?'

'Yes, heading north. Can't stop, we only have two weeks to complete it start to finish.'

'Wow, epic, that's huge miles every day.'

'Yes, between twenty-five and thirty every day. Might come in a bit ahead of schedule if we don't stop.' They disappear, enveloped by the landscape.

Hours later the tide has come all the way in. Moth jumps off the rock and swims out, floating in the syrup-smooth sea, buoyed by salt-dense water, as easy and weightless as a leaf skimming the surface. Time has no meaning here, there's only the sea, the rock and light passing over the mountainside. We would stay here, put the tent up and not leave until there isn't even a noodle left in the food bag, but we can't. Even though the right to wild camp is enshrined in the Land Reform Act, the landowner pays someone to herd all the campers on to the campsite. Apparently the sight of tents on the shoreline spoils the view from the big house.

The sea breeze drove the midges away when we were in the bay, but they've all collected at the campsite, where they rise in clouds of midge-fog. Moth's pegging down the tent and I'm doing CPR on the airbeds when three walkers sit down around us in a semi-circle.

'So where have you two come from? Have you parked at Kinloch Hourn?'

'No. Have you?' Moth sits down with them.

'No, we're doing LEJOG. We started out separately but met up along the way; now we're finishing it together.' They're an unusual group to be walking from Land's End to John O'Groats together, an epic walk of nearly nine hundred miles. A man who's just approaching his sixtieth birthday massages his feet, he looks tired but still fitter then most thirty-year-olds. A young woman of maybe thirty looks as if she could carry on walking, if only she hadn't taken her boots off, and a much younger man with a beard that seems surprised to have found itself out in the light wears a Hawaiian shirt with a face as burnt by the sun as our own.

'We're doing the Cape Wrath, heading south to Fort William – well, hopefully, if we don't run out of food on the way. You must have left Cornwall in April to get this far north, bet you were so cold in all the frost?'

'You should divert to Inverie, there's supposed to be a shop there. It was absolutely freezing when I set off and now it's so hot, such a contrast. How do you know it was so cold there, do you know Cornwall?' The woman doesn't look as if she's ever cold, or hot, or burnt. She just looks totally, unstoppably capable.

'That's where we live. So you've walked all this way in just a few weeks? How? Are you doing a marathon every day?'

'Yeah, just about, between about twenty-two and thirty miles a day. Pretty tiring, but okay if you just keep going. But we do start out at four a.m. every morning, and we eat this all the time, we have a huge sack of it and it just never runs out.' She shows me a bag of gruel, mainly dried grains and rice. 'Yeah, we don't even carry a stove, so super-lightweight, we just soak this in cold water every night, it contains all the nutrients we need, so really effective.'

I think back to our days with no tea when the stove broke and think I'll happily carry the extra weight of the stove and pan.

We retreat from the midges into the tiny bothy and tell trail stories, all of us happy to share our experiences. The man's still massaging his feet, but he has a theory.

'Something remarkable happens when you walk a long-distance path. I think you find an honesty that you don't see in normal life. It unites those who walk in a sort of trail-induced euphoria that gives you a sense of openness, where normally we're all so closed. I think that's the place where trail magic comes from.'

Trail magic is the wonderful theory that if you need help on the trail it will come from somewhere, as if by magic, or at the very least you'll experience something that makes you feel awe and gratitude. I promise myself I'll go to sleep hoping for more food and the boots that I left in the Tourist Information office in Fort William, while practising the gratitude I'll feel when they arrive.

The woman's nodding, happily agreeing. 'I've just read a book – if you're from Cornwall you should read it – it's called *The Salt Path*. It'll change how you think about walking – you'll believe in trail magic after that.'

I'm in a warm glow of communal experience, slightly in awe of these amazing athletes and their ability to cover so many miles each day and still laugh in the evening, but it seems Moth is suffering some kind of trail-induced honesty.

'Well, actually I know the woman who wrote that . . .'

At four in the morning, I'm startled awake by a hand reaching under the flysheet of the tent. I'm barely awake, confused and slightly scared, but as the hand puts chocolate bars and a packet of Haribo into the pan, I can just make out the outline of the older man in the dawn light. He puts his finger to his mouth and whispers.

'Shhh, it's trail magic.'

'I'm so hungry, shall I get the tea on?' I'd gone back to sleep after the hand under the flysheet, it's 7 a.m., our athlete friends are probably already beyond Kinloch Hourn and Moth has woken on his own. He gets out of his sleeping bag, squats in the door-way and lights the stove, pouring water into the pan without spilling it. I watch his hands as he opens a sachet of sugar and dips a teabag in a cup. He holds the spoon in his hand; it still shakes with a tremor, but reaches the mug and stirs the tea. Before we left Cornwall the same movements would have seen the water on the ground and the sugar anywhere but in the cup.

'How are your hands feeling this morning?'

'They're okay, why?'

'Just wondered, you haven't mentioned them hurting for a few days.'

Moth looks at his hands, turning them over. Just a slight tremor. 'There're not as painful as they were, not enough to complain about anyway.'

'What about the rest of you? You haven't complained of the dizziness for a while either.'

'No, it hasn't been as bad. Still there in the background, but not so bad that I need to lie down.'

I watch him devour the last remaining biscuits with his tea, followed by a cereal bar, and try not to allow myself to be too optimistic. If I were a scientist, I would approach this with reason and say everyone would be hungry after walking for miles with a limited food supply, and the dizziness could have been something to do with blood pressure, something corrected by the exercise.

'I was wondering if we should do what Ian suggested, and go over the bealach to Inverie, apparently there's a shop there. It might add a couple of days to the journey though. What do you think?'

'Definitely, great idea, decision made.'

We pack the tent away, as I add decision making to the list of things that have changed for Moth. In the misty, midge-filled light of early morning, I could try to rationalize these small changes with scientific reasoning. But as he tightens the fixing that holds the tent pegs to the side of his rucksack, then lifts mine for me to put my arms through the straps, just for a moment I don't need a scientific reason. For a moment I can just accept this as trail magic.

15

Climbing over the steep bealach we stop to look back at Barris-dale one last time, packing the white oyster-shell beach and blue reflective mountains into that space in our memories reserved for treasures never to be lost, before turning west and heading for the coast.

The wind drops, the heat of the day rises and our skin tightens to pink leather. Highland cows stand thigh deep in a treacle-smooth loch, barely acknowledging us as we pass through the heavy, midge-laden air. The sun gets higher in the sky, but the trail winds down into shady woodland and the shores of Loch Nevis. The loch dances and moves in the sunlight, distorting the view across the bay to the North Morar headland. Eventually a group of low white houses emerges from the heat haze, a small shop, a pub and a shed where people meet to chat, or so it says on a notice board, and (from the number of recycling bins along-side) to drink a lot too. Inverie.

Deckchairs line a grass patch outside the pub, facing out to sea. We drop the rucksacks and sit on them. This place already feels rare. A tiny community existing at the edge of the water, cut off from the modern world, with a road that leads nowhere and only the ferry to Mallaig to connect this hidden spot to the outside world. But this tiny hamlet doesn't feel alien in the wild landscape, the hills seem to fold around the houses as if they belong there. As the sun begins to dip and the tones of light soften, just being here somehow feels like a privilege. I relax into the chair in the warmth of the early evening, feeling noth-ing but gratitude that we've found ourselves in this place, in some kind of paradise. My eyes closed against the light, I float with the sound of oystercatchers skimming low, the swash and suck of water against shingle and understand that the rock climber was right. We've put ourselves in the way of hope and it's washing over me like the tide on the shore. It might dissipate on the ebb tide, but for now, the rising tide of possibility soothes me to the core.

We ask at the pub for directions to the campsite.

'You can't camp tonight, the midges are going to be really bad. Stay in my lodge; there's a room free.'

We take his word for it and head to his converted barn. It feels more like an African hunting lodge, with walls hung with animal-head trophies and a stuffed zebra outside our room.

I'm putting our stinking clothes in a washing machine when two men check in. They obviously think they're alone. A short man with dark hair holds an intense conversation on his mobile, while the taller one with long hair holds out notes for him to read.

'The MOD target is here and we're closing in on him, we're preparing the subsonic communications package now.'

Just for a moment, as I fill the washer with sweaty T-shirts, I wonder if I've nodded off and I'm dreaming, or maybe we've just walked on to the set of a spy movie. They go to their rooms and I head back to ours.

'Moth, did you hear that? What the hell was all that about?'

'I did. Sounded like they're looking for someone they want to sell something to.'

They leave and we follow them, at a distance, until they go into the pub to a pre-booked table and we sit on the deckchairs drinking tea. The sea continues to move in a slow rhythm of light, the tide starting to leave the short tidal zone. Moth takes off his boots and I pick a huge tick out of his leg.

'Ian was right, this almost feels like the perfect place to end the journey. It really has become the Sheigra Trail, something more spiritual than this yomping, ego-littered Cape Wrath Trail.' Our path hasn't been about covering miles and listing speeds, it seems as if our only ambitions have been to take in each moment and collect views. I really could just stop now, spend days soaking in this view and put my boots in the skip on the harbour.

'I know what you mean, but we've come this far, it would be good to finish it properly. There's hardly any food in the shop, but maybe we could get the Mallaig ferry, stock up on food there, then come back and finish it. Just three days from here and we'd be in Fort William.'

I watch Moth putting his sock back on and lacing his boot. Is he really the one saying let's keep going? Am I witnessing a change? Or has the ego-strewn Cape Wrath Trail got into his bones, and he secretly has a distance and time chart in his notebook?

'Shall we go into the pub before we're eaten alive by these midges, get a bowl of chips or something other than dried food?'

'Yeah, let's see what the spies are up to.'

The only available table is right next to them. It seems they aren't spies after all, but city traders talking about the climate.

'. . . the whole idea of a green future is nonsense. We all know that no policy comes into force simply because it's the right thing to do. Policy follows finance, not the other way around. We do the deals, then governments sell themselves as having a green agenda, but only when they're sure there's money to be made. So, I'm telling you, we need to get our foot in the door with hydrogen, choose the right company and you could be in the right place at the right time. I mean, look how we cashed in on carbon trading.'

I can feel a rising sense of outrage at what they're saying. The last remaining cuckoos that migrate to this remote corner of the country can't wait for 'policy to follow finance' before they're rescued. This is their Dunkirk and no small boats are coming to save them. The idea that a crisis that's imminent for birds and humans alike isn't a priority, but just another commodity to be traded, makes me fidget in my seat. But I catch Moth's eye and a look that says: Stay out of the conversation, so I take a deep breath and don't say anything. I'm not naïve enough to think that this isn't the way economies work, or governments view the climate crisis, but I'm still activist enough to believe that it's a crisis that can't be solved on the trading floor alone. Real change will take a consensus of humanity, ordinary people accepting that this is an existential crisis for us, as much as it is for the cuckoo. The climate crisis can't be solved by carbon off-setting – merely moving figures around the carbon chess board and allowing polluters to go on polluting – or by governments failing to implement their green agenda because the right deal hasn't been done. That time is over. Time now for us to look up from our balance sheets and see what's happening outside the window. The cuckoos can't wait any longer. How long, I wonder, before we become the cuckoos?

It seems the traders have the target in their sights, they're now deep in conversation with a man on the next table, who tells them he's ex-RAF, a member of his local mountain rescue team and also the heir to a large part of Scotland.

'Ah really, we're ex-Army Air Corps.' They've obviously found their MOD target. 'Interesting, so you're in the mountain rescue. How do you prefer to route-find?' The long-haired trader is completely calm. Just a casual conversation.

'Map and compass every time. Technology can always let you down in the field.'

It seems the mountain rescuer is being hunted like the zebra at the lodge, possibly as a potential and very lucrative investor. The long-haired trader puts his glass down. 'I've recently come across some technology that's super reliable and cuts out human error, it's known as subsonic communication . . .'

We leave them to deliver their package, whatever that might actually be, and go back to the lodge.

Late afternoon, with a bag full of food and blister plasters, we return on the late ferry from Mallaig. Cloud has moved in from the west, obscuring the mountains, cloaking the village in grey drizzle. Inverie looks very different in the grey light, more remote, more evidently dependent on the ferry. A local on the boat tells us the pub is for sale due to a dispute between the locals, who want to use it as a local pub, and the owner, whose livelihood comes from offering the tables to visitors who spend readily on their meals.

'Outsiders are the problem. People come in and before you know it the old ways of doing things are gone.'

I try to listen to her talking about the outsiders, but for a moment it's as if she stops talking and simply drifts into the mist. For a moment I don't know if I'm in a trinket shop listening to the argument for Scottish independence, or on a campsite listening to a trucker's view of Brexit. Maybe the shed with the recycling boxes isn't actually a sign of a close-knit community coming together, but actually the complete opposite – a sign of a community falling apart. We walk away from Inverie with a powerful sense that it could be a miniature diorama of the rest of Britain.

16

The mist lifts for a while, but quickly returns, creeping over the top of the Munro, Meall Buidhe, slipping down its sides and settling around the tent as wet white air. The light fades into night and the thickening mist mutes any sound. But the longer we spend hearing nothing, the more we begin to hear. The faint bubble of water just beneath the surface of the bog, an occasional higher note as it breaks out over rocks, then something lower, more animal. Deer. They're somewhere close by, enclosed in the fog, calling to each other in quiet, song-like calls, and that bird, the unknown bird, with the long single tone of its night-time call. And Moth, unable to sleep.

'This reminds me of the fog in the orchard in early May. Can't believe we're already into June. We'll be back before you know it; the Rough Bounds will be behind us and all of this will be over, just a memory.'

I listen to the bird calling, further away now. 'Do you want it to be that, just a memory?'

'No.'

We barely sleep and break camp with the light, pass over the bealach as the sun rises, and drink tea on the sand at the head of Loch Nevis, near the stone shelter of Sourlies Bothy. Grey clouds hang low, obscuring the mountains, but a pale light seems to emanate from the loch as we turn away into the hills at a time when we would normally be still sleeping. The fog lowers and thickens, suppressing conversation, forcing us to keep our eyes fixed on the faint path for fear of losing it, passing through Glen Dessary, then south until fog-grey becomes fog-dark and we pitch the tent at the edge of a forestry plantation.

Glenfinnan is heaving with tourists. Tourists in cars and coaches, on cycles, motorbikes, and us on foot. A place where Scotland's history sits directly alongside its present. The place where Bonnie Prince Charlie raised his standard on the shores of the loch and began the Jacobite Rebellion of 1745 (although some people believe the flag was actually raised further up the hillside, overlooking the railway viaduct that carried Harry Potter in the Hogwarts Express, not near the edge of Loch Shiel where the monument stands). Charlie came back through this glen, fleeing from the English soldiers, after his attempt to claim the throne ended in a disaster that left thousands of his clansman dead and their culture in tatters. He then made a swift exit to Italy, never to return. If he'd been here today, he'd possibly disguise himself in a wizard's hat, jump on a steam train and pretend his rebellion never happened. He'd probably have a much smoother escape, as that seems to be what most of the tourists are doing, passing right by the monument commemorating a momentous turning point in Scottish history and moving straight on to the tale of a fictitious wizard.

Oystercatchers skim low over the darkness of Loch Linnhe, flickering in the silver shards of moonlight caught by the rippling water. We're quiet; there doesn't seem much to say. One final loch to walk alongside, before we reach the ferry over the water to Fort William, and our Sheigra Trail will be over. Somehow we've walked through the most remote wilderness in the country, lived among deer, eagles and those annoying birds that make that single call all night, surviving torn feet, concussion and hunger. Lying under the sleeping bag, as even the mystery bird falls quiet, I drift into sleep with a sense of having found a place in myself that I haven't fully inhabited before. An empty space that hasn't been fought for through miles and times, but has simply grown as we've sheltered from the rain with the deer, or crossed the same hillsides as the eagles. A place within me that will always be wild, empty and free.

Yet one thing remains elusive: the thing I had hoped for the most, the thing I put Moth in jeopardy for, has only come in part. His health has improved in so many ways, but there hasn't been the complete overwhelming reversal of his symptoms that we saw on the South West Coast Path. As the climber at Sheigra said we would, we've put ourselves 'in the way of hope', but maybe hope and miles aren't enough any more. Maybe Moth has been right all along, maybe we finally have to accept that this illness can't be fully defeated. Maybe *I* finally need to accept that.

If we'd walked north our Cape Wrath Trail would have ended at a beacon of light on the storm-lashed, north-westerly corner of Britain. But we walked south, so our trail ends with a ferry ride across Loch Linnhe and a walk into the centre of Fort William. There didn't appear to be a marker for the start of the Cape Wrath Trail, so we find no official place to end it. We just sit on a bench and share what's left of a packet of digestive biscuits, next to a couple taking photos of each other on the seat. Photos taken, they pick up their bags and go, leaving us alone on the bench. Without them to block the view, what we thought was someone sitting next to them is actually a statue of a man with one leg crossed over the other, rubbing his foot. Moth gets up and sits next to it.

'Wow, I didn't notice this when we were here before. It's the end point for the West Highland Way. Must have been where all the walkers were heading when they passed us in the café.' He takes his boot off, strikes the same pose and I take a photograph.

'The West Highland Way?'

'Yeah, it ends right here.' He's putting his boot back on and slowly, methodically, lacing it up.

'It ends here?'

He looks at me with a changing expression, one I've watched slip across his face many times in our forty years together. But not one I thought I'd see here, not now, not when he's been so sure that he has that final corner in sight. 'Or begins.'

I pull off the huge black boots one last time and place them next to the bench. Their leather has barely changed shape; there's hardly any trace of more than two hundred miles of rocky, boggy terrain, or that my feet have been inside them for every one of those miles. I peel the socks off the blister plasters and drop those in the bin, followed by the plasters. My feet are swollen and deformed in parts, raw in others. The skin has changed texture after so much time under the plasters, as if the top layer has lifted into a spongy, pulpy sock, disconnected from the bone and muscle beneath. And my big toe has no sensation at all.

'I'm going to post these to Cornwall. I was going to put them in the bin, but I think I'll keep them, just to remind myself never to be so stupid again. And I don't want to carry them if we're catching the train.'

'I've been thinking about that.'

'What? Do you think we should call Tom?'

'No.'

'What then?'

That look again. I know what he's thinking. He holds my gaze, unwavering, those same blue eyes that drew me to him four decades ago. He knows I know.

'It's this place. I thought I'd lost the passion for it, after all those years of not returning, but I haven't; it's as strong as ever. And my body's changing, you've seen it, I don't have to explain.'

As he speaks I look down at my bare feet on the concrete path; they're raw and painful and could take weeks to heal, but as he continues a current of excitement raises the hair on my arms.

'I'm not ready to stop. How do you feel about the West

Highland Way? It's ninety-six miles, that's ten days at the most. I'm sure Tom wouldn't mind keeping Monty for another week or two. And maybe, just a few more miles . . . well, who knows what could happen.'

I put the plastic sandals on and look at the man who fell in the grass of the orchard, the man who was ready to stop, his face alight with hope as he picks up his rucksack and walks down the road, turning his back on that final corner.

West Highland Way

Fort William to Milngavie

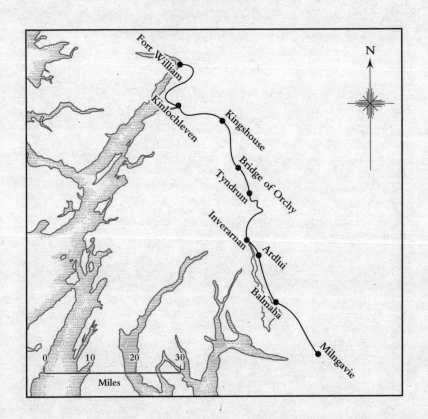

17

It's easy to spend time in Fort William. An hour can pass in the café of the outdoor shop, reading maps and guidebooks and drinking endless tea; time disappears in the tiny cinema, watching black and white projections on the wall of Highland life a century ago; and the evening winds down, despite the wincing and complaining, with my feet in a bowl of salt water.

Leaving the town the following morning, we walk slowly down the high street, past a wedding party putting their umbrellas away after a shower, stopping outside a shop with huge bikes in the windows, like the many we've seen heading over the bealachs of the wilderness. Moth ends a conversation with Dave and puts his phone into his pocket.

'Wow, look at those, they're incredible bikes. Maybe we should have thought about cycling instead of walking.' Moth didn't pass his driving test until he was nearly thirty. Even then, all those years ago, he was convinced cars were damaging the environment, so travelled everywhere on his bike, only finally passing his driving test two days before Tom was born. 'Let's go in and look.'

Moth wanders around the shop, stopping to stroke the handlebars of a silver bike that's in the sale. 'They're amazing. We were just saying we're about to walk the West Highland Way, but maybe we should be cycling it instead.'

A small, compact woman in a beanie hat looks at us with what seems like an 'at your age?' expression. But when she starts to talk it feels as if it comes more from experience, and on a closer look she's not that young herself. 'Don't cycle the Way. Parts would be okay, but if you're going all the way to Milngavie you've got the Loch Lomond section – believe me, you don't want to take a bike through that. Anyway, it's a good walk. But if you do want a bike, we've got it all in this shop.'

'Cycling's popular here then?'

'It's more than that. People here have a passion for the landscape, it's in our DNA. If you grow up here, you grow with the mountains in your every breath; even if you're not into the outdoors it's still part of who you are. The wilderness, the wildlife, it's ours, it's us. That's what we sell. A quicker way into the mountains than on foot, and it feeds the need for excitement and a bit of adrenaline in the young. People complain about the mountain bikers in the hills, say they don't belong there, but they're still appreciating our country, still connecting with it, so who cares how they do that? You've got to love it before you can fight for it, right? They're the future of the Highlands; I'll sell them all the bikes they want.'

'We'd need panniers for our stuff.' Moth's moved over to a used green bike in the corner, already kitted out for touring.

'We have panniers.'

It's early afternoon when we stand on a hillside on the opposite side of the glen to the broad flank of Ben Nevis, before turning south down the West Highland Way. My feet are swathed in plaster bootees inside boots so old and worn that they feel like slippers; our rucksacks are much lighter without the need to carry so much food. We're as ready as we can be.

We immediately meet far more people on this path, many of them coming towards the end of their walk from south to north. It seems, again, as if we're the only ones walking in the other direction.

'You know, thinking about it, we didn't meet a single person walking the Cape Wrath south, they were all going north.'

'Weird. I wonder if it's going to be the same here.'

'Well, it is so far, maybe we're the only ones moving against the tide.'

This is a changed landscape; softer, less rugged, less remote.

We've left the high mountains behind, we're in some other Scotland now, on a very different kind of path, walked by a very different kind of hiker.

The West Highland Way was opened in October 1980. Two weeks later I looked across a college canteen and saw a young man dipping a chocolate bar in a mug of tea. Even though I knew something momentous had happened on that Wednesday morning, even though I thought I'd just seen the man I'd spend the rest of my life with, I couldn't know that one of our first conversations would be about how exciting it would be to walk Scotland's first long-distance path. Or that this new, tenuous relationship would last as long as the West Highland Way. Or that our time together would be just as wild, rocky and totally breathtaking as this trail. Or that it would be forty years before we finally walked it and the map we'd looked at so many times would finally translate into a landscape I understood. This path was used for centuries before the ramblers of Scotland put a name to it. Unlike the Cape Wrath Trail, which incorporates many of the paths used by crofters and stalkers, the West Highland Way is built on the old drovers' roads, used to walk cattle to markets in the south long before road transportation, and old military roads built to control the rebellious Jacobites. It's a path intrinsically tied to Scottish history, a living connection to how man has lived and used this land, from drovers, to rebels, to walkers; our feet tread on the same ground, trace the same lines across this earth.

After the bogs and heather of the north, this solid well-trodden path feels like walking on a pavement. The mountains are lower, the weather gentler and the miles far easier to cross, all creating a powerful sense of heading south towards the lowlands. But with that a feeling is growing of the distance we've already covered, as if we've traced a line through the Highlands and the vastness of it follows us like a weightless balloon of knowing. The wild miles are imprinted on us and I can feel their remoteness just over my shoulder, made clearer, more defined, ever more precious as they reduce into the distance.

It rains steadily through the wide-open glen of Lairig Mor, Moth's early energy has faded with the light and we put the tent up near a ruined house in the rocky heather above the path. I boil water watching a ewe who has obviously lost her lamb and repeatedly lifts her head from grazing to call for it. Occasionally a faint response drifts on the wind, but it's hard to tell where from. We barely saw any sheep in the north, just the few scattered around the coastlines, the mountains belonged only to the deer. I look around the hillsides, but there are no deer to be seen. The ewe's standing on a rocky outcrop, still calling for her lamb as we close the tent zip on the rain.

I wake in the night to the sound of Moth struggling with his sleeping bag.

'What the fuck, I've broken the zip, fuck.' The zip split as he turned over, breaking the zip closure and pulling the teeth apart.

'You'll have to use it like a duvet.' He opens the bag and lays it over him as a quilt, but it's too small to cover him properly, so we swap bags and I wrap the broken bag around me. Sleep doesn't come. I lie awake listening to Moth's quiet breathing, the river, the wind and the faint replies of the lamb getting louder as it slowly gets closer to its mother.

In the grey morning light we pack the tent away and prepare to head towards Kinlochleven. It's raining steadily as we pass the ewe grazing close by, no longer calling, but the lamb is nowhere to be seen. Then we spot him, sitting behind a wall close to the path; he sees us but doesn't run away. Maybe he's exhausted from a night spent searching for his mother. Eventually he tries to go, but as his strong front legs haul him up his back half drags behind. I've lived a life with farm animals and it's immediately obvious he's seriously damaged his back. But there's no wasting in the back half of him; this is a new injury. It probably happened on the hillside, unnoticed by his mother until they were separated. He must have spent the night dragging himself down from the mountain, following the sound of her voice, until his painful broken body was reunited with the reassuring security of the ewe. She continues to graze, making small noises to encourage him towards her. There's nothing we can do and walk away with an overwhelming sense of helplessness at leaving him there in what must be incredible pain.

The miles pass but we barely notice them, hardly speaking during the morning. Moth walks with his head down, lost in his own thoughts. I know they're the same as mine. The instinct to survive was so powerful in the lamb that it drove him to crawl through the night in pain and fear until he reached his mother. No lying in the heather, wallowing in self-pity, just the raw will to survive, whatever that takes. Do we humans still have that? I follow Moth through the rain, down the steep, slippery mountainside into Kinlochleven. Maybe. Just possibly, when there is absolutely no other option, the will to survive is there in all of us.

Kinlochleven is a remote village sitting in a basin among the hills, a quiet hidden spot, but when the rain comes up the valley it stays in the basin. It's nearly mid-June, but the day is dark as the rain drives in horizontally on squalling wind and with nowhere to go just hangs in the basin, until it begins to fill with water. Water falling from the sky, pouring off the hillsides and rising from the river. Going any further in the storm makes no sense, so we put the tent up in the pub garden, eat chips in the bar and watch a repeat of the opening game of the Euros football tournament on their TV, while our clothes drip by an electric heater.

The following morning the storm still hangs in the basin. The rain has lessened, but the wind is even stronger. Moth's quiet and has barely spoken since he woke.

'Are you okay? Do you want to stay another night? I think

there's a Co-op in the village; we could get food, or hang out in the pub for the day.'

He packs his sleeping bag into its stuff sack, slowly, obviously preoccupied by his thoughts. 'I can't get the thought of that lamb out of my head. I should have done something. And there's no point staying, the barman said the forecast was for rain for the next few days.'

'What could we possibly have done about the lamb? We couldn't carry a half-grown lamb for five miles across a hillside. And you know if you'd taken it to a farmer, or a vet, they'd have put it down anyway.'

'I know, but there might have been a chance.'

'He's probably in pain, but he's got a greater chance left to his own devices. Do you remember my uncle's dog?'

'Which one? He had so many.'

'The skinny little whippet. It fell through the loft floor, and it looked just like that lamb – we all thought it had broken its back and should be put down, but Uncle wouldn't. He carried it around for six months because it couldn't walk and then one day it just jumped off the sofa and ran outside.'

'I suppose you're right. If they have the will to survive, you just never know.'

'Exactly, you just have to hope. Same as you. A few weeks ago you didn't want to leave the orchard; now you're here.'

We look out of the tent flaps at the storm that's still raging.

'You really can't compare me to a whippet.' He's in a pool of introspection and thoughts of mortality are weighing him down, but I can't shake the thought of the similarity between him and the dog.

We pack the tent and it hangs from the rucksack, water pouring from its bag, buy food from the shop, then follow the steep path out of the village. Rain falls relentlessly, filling our boots until they brim over with water, driving under the hoods of our waterproofs until we're soaked inside and out. The path continues to climb and we begin to pass people heading north. This is the second day of passing people at the same time; they must be leaving the stage point as dictated by the guidebook, then straggling out as the day passes. The path climbs up and up and we force ourselves forwards into the wind. The author of the guidebook says this is a 'short' and 'fairly relaxing' day. He was obviously heading north, going downhill in the sunshine, not trying to walk five miles uphill weighed down by water, in wind that drove him backwards. The trail finally levels out across a rocky patch of bare earth and stone, where suddenly the clouds break and we can see we're standing on the highest point of the West Highland Way, at the end of the Aonach Eagach Ridge. Straight ahead, rising up on the opposite side of Glencoe, is the iconic mountain Buachaille Etive Mòr. This is the landscape that adorns map covers, tourism leaflets, biscuit tins and just about every other item of Scottish trinketry. The clouds wisp and fade, leaving a grey-blue sky full of vapour, transforming Glencoe into a prism of water and light that could be anywhere, at any time. There's a noise rising through the mist and I can't quite work out what it is. It's an eerie sound, as if the history, battles and massacres that have played out in this glen are caught in the endless cycle of water. But as the mist clears there are no battles: the noise comes from the present day and the heavy traffic on the eternally busy A82 that runs between the mountains.

At the foot of the Devil's Staircase the glen opens out on to Rannoch Moor, over fifty square miles of boggy moorland. More bogs. I look around to tell Moth what I think about bogs and he isn't there. I wait and he doesn't come. I walk around the next bend in case he was ahead of me and I only thought he was behind. He isn't there. I retrace my steps and find him sitting on a boulder with his head in his hands.

'You disappeared! Are you okay?'

'My feet are killing me and I'm exhausted. I can't go on.'

I look around the wet glen. We're soaked, there's a strong wind blowing up the valley and there's nowhere to put the tent on the boulder-strewn boggy ground, but in the far distance is the Kingshouse Hotel. It's the end point for this stage of the Way, so there must be a campsite there. I begin to fantasize about warm beds and hot showers, then quickly remind myself that in this post-Covid summer the whole of the UK seems to have decided to take a staycation, and it's almost impossible to get a bed anywhere.

'We have to go on, there's nowhere to put the tent here.'

'I can't. Go on without me.'

I hesitate for a moment. What did he just say? Did I actually hear that? I look at him for a while, head still in his hands, ready to give up.

'What the fuck! What do you mean "go on without me"? As if I'd go on without you!' I can hear myself, but it sounds like someone else.

'I mean I'm done. I can't go on.'

'What's all this drama queen nonsense? Just get up.' I almost don't believe it's me saying the words, but he can't stay here, he's wet through and exhausted in a howling wind. *We* can't stay here. I feel panic rising like a pulse in my head. 'I think if that lamb could drag itself off the hill with a broken back, you can probably make it as far as the hotel, then we can at least put the tent up.'

'Are you going to start comparing me to that whippet again?'

'I might, but we can't wait for six months to see if you can get up.'

He gets up and we trudge on across a bog-covered landscape: no deer, no eagles, not even any potentilla, as if every wild thing has retreated away from the traffic. There's nowhere to camp. The only flat spots by the rapidly rising river already have tents on them. But there are two beds left in the bunkhouse and Moth desperately needs to sleep, so we take them.

He barely moves for twelve hours, submerged in a deep sleep, on a narrow mattress, on a DIY bunkbed, in a room that has the dimensions and feel of a cell. I perch on the high top bunk, like the eagle in the rock crevice at Loch an Nid: cold and wet, but in a safe haven. I can spread my wings when the storm passes. The room glows orange from the car-park lighting, the light falling on Moth, turning his face and the white bedcover orange. I watch him breathing quietly, emanating a peaceful, Buddha-like orange aura, and feel nothing but the familiar crushing sense of guilt.

18

I glance back at the view one more time as we climb over the shoulder of Black Mount, a final glimpse of Glencoe before we follow the path across the edge of the moor, leaving the high Highlands behind. An old military road stretches out for miles ahead, dark mountains rising to the west and to the east a vast moor of bogs, rivers and lochans stretching towards lower mountains in the far distance. This was once part of the great Caledonian Pine Forest, but now the only trees are occasional conifer plantations and groups of deciduous trees around the rivers. We head downhill as the day's section walkers begin to appear heading uphill, straggled out and looking exhausted. For once we're going in the right direction. They've already walked uphill for miles, on what initially appeared easy cobbles, but has quickly become a painful, foot-aching, ankle-twisting surface. I can feel the weariness of thousands of feet that have trodden this path. From foot-sore soldiers heading north to quell the Jacobites, through mountainous terrain they were unprepared for, to cattle drovers heading south with their animals in the hope of selling them for a fortune in the markets of the wealthier borderlands, and modern-day walkers treading this same path in the hope of finding some kind of meaning to life, or just a great view. For centuries people have walked along this well-worn line as it passes through the hills, connecting us all through time and weather, connecting us all to this land.

After a day on the cobbles Moth's feet are almost too painful for him to keep walking. Loch Tulla appears ahead, an idyllic scene of grazing cattle and still water backed by dark mountains that could come straight from a nineteenth-century oil painting. But as we enter the estate 'Keep off', 'Keep out' and 'Keep away' signs make me think the landowners aren't too keen on the West Highland Way passing over their land. Moth needs to stop and we thought we'd camp here, but we'd definitely be moved on if we did, so walk on through midge-fog rising in the evening air, passing a closely pitched cluster of tents by a bridge, until finally reaching a pub on the opposite side of the loch. We can't camp there either. Instead, we're directed back to the bridge we've just crossed, where apparently all the wild campers are sent.

There's a moment while you're backpacking when you know that your night's camping isn't going to go well, but there's absolutely nothing you can do about it. We know we're at that moment when we sit in the bar with a pot of tea and watch the people in there. There are no cars outside, so they must either be staying in the pub, or in the tents by the bridge. A group of young women playing cards and on their second bottle of gin. Students who have just finished their degrees, so are walking to release the steam of the last six months. A young man who said he left Milngavie with a twenty-two-kilogram pack, but now it only weighs ten. And a group of boys who're buying the girls a third bottle of gin.

We pitch the tent on the outer edge of the camp by the bridge as the midges thicken, filling the air until it's hard to breathe without inhaling them. I can barely see through my midge-proof head-net that's shrouded in insects trying to get through the tiny holes, but I see the stag. A large stag with shaggy wet hair and long four-pointed velvet-covered antlers. He's grazing quietly among the tents, unconcerned by our presence. After weeks of trying to stalk deer and get close enough to take a decent photo, this one virtually sits down by the tent and asks for a cup of tea, and I can't even see my camera screen to tell if I've taken a photo of him or not. He's so out of place among the tents, powerful, docile, but completely wild. I watch him cross the river then head away and I realize he's completely in place;

we and the tents are the ones that don't belong in his world, not the other way around.

I wake to the sound of shrieking. The pub has closed and I can tell from the voices that the group from the bar are back at their tents.

'These fucking midges, they're fucking mental.'

'Fire, we need a fire to keep them off.'

'I'll get wood. I'm good at fires.' Someone clatters off to the river and there's a sound of branches being ripped off trees as music starts playing from someone's phone, the bass beat getting louder and louder. The wood collector comes back and there's a commotion while they try to light the fire, eventually getting a few sparks from the wet wood. Then we realize why we can hear them so clearly. They're lighting a fire two feet from the back of our tent. Moth's out of his sleeping bag in seconds, with his head out of the tent.

'Guys, guys, don't light a fire right next to my tent, if a spark gets on it I'm toast.'

'Your tent won't burn, mate, I'm great at fires.'

Moth gets back in, spitting out midges as he closes the zip and sparks start to fly from the fire. We hold our breath and cross our fingers, but the fire gets brighter and the voices louder.

'I tell you, mate, you are not Scottish if you don't want independence. If you don't want to stand alone, you're betraying our history and all those who fought for it.'

'Bollocks, man. Modern Scotland's not just about its history, and independence won't change our lives.'

'How can you say that? Of course it will.'

The argument heats up, glass gets broken, the girls fall quiet, then the rain ends it all as the fire hisses out and they run to their tents. We try to sleep, but I can't, my thoughts keep running through the argument around the fire. I think of the stag, grazing, moving on, unconcerned about borders or boundaries, yet inhabiting these hills, this bogland, without a thought or question of power and ownership. When did humans start to believe our existence on the land required ownership and borders – was it when we stopped moving and started to build? Was that the moment we began to disconnect from the land and each other and in doing so created a world so complex that, even as drunk as they were, these young people were still arguing over how to rearrange the puzzle? Yet all the time, while even in the wilderness we argue about who wields the power, the climate is heating up and the very land over which we're arguing is beginning to burn.

19

'Can you hear bagpipes?' Moth's stopped to listen to music drifting through the midge-fog and drizzle. Definitely bagpipes. Suddenly a large group of men in vests and kilts appear out of the trees. Bare arms and legs despite the midges, one carrying a CD player on his shoulder blasting out a bagpipe version of 'Flower of Scotland' across the hillside.

'Great music, guys.'

'Aye, it's the Scotland v England game in a couple of days, hoping to catch it in Kinlochleven, but we need "Flower of Scotland" to prepare us for that.' The Scotland football team are hoping to get through to the next round of the Euros, and even here no one wants to miss a game.

The pipes fade into the distance as we reach the pub at Bridge of Orchy and drink tea on a bench. It's only ten in the morning and it already feels like we've walked miles. We're about to leave when a group of women come and sit nearby.

'Are you Raynor Winn? We're from Cornwall. We're only walking because I read your book.' The smaller woman tells us she's walking the West Highland Way to celebrate her fiftieth birthday.

The taller of the group is clearly not as happy to be here. 'You're Raynor Winn? Is it really you? I hate you.'

I'm quite taken aback for a moment. How can this stranger feel so strongly about me? 'Oh no. Why?'

'I didn't want to come here, I wanted to go to a spa.' The birthday girl picks up her friend's rucksack, helping her put it on her back.

'Yes, but it's not your birthday.'

This trail has such a different character to the Cape Wrath. It's a social path; walking it feels like being part of a day-long party. Groups of people enjoying time in the natural world, but mainly just enjoying being together after being locked down for such a long time. Rubbish can be collected, hangovers will recede, but their memories of being here in this wild landscape and the adventure of covering so many miles on foot will stay with them forever. In a time when we're trying to work out how people should reconnect with the land, we pass tens of people doing just that. And women, there are women everywhere. Groups of young women straight out of university, groups of middle-aged women looking for something new. So unexpected after the very male atmosphere of the north.

Along the broad open hillside below Beinn Dorain and Beinn Odhar, we walk parallel to the main road that runs along the opposite side of the glen. It's a wide empty landscape where the only things that move are humans on foot and in cars, a landscape where eagles should soar and deer should graze. But the skies and the hills are empty of all but crows and sheep, and despite the treeline beyond the road, there's no sound of cuckoos. Moth sits on the hot dry hillside and strains to hear the low woody call of the large grey bird, but there's nothing.

'Now I think about it, I don't think I've heard a cuckoo since we left Kinlochleven.'

'No, me neither. And not a single deer since the stag at the bridge. It's almost as if we stopped seeing much wildlife after we came down from the Aonach Eagach Ridge into Glencoe, as if it was some kind of barrier.'

'Still heard that bird that wakes us up in the night though.'

'Oh yeah, still that. I wish I knew what it was.'

Moth gets up stiffly, he's tiring and his feet are hurting, but we carry on.

We pitch the tent on a midge-thick patch of turf by the stream in Tyndrum, a place where travellers have stopped for centuries. Once the staging post for cattle drovers, it still serves the needs of the Highland traveller with the only petrol station for miles. But there's a power cut, so no petrol and the cars are backing up, the drivers getting out and arguing with the pump attendant. We buy some sandwiches that they're selling for a few pence in the petrol station because the fridges have no power and the food's going off in the heat, and retreat into the tent away from the midges. Moth is asleep as soon as it's dark and doesn't wake for twelve hours. The night crawls by, minutes stretch out as if time has become elastic. I'm sleeping less and less as the days pass, as if every movement on the airbeds creates a noise that stops sleep and leaves me wide awake. I try to focus on Moth's breathing, allowing that to lull me to sleep, but even that's quiet and not having the usual effect. He's exhausted and sleep comes like a warm blanket of relief whenever he lies down, or sits, or even stands still for too long. But my body's beginning to run on less and less. Less food, less sleep, my days pass in a metronome of walking, without even painful feet to ground me. The trees block any light from the moon, leaving the tent in extreme darkness, and I feel totally alone, even though Moth lies next to me.

Is this how life will be without him? Our greatest fears always greet us in their ugliest form in the quiet of the night, and in the darkness of the Highlands I'm forced to see mine for what they are. This cocoon of darkness is what my life will be without him. This man, who has filled every corner of my life with light and noise, will leave me with nothing but empty quiet darkness and I know I'll retreat into it, consumed by the emptiness. These endless sleepless nights feel like a forerunner of my future. Even at my most optimistic, I can't convince myself that this walk is having the effect I hoped. Moth's thoughts are clearer, he's stronger and more dexterous, but it's as if his health has hit a point that he can't pass.

At the head of Loch Lomond a herd of black goats sleeps among the rocks, occasionally standing to wade ankle-deep in the gently lapping water. Evening sun bounces from the loch, turning its surface into a field of light between the dark hills rising either side. The soft evening air hangs warm and still, hardly a breath of wind moving the water, and we're caught with nowhere to camp by a midge-infested loch, surrounded by signs warning of camping restrictions and warden patrols. I can barely see through the head net and I'm dripping in insect repellent, but tiny red bites still appear on every patch of exposed skin. Our only hope is to climb higher and hope for a breeze, but there's no guarantee of a flat patch even if the wind saves us from the insects. Then suddenly a ferry appears through the midge-dark air, a passenger ferry for the hotel on the opposite shore. We jump on, in the hope that there might be some kind of midge-refuge on the other side.

'No, we're fully booked, and there's no camping here. That's why walkers walk the full twenty miles from Rowardennan to Crianlarich. You haven't timed your day very well, have you?' The hotel receptionist is about to go back into the office when he has a moment's inspiration. 'Tell you what we do have though. There's a pod at the back of the caravan park – you can use that if you want.'

Yes, we'll take the pod; yes, we'll take refuge from the biting beasts; and yes, without a doubt we'll use your shower block. We thank the man so profusely he probably thinks he's undercharged us, and lock the door of the pod behind us. The midges throw themselves against the glass of the door like zombies in a horror film, as we watch them from the safety of the plastic mattresses. We don't get anywhere near the showers until morning.

20

'Are you heading north? At least you have the worst section behind you now.' We hand the key in to the same receptionist as we leave.

'No, we're heading south. Worst section, what do you mean?' I'm starting to feel uneasy: didn't the woman in the bike shop mention something about this section?

'The Way follows about twenty miles down the side of the loch and a long stretch of that is a boulder field – it's hell to cross. If people are going to give up on the Way, then here's where they do it.'

We sit on the bench outside the hotel in already hot sun and read the guidebook.

'It says "a tortuous up-and-down route". Maybe we should call it a day, and just catch the bus.' Moth's feet have caused him so much pain on the relatively easy path from Fort William that I can't see how he can carry on. I close the book and resign myself to this being the end. But he's already putting his rucksack on.

'No, I'll just go to the bar and buy a few more Mars bars, then we'll catch the next ferry. Unless of course *you* want to give up.'

The boulders are scattered but then quickly become a continual up-and-down scramble over, around and between the rocks. It's hard going, but maybe it's easier going south, or maybe it's downhill, because as the section-walkers heading north begin to pass they're in every stage of exhaustion: sweating, swearing, crawling and moaning. But we're alongside a loch so we can't be going downhill, it's actually flat, just boulder strewn. Maybe, just possibly, our legs are finally feeling some benefit from having dragged us through the bogs of the north. I watch Moth climbing up, over and through the boulders, sure-footed, not losing his balance, with enough breath to stop and chat. *Maybe, just maybe.*

A group of girls stop at some steps, waiting for us to come down.

'Have you seen Rob Roy's cave?'

'No.'

Rob Roy was part of the first Jacobite uprising and lived most of his life as an outlaw and a rebel, until, by then in his fifties, he was finally pardoned. Now, his story is one of the many legends of folk heroes that echo around these hills, drawing people to scramble across boulder fields in search of caves where he's said to have hung out during one of his exploits.

We continue south as the party heads north. Men in kilts, girls in Lycra, grannies with CD players blasting 'Flower of Scotland' across the loch, a man dressed head to toe in shiny blue synthetic fabric, who stops us halfway over a boulder.

'Have you seen Rob Roy's cave?'

'No.'

Through the tree canopy the sun rises high above the mountains, it's warm even in the shade and the boulders go on and on, for mile after mile. Two men struggle by, carrying huge mountain bikes over their shoulders.

'He said we can cycle the Way in two days, said he'd done it before, said we'd have a great weekend. He didn't tell me about this though.' The older Lycra-clad man doesn't look as if he's joking.

'I told you, it was fifteen years ago, I think I just remembered the long downhill into Bridge of Orchy.'

'And you said it was worth doing this bit because we'd see Rob Roy's cave.' The older man looks at us. 'Have you seen Rob Roy's cave?

'No.' We shake our heads as they struggle on, trying to run

with their bikes as the wheels and pedals catch and bang against the boulders.

'This must have been what the woman in the bike shop in Fort William meant when she said this would be harder on a bike than on foot.' Moth carries on ahead of me but looks back over his shoulder. 'I've been thinking about those bikes.'

The boulders eventually thin out near a huge hotel, heaving with coachloads of tourists and surrounded by no-camping signs. Unsure what to do, we sit on a bench near a group of ladies in their seventies, who immediately start a conversation with Moth.

'We've walked up from Rowardennan, we live on the other side of the loch, but our friend fell in the rocks. She still hasn't got here and now we've missed the last ferry over.'

'Oh dear, what are you going to do?'

'Just sit here and drink wine and watch the sunset. I'm sure some nice young man on a boat will take pity on us.'

'Did you notice anywhere to camp to the south of here?'

'No. You should call Les.'

'Les?'

'Yes, he runs a bunkhouse up over the hill. I've got his number somewhere.'

The bunkhouse is heaving, even though Les tells us they're only half full. Mainly young people heading north on the path, laughing, arguing, talking. Moth starts a conversation with a man sitting alone on a battered leather sofa.

'This seems like a really popular path. Great to see so many young people walking.'

'That's because it's so close to Glasgow. And it's the end of term for the universities, lots of us come and do the West Highland Way before we go off for the summer. It connects us – reconnects us.'

'Reconnects? Surely most of the uni students are from outside Scotland?'

'They are, but lots of us are Scottish. And to be Scottish

means the nature, the mountains, all of this wild open space – it feels like ours. It might well belong to foreign millionaires, but that's only on paper. Really, this land is ours, it's our birthright. That's what we're reconnecting to.'

The late-evening light is shining through the chapel window, highlighting the rips in the battered leather of the sofa. I look at the ordinary young man, curled up at the end of it with a book in his hand, and wonder how many young people in England think its few remaining wild corners are their birthright? I know the answer; maybe that's why the wild corners are getting smaller by the day.

'I'm going to try to visit Rob Roy's Cave on the way north tomorrow. Did you see it?'

'No.'

The morning's warm without a breath of wind and even though the midges normally drop a little during the heat of the day, on this day they continue to increase. The boulders behind us, we follow a flat loch-side path, but can't stop to enjoy it for even a moment. Even the seemingly obligatory accompaniment of 'Flower of Scotland' can't distract us from the remorseless biting. The only way to avoid being crusted in the black beasts is to keep moving, even eating and drinking while walking.

Arriving from the south, Balmaha might be no more than a small boating village on the loch, but from the midge-infested banks of the north it appears like a tranquil oasis, at the point where the path bends away from the end of the loch. We hang out under a huge oak tree drinking ice-cold water from the pub, before camping in the midge-free wind on the side of Conic Hill. Moth traces the line on the map, backwards and forwards through the guidebook.

'I can't believe this will be over tomorrow. But it could still be another eighteen miles to Milngavie. I think it's going to be too far. Maybe we should have tried to go further today?'

'I don't think I could have gone another step tonight, but it's easy going tomorrow, I'm sure we'll make it. We'll have to leave early though.' I'm sounding confident, but I don't think we stand a chance of getting to the end of the Way tomorrow, although I know we have to try. The person we need to meet can't wait and we can't miss him.

The day's warm, overcast and still – a day made for midges. But as we head further away from the loch they begin to lessen. Finally we can stop occasionally without breathing them in. The path becomes a road and even more of a party route as we hit group after group of people coming the other way, fresh off the train, on the first day of the West Highland Way. They're all happy and excited, no one asks what the path's actually like and we don't tell them about the boulders. We've passed the watershed, the place where Highland becomes Lowland and the mountains are behind us. We should be celebrating the fact that we've walked so far and are still standing, but with our backs to the high wild places we're filled with a sense of loss.

'We shouldn't be down, we know what's coming, let's just look forward to that.' As usual I'm trying to lift the mood even though I'm feeling as flat as Moth.

'I know, and I am. I just feel we've experienced something so special and I might never come here again.'

'Then let's promise ourselves we will.' We make the promises we all make at the end of a holiday, with no idea if we'll be able to keep them.

Through lanes and villages, woods and fields, scratched by patches of tall thistles and bracken uncurling to a foot high. Moth's exhausted, his feet painful, his shoulders aching from carrying the rucksack for twelve hours, and we're close to stopping, putting the tent up and acknowledging that we won't make it to the meeting tomorrow, when we reach the edge of Mugdock Country Park. There's no stopping now in this wildlife-sensitive area; we have to keep going. The air is dense with birdsong, through oak woodlands and swathes of wild flowers. The park holds the remains of Mugdock Castle and I let my imagination run with the deer through what was once a site of barons and serfs, of feudal rights and suffering, before finally being gifted to the people of Glasgow in 1980. Now it's just a pleasant walk in the woods without a deer in sight – but not that pleasant as my legs are in spasms of cramp and Moth takes his boots off every twenty minutes to massage his feet. But suddenly, as if the Highlands are just in our imagination, buildings begin to appear and we're passing rusted steel sheets that line the final metres of the path, each one engraved with a highlight of the Way. We walk past them and know each one, as if the memory of it is somehow tattooed on to us, indelible, constant, something we will feel infinitely rather than remember – Ben Nevis, Buachaille Etive Mòr, Ben Lomond . . .

A concrete obelisk marks the start of the West Highland Way and our end. As we dance around the pillar, there's finally a glow of appreciation of what we've done. Our feet have traced a path through the wilderness of this country and it's ingrained in us. We've loved the Highlands since life-changing trips in our early twenties, but this is different. Now we feel as if each step across bog, heather and boulder has created another strand of DNA, something that will always be a part of who we are.

'I'm starving. Shall we get some chips?'

'Oh yes, please, with loads of salt, then we'll see if we can find a taxi.'

We eat the chips on a bench by the obelisk, marvelling at the fact that we're finally here. I don't say it, but I'm really marvelling at something much bigger than that. Moth has walked eighteen miles from Conic Hill. His feet are painful and his shoulders ache, but he's here, laughing and dancing around the pillar, chips in hand, singing 'Flower of Scotland', with nothing but sheer joy written on his face. I still don't know how it's possible, I may never know how, but I don't need to. In this moment I'm happy to join in the chorus and accept it as a miracle.

★

The taxi drops us a few miles outside the town at a guest house on the hill. The only bed available in the district. We're met by an elegant woman with bright silver hair.

'Oh, you're here! What a shame you didn't get here an hour ago; he's been and gone.'

'Oh no. He said he was coming tomorrow morning. We thought we'd be here to meet him.' I see Moth's shoulders drop as he blows air out through puffed cheeks. 'What are we going to do now?'

'It's not a problem, I was here so he left them with me. Come and look, they're in the garage.' We follow her to a neat garage behind an up-and-over door, and they're there. The shiny bikes from the back of the shop in Fort William, dropped off by their driver a day earlier than expected.

'Wow, I can't believe they're here.' Moth's immediately unwinding the bubble wrap, helped by the silver lady.

'Where are you going on them?'

'We're going to follow the canal towpath from Glasgow to Edinburgh, then on through the borders until we reach England. I can't walk any further, my feet are agony, but this way we'll have travelled the length of Scotland under our own steam.'

I watch him enthusiastically ripping off the plastic and find it hard to believe I'm hearing him say these words, but since the moment Dave phoned as we stood outside the bike shop and said, 'Well, are you meeting us in Kirk Yetholm then?' it had felt almost inevitable.

The Borders

Milngavie to Kirk Yetholm

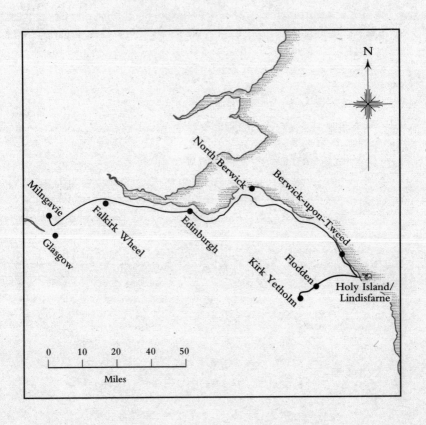

21

Glasgow is buzzing with pre-match excitement. The streets heave with football supporters all heading to the pubs to communally watch Scotland play Croatia in the final group game of the Euros. The excitement in the air makes it seem beyond doubt that Scotland will win and go through to the knockout stages. There's tartan everywhere, kilts and cockades, exuberant feathered bonnets and blue face paint, all creating a feeling of carnival and joy. We've collected the things we need for the bikes, posted our rucksacks to Kirk Yetholm and got back to the guest house before kick-off, so don't stay to see the party fizzle out as Scotland's hopes are dashed and they lose 3–0. But the next day there's no sense of failure in any of the supporters; people are still wearing their tartan, still singing 'Flower of Scotland' and feeling nothing but pride that their team got as far as it did.

It's been fifteen years since I last rode a bike, so I should have known better when Moth said we'd be fine to cycle all the way from Milngavie to Edinburgh in a day. After all: 'The towpath's completely flat and the bikes have loads of gears, we'll fly, it's only about fifty miles, we'll be there in time for tea.'

But cycling isn't walking. It uses an entirely different set of muscles, and those that brought us all the way from Sheigra are being stretched in ways I didn't think possible. Maybe I should have posted my walking boots to Kirk Yetholm too, and the stove, and the airbed, instead of adding all that extra weight to the panniers and causing the bike to overbalance every time I stop.

'We're never going to make it.' It's late afternoon, we've just passed the Falkirk Wheel, swapping from the Forth and Clyde to the Union Canal, where the immense rotating boatlift takes boats from the lower canal to the higher one further up the hill. It has a huge, dominating, almost alien presence and I'm happy to leave it behind as we push the bikes through a slimy, stalactite-encrusted tunnel to return to the towpath. The path is wet, cobbled and, despite faint lights, very dark in the middle. I fall over twice, clattering the bike down on top of me and nearly sliding into the canal.

'We'll be fine, we've got hours before it's dark.'

Can it really be me begging to stop and Moth saying carry on? I keep the wheels turning, my legs throbbing in hot pain. I try to distract myself by counting ducks, swans and moorhens along this wildlife corridor, enjoying the warm wind in my face, but it only works for a mile before my head's once more full of pain and impossibility. Eventually, after what feels like half a lifetime of agony, Edinburgh appears in the glow of a midsummer sunset. We push the bikes down Princes Street at nearly 11 p.m., in the twilight of midsummer's eve. Each step feels like the last I'll ever have the energy to take, but inexplicably Moth is bright, alert and marvelling at the peach streaks in the sky above the silhouetted outline of the castle on the hill.

As if from nowhere, a memory breaks through my exhaustion. 'You know we were in Scotland thirty-five years ago today?'

'Were we? Where were we, what were we doing?'

I know he's losing his memory, but he can't have forgotten this. I'm about to get annoyed, then I remember it's taken me until nearly midnight to remember myself.

'We were on the Isle of Skye.' I watch him as he stops walking and puts his hand to his face, shaking his head. 'We were getting married.'

Edinburgh's built on history, the history of the rocks on which it stands and the people that settled here. There are traces of habitation from the Mesolithic period, around 8000 BC, and after that through the Bronze and Iron Ages, where humans sought out the protective rocky heights that still surround the modern city. Sites where they could see for miles and defend themselves from whatever might come from the hills beyond. The city still seems to hold the weight of millennia of connections between this landscape and the people who have inhabited it. The stone buildings that dominate the Old Town on one hill and the undulating New Town that rises from the valley are hewn from stone from the hills that surround the city. Modern Edinburgh may house industry, technology and the Scottish Parliament but, as with the rest of Scotland, the modern fabric is almost inseparable from its historic past and the landscape from which it grew.

'Think I've seen enough architecture for now. Shall we look for a new sleeping bag? I'll have the new one and you can get rid of the broken one and have your old one back.'

'Could do.'

We go into the outdoor shop that seems to have the greatest selection, choose one and go to the counter. The huge bundle of green fabric and feathers is loosely stuffed in its big storage bag, but the girl at the till says she'll quickly put it into its tiny stuff sack.

'It'll only take a moment, I'm the world champion sleeping-bag stuffer.'

'What? Is there such a thing?' Looking at this smart young woman, with her straightened hair and perfect make-up, I can only wonder how she could possibly have found herself at the sleeping-bag stuffing world championships. Perhaps she's having a particularly boring afternoon and has just made it up. But as she begins to demonstrate the technique of a world champion sleeping-bag stuffer, I think it could be real. Her hands move in a flurry of stuff sack and down bag, compressing the one into the other in seconds.

'How did you do that? And why would you even dream of becoming a world champion sleeping-bag stuffer?'

'Well, to tell you the truth, the rest of the competitors were under ten and most of them were boy scouts.'

'Still, I don't know how you did that.'

We go back to our room and repack the panniers ready to leave the next morning. Rather than packing it, Moth unstuffs the new bag.

'I've got to try and stuff it the way she did. It was so quick.' He takes the sack in one hand and the bag in the other and begins grabbing handfuls of bag, stuffing them rapidly into the sack. For a moment I think back to the trembling hand in Cornwall and wonder at the control of this hand filling the sack, but only for a moment.

'Oh shit.'

'What? What have you done?'

'Oh fuck, I've done something to my hand.' He drops the sack and examines his hand. 'Jeez, my whole hand hurts, but this finger, something's happened to it, I think I've broken it.'

'You can't have broken it stuffing a sleeping bag.' I look at his ring finger, which is already changing colour and looks strangely rigid. 'You're right, I think you have. Shall we go to the hospital?'

'There's no point, it's only a finger, they'd just tape it to the next one anyway.'

'Take your ring off at least, it's going to swell.'

'I'm not taking my wedding ring off. I'm going to have a shower then can you tape it up?'

'Well, doesn't it hurt? Do you want some painkillers?'

'It hurt for a moment, but it's okay now. Maybe it's not broken, perhaps I've just twisted it or something.'

Obviously there are some benefits to losing the feeling in his hands. But the finger's already swelling by the time I wrap the tape around it, a large bruise beginning to spread down his hand.

Leaving Edinburgh on the bikes is a nightmare of traffic and busy roads, but it's a relief to find that two days of hot and cold baths have soothed muscles that I'd thought might never recover, for now at least. Moth's cycling with his fingers pointing out, steering with his thumb and braking with his little finger, but still insisting it doesn't hurt. Thirty miles out of the city and we're into a landscape dominated by Torness nuclear power station on one side and the North Sea on the other; they seem to be all I see. It's not until two days later, as we head on to a coast path south of Berwick-upon-Tweed, that I begin to realize how much less observant I am on wheels, compared to when I'm on foot. There could be so much of note in North Berwick, I should be excited about being back near the coast, but my focus is on the traffic and the power station.

Then suddenly, as we hit the bumpy dried grass of the coast the light changes, the sea fills the horizon and my lips taste of salt. My senses are rebooted as the song of skylarks fills the air. The call of this little brown bird is the iconic sound of our uplands, moorlands and coasts, but in the last twenty-five years their breeding numbers have fallen by 50 per cent, putting the beloved skylark on to the UK Conservation Red List. We drop the bikes on the ground and lie on the dry grass, trying to spot them in the bright blue sky. They're all around, their trilling song rising with them into the salted air, only stopping as they fall back down to earth to take a deep breath before rising again. A musical attempt to distract us from what must be a prized nesting site.

'Listening to that sound, it's like the backing track of our time in the hills. They've always been there, in the Staffordshire moorlands when we were in our twenties, through all our time in Wales, but when you really think about it, we've barely heard them in recent years. On the coast in Cornwall, in the grass meadows on the farm, but not in numbers, not like this, not like they always used to be.' Moth's shielding his eyes from the sun, trying to count the birds.

Maybe that's how we've slipped into this biodiversity crisis? We don't notice things until suddenly we don't notice them.

The skylarks, like the cuckoos, driven to the few remaining patches of habitat that can still support them. But very soon it will be the same as when the swallows leave. You don't see them go, you just look up one day and they're not there.

We doze on the headland, lulled to sleep by the song of the birds, until suddenly Moth sits up with a jump.

'Oh fuck, look at the time, if we're going to get to Lindisfarne we've got to go, the tide's coming in.' He looks over at the tiny island in the distance. 'We'll be lucky if we make it.'

Lindisfarne is also known as Holy Island, a pseudonym drawn from the centuries of saints and Celtic Christians who've inhabited it. But it's also tidal, approached by a causeway that disappears as the tide comes in, and we have only an hour to cycle four miles to the beginning of the strip of tarmac that crosses the soft sand, then a mile and a half to the other side of the causeway, before it disappears underwater. Camping isn't allowed on the island, so we've booked the last remaining hotel bed, but as we hit the causeway the tide is racing in like a wall in the distance as we pedal into a strong headwind. However hard I try to push I'm moving forward at a snail's pace, the distance between Moth's back wheel and my front one becoming greater by the minute. I put my head down in an attempt to become more streamlined, hope all the saints are on my side, and pedal until my legs refuse to do as I ask. There's an unending stream of people driving in the opposite direction, lots gesticulating through their car windows as they fly past, or opening them and shouting: 'Get off the causeway, it's closing.'

'I'm trying.' I feel as if I'm in one of those dreams where you run as fast as you can but go nowhere.

Eventually Moth comes back into view. He's lying flat out on the grass at the edge of a lay-by, at the foot of a hill of sand dunes. I fall down next to him, trying hard to breathe as the water closes across the causeway and we and the island are cut off. The island rises just far enough above sea level for the miles of dunes to stay above water level, but it wouldn't take much of a sea-level rise for half the island to disappear underwater, for the dunes to become flat seabed. Two cyclists at the other end of the lay-by are mending a puncture. He's swearing and she's crying.

'Are you okay? Can we help?' I've dragged myself back on to my feet and walked over to them, while Moth is still lying flat on the grass in a stupor.

'Fucking puncture.' He's just feeding a new inner tube into the tyre.

'We've missed the causeway – it's going to be hours before it opens again.' The girl's crying in despair.

'What are you going to do?'

'Fucking wait, what else can we do?' The man glares at the woman. 'It's your fault for going back into that bloody trinket shop.' He flips the tyre back into place. I don't know why he's rushing, it's not as if they're going anywhere.

'Have you got any food?'

'No, we were going to eat on the other side.'

Moth wanders over with chocolate bars and a banana and we leave them to watch the tide, thankful they're the ones with the puncture, not us.

We catch the ice cream van as he's closing for the evening and ride slowly across the island. Somewhere in the west, the sun will be dipping. Facing east there is no sun, but the deep rare colours of a sunset smudge the horizon between sky and water, an ink stain of colour running through a line of least resistance. On a promontory at the edge of the island, a castle stands silhouetted against the colour, disconnecting it from reality. It's not hard to see why Henry VIII thought it was a good idea to take the stone from the priory and rebuild it as a castle out on the edge of the land, where the views are infinite and defence easy. But I doubt if the monks, who for nearly a thousand years had rubbed shoulders with saints and shared plates of fish in the priory, felt the same. I doubt, too, if Henry would have expected his defensive building to be re-imagined by Edward Lutyens in the style of the Arts and Crafts movement, or for Gertrude Jeykll to design a garden where his armaments had stood.

I have no religious belief and we didn't come here on a spiritual quest – it was more out of curiosity – yet there's a sense of something other-worldly here. The tide still cuts the island off from the mainland, just as it would have when the first monks came here from Iona on the west coast of Scotland, just as it did when Henry and his soldiers left, having completely changed island life. It still feels as if the tide is the perfect defence, although no longer against marauding armies – now it's just against the many visitors who flock here every day. There's a strange, almost palpable feeling of human connection that hangs in the air, as if a thousand years of time and lives are compressed into the flight of an oystercatcher calling in the dying light as it skims the water between the island and Bamburgh Castle, fading into a haze in the south. The same scene that will have replayed for hundreds of years.

Moth's leaning against the stone wall of a ruined building. He seems to be watching the last of the light, but he's not really here; his thoughts are beyond the horizon.

'Are you okay? What's on your mind? Shall we go now and just get some sleep? I don't know about you, but I'm exhausted.'

'Me too, but lately I've realized that it doesn't matter how tired I am, I can't miss times like this. I have to hold on to every moment I can.'

'But if you get too tired you won't be able to, you'll be sleeping through all the moments.' As I say it, the memory of his endless sleeping before we left Cornwall floods my mind. The days lost in a fog of exhaustion and the doctor's warnings of 'don't get too tired'. It's taken every ounce of his willpower to get him to where we are now; I fear that extra hour of physical effort, or even the wind in the wrong direction, will be enough to send him right back to where he started from, or even further down.

'I might have said the same before we left, but this trip has taught me something about all of this – the living, the dying, the void in between. It's not about how long it lasts, it's about the value of each moment. It's like one of your pans of mushroom soup.'

It's almost completely dark, on the edge of an island stuck out in the North Sea, a chilly north-easterly wind blowing in from Scandinavia, and he's comparing life and death to a pan of soup.

'What?'

'It takes loads of mushrooms, so you only ever make enough for two bowls, but it's full of such deep and complex flavours – thyme and garlic, and earth – that it doesn't matter. That one bowl is enough, because it holds so much.'

'Earth? That's probably the compost I haven't washed off the mushrooms.'

'You don't have to do that.'

'Do what?'

'Whenever I mention death, you joke about it, or change the subject. Don't you get it? It's part of the soup. There's always more flavour when the mushrooms are about to go off: it makes the soup so much richer.'

'I might not make that soup again, not if it makes you think of earth and death, it's tomato from now on.'

'You know I see right through you, don't you?'

'I know. But you also know this trip's always been about gathering the ingredients for a great soup.'

'It's already good soup.'

'The very best soup.'

We walk away as darkness falls, somewhere in the void between life and death, that place where we all exist.

Cycling out of the village the following morning a tide is coming towards us, not of water, but people. It's only 10 a.m., but the car park is full, coachloads of people are being disgorged on to the road and the causeway is nose to tail with traffic. The peace of the island disappears under a tsunami of people. I could be outside a football stadium on the day of a cup match. How does such a tiny island sustain this many visitors?

Back on the mainland we stop in a café, drink tea and read a map. From here we turn west and follow the borderlands towards Kirk Yetholm. Leaving the tea room there's a cool wind blowing the chance of rain and my bike has a puncture; the tyre is completely flat. Pre-CBD Moth could change an inner tube in his sleep; I cross my fingers and hope that the memory hasn't left him. He takes the pump off his bike and tries to pump my tyre up, but the nozzle doesn't fit the valve; it fits Moth's but not mine. Without a pump we can't change the inner tube; if we can't change the inner tube we can't go anywhere. We order more tea and think about finding a taxi to take us to a bike shop, but there's no mobile reception. I retape Moth's finger. It's now blue and the flesh has swollen over his ring.

'I knew you should have taken it off.'

'It's fine, it doesn't hurt, retape it and I'm sure it'll go down in a day or two.'

We walk around trying to get reception, but there is none, so drink even more tea and listen to an argument about Brexit, which feeds into a conversation about Scottish independence. Both votes are in the past, but the repercussions from them are still reverberating, especially here in the Borders, where few people seem to identify themselves as either Scottish or English, but more as residents of some sort of liminal transitional country of its own. They look as if at any minute cakes will be thrown, but eventually the mood calms and their discussion leads to a conclusion.

'I voted for Brexit, but I didn't want to leave Europe, I wanted to feel as if we were truly independent within it. I just thought it would shake things up – I didn't really expect it to happen.' The old lady has finished her tea and her anger is subsiding.

'And I don't want independence, but I'm Scottish, not

British.' The young man in his sports shorts picks up the napkin the old lady has dropped and passes it back to her. 'I'd say we're both the same – we want to be married but keep our own names. To be team players, but still individuals.'

'I wouldn't marry you, dear, I couldn't live with a man who wears shorts.'

We leave them to exchange phone numbers and return to our own crisis. A couple are taking bikes out of the back of a car on the opposite side of the car park. She holds them while he comes up to the public toilets next to where our bikes are standing.

'Are you okay? That's very flat.'

'We would be, but the pump doesn't fit.' Moth keeps retrying the pump in the hope that he simply hasn't attached it correctly. 'And the inner tube fits my bike but not this one. So not okay really.'

'Come down to the car with me, I've got a tube and a pump that'll fit that.'

Moth follows him across the car park, then I watch the couple cycle away as he walks back.

'They said just put the pump under their car when we go.'

'That's so generous.'

After hours of sitting around and wondering what to do, and despite his taped-up fingers, the inner tube is changed in minutes and we're ready to go. Obviously some memories never leave. But while we've been focused on the wheel a number of cars have arrived and others have left.

'Oh fuck.'

'What? What's happened?'

'I can't remember which car it was. It was next to a red one, but there aren't any red ones.'

We walk up and down the row of cars, eventually leaving the pump and a note under the only car with its back seats folded down and cycle away with our fingers crossed.

★

We take the tent down from behind a hedge and push the bikes out on to the road, into a cold wind blowing in from the west. We're hungry when we stop at Flodden Field, but it seems almost disrespectful to eat Mars bars here, in the place where so many people died. In the sixteenth century the people of this area were used to unrest; skirmishes with the border reivers were part of life here for years. These raiders from both north and south of the disputed border made regular incursions into their opponents' lands, stealing goods, rustling cattle, taking prisoners, but what came to these fields in 1513 was so much more than a skirmish. The battle between the Scots and English left James IV of Scotland and between ten and twenty thousand soldiers dead in the mud of these border farmlands. Such a momentous and horrendous battle, now marked only by a stone cross and a tiny car park. We unlock the bikes and cycle away, the weight of the death of thousands hanging heavily over us. Since the sixteenth century humans have changed the world beyond recognition. We've revolutionized the way we live, made breathtaking and miraculous discoveries, and yet we seem totally incapable of changing ourselves. We haven't evolved a step beyond that day in 1513, which saw so many people die. Centuries in which we could have worked together to find a way of life where no one is hungry, or without shelter, a world where we don't destroy the climate, but instead all we've done is waste precious time fighting over a line on a map. I cycle on, imagining a world without borders.

'You sound like John Lennon, just pedal or we'll never get there.'

It's late afternoon when we cross the bridge over the River Bowmont and cycle on to the gravel forecourt of a guest house in Kirk Yetholm. A couple are drinking tea in the garden. The man, big, loud and northern, stands up; he's holding a teapot.

'Thought you'd never get here. We've eaten all the cakes.'

PART THREE

The Spine

Our unfenced country
Is bog that keeps crusting
Between the sights of the sun.

'Bogland', Seamus Heaney

The Pennine Way

Kirk Yetholm to Edale

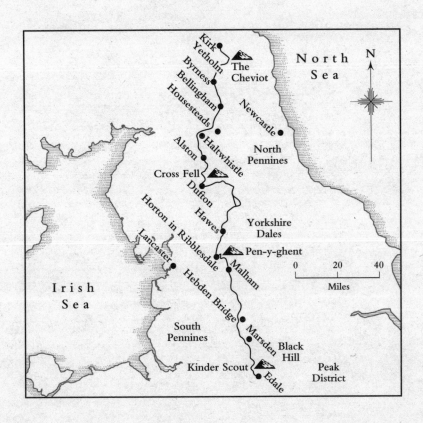

22

'Don't know why we're doing this, you could have just cycled home.' Dave's leaning over my bike, trying to take the pedals off so it will fit into a huge cardboard box to be delivered to Cornwall.

'We wouldn't have made it – it's too far. I thought backpacking was tough, but cycling's a whole other league of pain.' I take the pedal from him and drop it into the box. 'No, like we said on the phone, we'll rest up here then walk with you two until you have to go back to work, then we'll get the train south. I don't know why you wanted us to come anyway – oh I do, you need us to read the map.'

'Now don't tell lies. You know you wanted us to come cos life's just too dull without us.'

I throw the panniers at him. He stuffs them down the side of the bike and we seal the box.

'Are you finished?' Julie's closing the box on Moth's bike.

'Yep, all done.'

'Pub then?'

Moth's headed off through a maze of rooms to find the toilet and Julie chooses her moment.

'How's he been? We were quite worried about him when you left us, but I have to say he's looking different.'

'Cape Wrath was tough, in so many ways, but since then he seems stronger, more flexible, in his thinking as well as his movements. But who knows? I go to sleep every night with my fingers crossed and every morning I hold my breath, expecting him to wake up feeling worse not better.'

'And has he?'

'No, now I think about it, not for a while.'

'I read something recently about multi-surface training being more effective than flat in physio for people with a Parkinsonism, and it certainly hasn't been flat where you've been.'

It's a fact: the bogs and the boulder fields were anything but flat. My mind wanders to the South West Coast Path and how Moth's health had miraculously improved as we walked on a path that's constantly uneven, constantly undulating, and wonder if the wild places we're drawn to actually hold the key to Moth's health, in far simpler ways than I imagined.

'Here he is. Thought you'd got lost out there.' Dave's immediately changing the subject as Moth finally reappears from the toilets.

'Well, you know how it is, when you've been away from flushing toilets for a few weeks, can't drag yourself away from running water.'

'We were just saying, by the time we go home you'll be well on down the Pennines, you might as well carry on after we go, just finish it off while you're here.'

'No chance. Do you know how long the Pennine Way is?' But a faint light crosses Moth's face, a slight change of expression others wouldn't notice, but I've seen a thousand times before. He looks up and catches my eye and we both know what's happening.

The Pennines cover 268 miles of moorland along the spine of England, from Edale in the Dark Peak to the pub in Kirk Yetholm. Two hundred and sixty-eight miles of big skies, bogs and wild weather. When it opened in 1965 it was the UK's very first national trail, and most people didn't know what to do with it. But Tom Stephenson, a writer who had championed its creation, had a dream of what it would become – 'a faint line on the Ordnance Maps which the feet of grateful pilgrims would, with the passing years, engrave on the face of the land'. I close the guidebook to the Pennine Way, and consider those lines, quoted by my friend Paddy Dillon. I feel as if that's what we've been doing for weeks now, following in the footsteps of those who've gone before, tracing lines across the land.

After a few nights with the luxury of a bed and hot water we're reluctant to leave, but by the early afternoon when the truck finally comes to collect the bikes we're ready to go. I put my rucksack on my back, content with its familiarity. It's going to be okay, we're safe in Paddy's hands; after all, the Pennines are his home ground, so we'll be fine. But within a couple of hours, in the heat of the day, I realize he's missed something very fundamental from his guidebook. Where Scotland is terrorized by midges, the Pennines are home to the horsefly. Within five miles every bare piece of skin has huge, swollen bites. Unlike the small red irritating bite of the midge, these bites make the skin swell in a red lump the size of a penny if you're lucky, or two pence if you're not, they itch unbearably at night and take days to subside. Even though it's hot and still, we cover up with sleeves and long trousers and sweat our way up towards a tiny wooden shed we can see in the distance, the first of a series of refuge huts. But it's not as close as we think. A dip in the path leads us through a bog that had been obscured by the hill, and a group of women crossing from the other side, laughing and singing with dripping wet hair.

'Well, hello, amazing, there are people up here, you're the first people we've seen all day. Where have you come from?' The women seem so alight, as if they could spontaneously combust with joy.

'Just up from Kirk Yetholm, like. We're going south. Are you walking the Pennine Way?' Dave shuffles awkwardly in the presence of these very alive women.

'Oh no, we wouldn't do that, too much hard work and not enough water. We came up from a car park, over there somewhere. We've been swimming under the waterfall at Hen Hole. That's what we do. We're the Northumbrian Mermaids, swimming the Pennines and having a wonderful time.' They look at each other and burst into another round of infectious laughter.

'A waterfall, fantastic, I'd love to wash these bites.' I look around but there's no sign of water, even less of a waterfall.

'You'll find it, it's where the nearest water is, so you'll have to.'

As we watch them head away, we realize we hadn't thought about water. We left the village with enough for the day, but now we need to refill our bottles for tonight and the next day. We hadn't expected finding water to be a problem in a place that is essentially just one vast bog. But there are no streams; the only water is held in the peat-brown bogs and that's completely undrinkable, unless you filter it, then sterilize it, then boil it and are totally desperate.

We reach the refuge hut with plenty of time to make food before darkness falls, if we had enough water to cook with. Refuge huts are just that: huts. Made of stronger timber than a garden shed, but simply wooden huts all the same. Hen Hole Hut sits near the brow of a hill, with views to the north and up the flanks of the Cheviot. A man in his seventies appears in the doorway, a wool hat pulled low over straggling grey hair; it feels as if he's welcoming us into his home. Inside, his sleeping mat and bag are already laid out: Tam has definitely moved in for the night. The dark oppressive interior isn't for me; we put our tent up on the moor, facing towards the sunset.

'Do you know where there's any water, Tam?' Moth's shaking the water bottles; there's hardly any left.

'You have to go down there – it's quite steep for about half a mile. But you'll have to do it, there's nowhere else.'

We argue between ourselves for a moment, but Dave's boy scout need to protect the group wins out. Julie's laughing at him, with no intention of going down the hill.

'Let him go, he loves doing camp duties.' She's already got her boots off, so I join her, but Moth follows him down the hill.

'Hold on, mate, you can't carry all the bottles on your own.'

'Took you long enough. I thought I really was going to have to do it on my own.'

We sit on a bench outside the hut and watch the sunset, while Tam tells us he's been walking the Pennine Way in sections and tomorrow will be his last day. He walks alone and seems very self-contained.

'I don't worry about time and distance, I just walk each day and appreciate where I am. Everyone should do it at their own pace.' He's adjusting an electrical device on his knee.

'What is that?' Julie has been having the conversation; always curious, the counsellor in her can never stop asking questions.

'It's a GPS tracker. It tells me exactly where I am and how far I've walked and at what speed. I usually do a steady two point one miles per hour, so I know exactly when I'll reach my destination and where that is.'

I look at the already scruffy paper pages of Paddy Dillon's guidebook and realize how little we've considered time and distance since we began walking. As the weeks have passed, we've fallen into a rhythm of walking from one page to another of whatever guidebook or map we're using, rarely looking beyond the fold on the paper or the next couple of pages. They carry on talking as the light fades to twilight and the wind begins to chill, and Moth and Dave still aren't back. They finally reappear, laden down with water containers and looking unexpectedly clean. We boil water for noodles by torchlight, in a wind that's obviously blowing some weather our way.

The wind roars across the open moorland, the wide-open views of yesterday lost in swirling low cloud, nothing to see now except bog and path. Paddy tells me this stretch, like many other stretches of the Pennine Way, used to be a wide path of exposed black peat: a broad stripe where thousands of feet had worn the vegetation away, turning the peat into a thigh-deep, almost unpassable bog, where some say even horses have drowned. But over the years, as on many other parts of the Way, flagstones were laid across the bogs. As a result the bog-grass has returned to cover the peat, restoring it to its natural condition and allowing walkers to pass safely.

Blanket bogs like this cover vast tracts of the coolest, wettest parts of the UK, from Shetland through the north of Scotland, across the Pennines, over parts of Wales and the moors of the south of England. An immense area of over two and a half million hectares that forms around 13 per cent of the world's blanket bog. They're expansive, unwooded areas of deep peat that hold huge amounts of rainwater in pools, covered in vital vegetation of mosses and tussock grass. Peat is made from dead plant matter, which in these wet conditions doesn't completely decay, but is held locked in the ground, where all the carbon each plant has stored in its lifetime is locked in with it. Healthy bogs hold that carbon and as the vegetation on them dies it adds to the peat, holding even more carbon. In this time of climate crisis, a healthy bog is an incredible asset and it's estimated that healthy UK peatlands contain over three billion tonnes of carbon. But when those boglands are degraded, their vegetation lost through agriculture, peat extraction, or burning, they become a huge, unsustainable climate hazard. Degraded peatland in England alone releases something in the region of ten million tonnes of CO_2 into the atmosphere every year, making the restoration of our boglands essential in our attempts to slow climate change. But they're also part of our culture, they connect this island from north to south, exist in our everyday thinking without us even knowing it and their health has now become intrinsically linked to our own. Nancy Campbell wrote a book about fifty words that describe snow; I'm sure we could find fifty words for bog, although the book would have a far less romantic quality.

We walk through miles of rain and cloud, passing Windy Gyle, supposedly one of the greatest vantage points of the Way. We can't see anything beyond a twenty-metre circle around us, before the fog forms a wall, so continue down the path while trying to make a lexicon for boglands – swamp, mire, fen, marsh, sump, quagmire – and trying very hard to stay on the flagstones.

We reach the next refuge hut and sit inside for a while out of the rain. Three teenage boys have already made camp inside, all wearing shorts and white hotel slippers, their walking clothes and boots neatly piled on the bench. They're walking the Pennine Way for a children's charity.

'We've only got two weeks then we need to be back at work, but we're going to make it, I know we are.'

'What's with the slippers?'

One boy holds his feet up, admiring his dazzling white slippers. 'My mum gave us them to use in the huts. I don't think she quite understood what sort of huts they would be.'

I'm wondering how long the slippers will remain white when the door bursts open and two men pile in, followed by another man and a dog. The dog stands facing the corner with a sad, dejected expression. The ten-foot-by-six wooden shed is getting very crowded; steam's rising; the boys' slippers are getting muddy; and the others have pushed their sleeping bags off the benches. We're about to leave, to put the tents up in the rain, when another man and a boy come in, and suddenly it's all too interesting to head away just yet. They're all talking about the rain and riding their bikes through the boglands. The man with the dog, that apparently isn't his but his neighbour's, says he's going to camp, but the other three men and the boy aren't going anywhere.

'You'll have to squeeze up or get out, boys. We'd planned on coming here and haven't brought tents, so looks like the shed's ours as I see you have tents.' The large, loud, wet man looks at the teenagers' rucksacks and nods towards the door.

'Yeah, get out, the shed's ours.' The boy's like a miniaturized version of the man, and not only in the way he's dressed. It's strange to see a territorial fight in a wooden shed in the middle of a fog-bound bog. Stranger still to see both the man and boy being so rude, but unreprimanded. We put our tents up and cook inside them out of the rain.

We're packing in the morning as the man drags the reluctant dog away down the path and the teenagers are getting out of their tents, their slippers brown with peat. I spend the next few hours wondering if the idea of borders, countries and wars all started this way – with some large Neanderthal claiming the cave as his and throwing the smaller one out, along the way teaching his children how to do the same.

Despite the rain of yesterday, there's still no water to drink. A single small deer races across the horizon, the only one we've seen since the stag on the West Highland Way, and now I think about it, there's very little wildlife of any kind. An occasional skylark, the odd stonechat, but other than that, nothing. What there is, is sheep. Every patch of dry ground is a carpet of sheep dung, the grass grazed down to almost soil level, and more sheep than we saw on the whole Cape Wrath Trail.

The rain stops and the day heats up as we walk across flat-topped moors of tufted bog-grass, sheep and sky. But dark towering cumuli are building again in the south, growing darker by the hour. Then it hits us. Fork lightning striking the moors all around, dazzling phosphorescent streaks against the darkening landscape, the air booming with pulses of continual rolling thunder. Then the rain, huge pounding drops of water that echo through the hoods of waterproofs, until the whole day is filled with light and sound. The noise is continual, explosive, crashing, deafening: the sound of the end of the world. We don't know whether to stand in awe or run in fear, eventually finding a way to do both, until the moorland gives way to conifer forests and a steep path of stone and muddy water running downhill.

We stop in the woods as an old man walks slowly up the path towards us through the torrential rain and mud. A thick white beard sticks out from under his hood, his rucksack is wrapped in bin bags and running with water.

'I'm sure one of us has got a spare rucksack cover, do you want one? I bet your stuff's wet through.' Moth's already looking through his pack for the cover.

'No, lad, I'm fine. I'm just walking slow, taking my time, don't do much more than five miles a day, so rain or shine, wet or dry, doesn't make much difference. The sun'll be back tomorrow and everything'll dry out then. There's supposed to be a guest house at the bottom; I was going to stay there to dry off and get some food, but I couldn't find it. I'll be fine, I'm just going to find a place to camp in the forest. The trees'll protect me.'

We leave him, hoping he finds shelter and a patch of dry pine needles.

We slip and slide to the bottom of the hill, spot the sign for the guest house and head there to avoid the storm. A young couple greet us: they have two rooms left and they're just dishing up shepherd's pie, do we want any? The man takes our kit, puts it in a drying room and within minutes we're eating hot food in their conservatory. The guest house is created from what appears to be two ex-council houses, a place where wet travellers are rescued, where people use their rooms or, if there are none left, put their tents up in the garden, but still dry their clothes and eat hot food. It's an oasis. I wish the old man had found it; I'd rather he had my room tonight.

23

Coniferous forests spread for miles beyond Byrness. Miles of silent dark green air, where little moves except other hikers heading north. Coniferous woodlands hold most of the timber that our human world is made of, from tables to book pages, but for the natural world they're a dead zone, where little wildlife lives and even less thrives. But pine trees have an irreplaceable value to human life (beyond the toilet rolls that we've all been fighting over), their true value is invisible, except on very hot days when a blue haze hangs over the trees and we actually see their most precious offering. The trees emit a chemical known as pinene: for the trees it forms the haze that protects them from the heat of the sun; for us it has an equally protective effect. Scientists have found that when we inhale pinene it chemically interacts with our bodies, lowering levels of the stress hormone cortisol, and enhancing the activity of our anti-cancer killer cells. It's not surprising that by the end of the day we're all feeling very relaxed. I'm beginning to wonder if we can find a way to leave these stress-busting, carbon-locking monsters to grow and thrive, if it's possible to wean the world off its obsession with toilet rolls made from wood pulp without carpeting the earth in bamboo.

The skies clear above Whitley Pike, leaving a dark blue evening stretching from west to east over seemingly endless moorland. But there's nowhere to camp. The bogland is covered in tufted grass and low shrubby growth that bounces on water-soaked peat, and oozes like a sponge with each footstep – until we reach the summit of Deer Play and a tiny patch of dry ground beneath the cairn and the Pennine Way signpost. Dave and Julie squeeze their small tent under the post, but there's nowhere for ours other than right on the path. It doesn't matter, we're so high on pinene after our day of forest bathing that nothing matters.

The sun disappears, but the skyline from south to north is lit in deep, dark, wine-gum colours. We sit on the cairn, each lost in our own thoughts. Then we hear it, that bird we never see but we've heard all the way from the north of Scotland. There are no more deer or eagles, orchids or cuckoos, but this bird that we don't know has called all the way.

'There it is again, that bird. We just never see it, so there's no way of telling what it is.'

'Oh, come off it, Moth, don't tell me you don't know what that is?' I can tell by the smirk on Dave's face that he knows but he'll string it out. 'What beautiful bird have we got up here in the cold, wet north that you soft southerners don't have? Can't believe you don't know what that is.'

'Go on then, just tell me.'

'No, but I'll give you a clue: it's golden.'

I still have no idea what Dave's talking about. I'm trying to imagine a golden bird but can't picture anything other than a budgie.

'Oh, you're kidding, how did I not think of that? A golden plover.'

'See, you knew all the time.' Julie looks at me, smiling. We've sat in the sunset watching Moth drag a memory from a box that had been locked, until Dave gave him the key.

We fall asleep under a sky encrusted with stars, listening to the calls of the bird that now has a name.

Moth peels the black muddy strapping off his hand to reveal swollen flesh extending over the sides of his ring. It looks more like a purple and yellow sausage than a finger. We stand around in a circle, prodding and squeezing it.

'Does it hurt?' Julie seems to be the only one showing him any sympathy.

'It feels a bit hot, but otherwise it's okay.'

'You know they'll have to cut it off, don't you? Why didn't you take the ring off, you idiot? I might have a saw on my penknife that'd do it.' Dave's fiddling about with his multi-headed boy scout's knife. It has scissors, a file, a toothpick and a compass, but thankfully not a saw.

I rebind the fingers before Dave has a chance to start filing through the ring with a nail file, just as large drops of rain start to bounce off our waterproofs.

'Great northern weather. Let's get on, we might get to Bellingham in time for pie and mash in the pub.' Dave puts his penknife away and picks up his rucksack.

Julie's rolling her eyes. 'Even you're not that northern, Dave.'

We pass a few people heading north, all of them asking about mileage and days taken, most of them scoffing when we say we're not sure, and the rain keeps falling. A person in a Union Jack cap tells us that England beat Denmark in the Euros semi-finals, so they're through to the final, but there's not as much joy and celebration as we saw in Glasgow when Scotland had lost and we walk on through the rain, missing the sheer exuberance of the Tartan Army. Only one person, among the many waterproof-clad walkers, mentions anything about the path or the landscape.

'Aye, we're well in the clag today. It'll get better though. Wait 'til you get to Dufton, the bit from there to Middleton-in-Teesdale, wow, makes it all worthwhile.' As the man in the blue waterproof walks away, we realize how very few people actually mention the land they're walking through. The Cape Wrath Trail was filled with walkers whose main focus was statistics, but at least a few of them noticed something of the grandeur as they sped by. But the Pennine Way appears to be all about mileage, time and weather.

We head into Bellingham, past a wedding party running down the road under umbrellas, the bride holding a bundle of white dress above her mud-covered knees, as she splashes through the rivers of rainwater. But suddenly we stop noticing how wet it is as other senses take over. We're surrounded by food and the smell and sight of it fills our thoughts. Fruit, bread, pies, cakes, food oozing from every outlet; shops, cafés, pubs. We choose the pub. Three of us order pie and mash. Dave eats a dainty portion of salmon and salad in an attempt to prove to Julie just how sophisticated he can be. On the table next to us four men in their upper sixties are finishing food. Clearly walkers who are staying in the pub, they're discussing their day, congratulating themselves on covering twenty miles, six miles further than the fourteen-mile day Paddy describes in the guidebook. And it's only mid-afternoon.

'I'm not too stiff, don't think twenty miles has been too much of an issue.' The bald man looks exhausted, as if it's been a very big issue.

'Me too, feeling good.' The other three are nodding in unison.

'Let's order sandwiches for tomorrow. Cheese or ham?' The bald man seems in control.

'No, I want tuna.' The small man seems very specific in his needs.

'They don't have tuna, just cheese and ham.'

'But I want tuna.'

'But they only have cheese and ham.'

'I'll go to the Co-op in the morning and get tuna.'

'But what if they don't have tuna, then you won't have a sandwich?'

'If you're going to the Co-op, I want jelly babies.' I can tell from his expression that the man in the blue jumper really needs jelly babies.

'And me.'

'And me.'

'Me too.' They all need jelly babies. 'But I might not go to the Co-op.'

'You have to, you need a tuna sandwich.'

'Yes, you have to.'

'You do, you need tuna.'

They get up and go to the bar to order their sandwiches with the stiff, awkward movements of someone who's sixty-something and has just walked twenty miles. I get up to leave with the stiff, awkward movements of someone who's fifty-something and has no idea how many miles they've covered, but now really needs a bag of jelly babies.

We stock up on food from the Co-op and I see Julie putting a large bag of sausage rolls in her basket.

'That's going to be so heavy to carry.'

'I know, but he's going to be really hungry later and I can produce them just when he's starting to feel sorry for himself.'

I look at the bag of sweets in my basket and realize walkers are all the same. Yompers or not, we all ache and we're all obsessed with food.

Endless farmland slips by in a blur of gateways, stiles, stone walls and angry farm dogs. Sheep fill every field and the grass, what remains of it, is barely visible beneath their droppings. Far too many sheep on far too little land. As the sheep numbers increase, so the wildlife decreases. It reminds me of the farm in Cornwall and how overgrazed the fields were when we moved there, but how a few years of fewer animals and fewer chemicals changed everything. It's early July now, the fields of grass will be going to seed, ready to be mown for hay, the air above will be thick with insects feeding on the grass heads, and the skies full of swallows swooping low, gorging on the endless food supply. Moth walks ahead of me, his gait uneven on the dusty ground. I know it's his feet, the pain seems to start every day after he's walked about five miles, then continues until he's in his sleeping bag. For a moment I want to stop walking altogether, get on the train and head back to the orchards and the grass fields. Just for a moment.

Then suddenly, in late afternoon, there's a vision of what this landscape could be. A whole valley filled with wild flowers and the rich smell of honey rising from acres of lady's bedstraw, the air thick with insects. It's intoxicating. But the path draws us out of the valley and very soon we're back into fields of sheep and horseflies. An old man appears ahead. He has the wiry look of a fell runner but is dressed in Lycra: he could be a cyclist. As we get closer I can see he's almost in tears.

'Hi, are you walking the Pennine Way?' I'm sure he isn't, his rucksack isn't much bigger than a daysack, but I don't know what else to say.

'Well, I am, if you can call it that.'

'Oh, are you just doing part of it?'

He looks at me as if I've suggested something sacrilegious. 'I've walked this whole path four times before; this is the fifth. But I'll never walk it again, this or any other long-distance path.'

'Why, what's the problem?' We all look at him, expecting him to say he has some kind of terminal disease.

'I'm seventy-two, it's always taken me ten days, but I just can't do it this time.' He scuffs the ground with his foot, shaking his head. 'I'm embarrassed – in fact I'm ashamed of myself. I'm not what I was. I just can't come to terms with it.'

I wonder if this is the fate of all those yompers whose focus is only on time and distance. Does their time spent in these remarkable landscapes become worthless when they can no longer keep to the schedule? I offer him a jelly baby, but he shakes his head, turns and walks away, dashing along the path like a whippet through the horseflies. I wonder what the old man in the woods above Byrness would have said to him, and hope again that he had a peaceful night in the pine needles. He didn't care about miles, but I know he will walk again, and again, and again, until he can't walk any more. His only desire was to feel the earth beneath his feet for as long as he could.

The night closes in around tents pitched on open moorland, where the endless views of dark skies are only broken by the occasional dots of farm lights. I can't see them, but I know Dave and Julie are sitting in their tent flaps too, looking out at the night.

'Don't know why I had that salmon, I'm bloody starving.'

'Bet you could eat a sausage roll?'

'What's the matter with you, woman, do you just enjoy torturing me?'

'Well, yes, but I do have a sausage roll if you want one.'

'What, oh yes, I bloody love you.'

We're about to close the zip when they start falling from the sky. On the far horizon, lights begin to fall to the ground. One by one they appear in the sky, then fall down to earth. We count ten, eleven, twelve: they just keep coming. No sooner is one on the ground than another appears in the sky. Each time, just one single light.

'Guys, guys, you've got to see this, it's a fucking alien attack.' Moth is excited, trying to spy on the lights with his monocular, convinced he's witnessing the start of an invasion. A zip rips open nearby and I know Dave will be hanging out of his tent.

'Bloody hell, what is that?' The lights continue to fall. 'Do you think they're helicopters?'

'Don't know what else they can be.' Eventually the lights stop and we think it's over, but then it starts again from a point further west. More and more lights falling from the sky.

'Is there a military base up there?'

'Don't know, but I've never seen anything like it.'

After thirty minutes the lights finally stop and we're all preparing to fight the aliens, who will imminently be pouring over the brow of the hill, when we hear Julie's voice of reason from the other tent.

'It's probably military manoeuvres. If not, I did read that Tom Cruise is filming nearby – maybe his helicopter landing needs a few takes to get right.'

We all stand down from high alert and try to sleep.

When we open the tent the next day there are no aliens, not even Tom Cruise, just a moorland of horseflies and sheep.

24

After three hours in a conifer plantation, ducking fallen trees and avoiding knee-deep mud, we finally leave the trees behind and head out into daylight and rolling hills of farmland. The day winds on, until we climb over a stone wall and are suddenly confronted with the biggest boundary of second century Britain – Hadrian's Wall. The wall began life in AD 122, in the reign of Hadrian, as a defensive line that marked the edge of the Roman Empire in Britain and held back the marauding tribes of the north. When it was finished it stretched for seventy-three miles across the full width of northern England from west to east. It's now a UNESCO world heritage site, visited by thousands of tourists every year, although only parts of it still exist. After the Romans left the annoying northern tribes to fight among themselves, they obviously called a truce for long enough for both sides to re-imagine the wall, taking much of the stone away to build farms, houses and mile upon mile of field boundaries. Looking across the landscape now, it's as if the wall has leaked into the surrounding countryside, like watercolours on wet paper. But the wall was built on a natural barrier and what remains still sits on top of the escarpment, creating an imposing outcrop on the southern skyline.

Having come from the farthest north-western reaches of Britain, we feel like wild tribesmen attacking from the snow-line, about to forge our way through to the soft lands of the south. We break on to the wall, a ragged, smelly, rucksack-wielding army of four striking from the north, enough to terrify tourists, if not centurions. We march on Housesteads Fort, then break formation and raid the English Heritage trinket shop for ice creams. Our attack on the fort ends here, as it's already closed and even marauding tribesmen aren't allowed in, so we kick sheep shit aside and sit on the wall to eat ice creams.

The air cools and damp rises in a mist that hangs beneath the wall on both sides, until we're following the line of it in near darkness, dipping occasionally to disappear in the mist, only to reappear as silent centurions marching through the sky. The wall follows a deep notch in the landscape down to Sycamore Gap, where a lone sycamore tree stands guard. According to the Visit Northumberland website, it's 'one of the most photo-graphed trees' in the country. I only know it from a 1990s film about Robin Hood, as the tree where Kevin Costner hung out with Morgan Freeman. We hide our tents, in sight of the tree, but out of sight of anyone else, conscious now that we're in the land where wild camping is soon to become criminal.

'So that's it, we're home tomorrow, have you decided what you're going to do?' Julie, questions, always questions, always pushing us towards a decision. I remind myself why I've never considered therapy; counsellors just ask so many questions.

'We're going to Newcastle.' There, I've said it, it's happening.

'Why Newcastle?'

'Because my rucksack strap's broken, the waist buckle has snapped on Moth's, and I've booked our second Covid vaccine while we're there.'

'Why not wait until you get back to Cornwall? I thought you said you were finishing here? It doesn't matter that your ruck-sacks have broken now if you are.'

'Because we're going to carry on, finish the Pennine Way. It seems a shame not to.'

'I knew it! I knew you would.' Dave's laughing, content that his prediction is playing out. 'You know what you'll do after that, don't you?'

'What, Dave, tell us?'

'You'll just walk home.'

★

Haltwhistle railway station is small but mainline enough to take Dave and Julie west while we head east. They're already on the train and we're waiting for it to leave, but Dave leans out of the door.

'I tell you, you'll just walk home, I know you will.'

'Don't be daft, that's impossible.'

Newcastle is a shock to the senses. After weeks spent in the wild, punctuated by only a few days in towns or cities, we walk out of the station into a slew of humanity. The broad paved entrance to the station is filled by a street fight: young men who, despite the police arrests, sirens and onlookers, are so lost in their anger that they won't stop. Distracted by the fight, I almost fall over a homeless girl sitting by a column. Her face is drawn and grey, drained of enthusiasm and completely unmoved by the scene playing out in front of her. Long brown hair hangs around a life-worn expressionless stare and bruised arm; she looks no more than twenty-five so she's probably younger. Our own children were in their early twenties when we lost our house; in their last years at university when the security of the family home was pulled from beneath them. So young, so vulnerable, so in danger of their lives taking a wrong turn. The fighters are bundled into police vans; the onlookers start to disperse. I take a deep breath, prop my rucksack against the wall and phone each of the children. Not so young now, but I need to know they're okay. Moth's talking to the girl.

'Hi, are you all right? Is there anything you need?'

She doesn't reply, doesn't even look up.

Later, when the shops are closed and darkness is creeping between the street lights, the girl with brown hair is standing with two other men. One older, more street-worn; one young and clean with a rucksack. They hang around a piece of street art, as if they're waiting for something. Eventually a tall man appears; dressed in black, he looks like a bouncer, but they're all attentive to what he has to say. He takes the boy with the rucksack, telling the other two to stay there, he'll be back. The girl with brown hair stays, but the older man immediately leaves, heading to the railway station.

An hour later we're about to leave the café near where the girl is still waiting when the bouncer returns.

'Sorry, hen, there's nothing more tonight. Here, take this and get yourself some food.'

'Shit, Paul, can't you get me in somewhere?'

'There's nowhere left, hen, I'm sorry.'

The girl walks slowly away, back to the railway station. Paul's turning to leave when Moth speaks to him.

'Hi, Paul, I gather you're trying to get the guys into hostels for the night.'

'Yeah, why?'

'I just wondered why you chose to take the boy, not the young woman?'

'He's new, first time I've seen him, says he's been on the street for two days.'

'But why him and not the girl? Surely she's more vulnerable?'

'They're all vulnerable. The girl's been here for a few months, but he's new. If we get them into the hostels straight away, then they've got a better chance.'

'Better chance?' I don't understand what he's saying.

'Better chance of getting straight back into normality, before the street takes them over. It's about outcomes. The girl knows she's top of my list unless there's someone new.'

Paul walks away to continue his night. Making difficult choices in a job without end.

We sleep in a bed, safe in a room, away from the perils of the city. I message Rowan one more time, thanking the stars again that we made it through the loss of our home without there being a girl with blonde hair on the street, waiting for the chance of a night of safety.

★

The rain beats against the window of the pub, almost obscuring the view of the bridge. I wipe the condensation away and look again; I'm not imagining it.

'Can you see them? When you look closely, you can see them everywhere. I can't quite tell what they are. Some sort of small gull, I think.'

The steel arches beneath the Tyne bridge are filled on every ledge and corner with bird's nests. Small gulls swoop and call beneath the girders, splatting the pavement and passers-by with droppings. Moth presses the monocular against the steam of the pub window. 'They're kittiwakes.'

'But I thought they nested on sea cliffs, not inland.'

'Me too.'

It seems these kittiwakes are the furthest inland breeding colony of kittiwakes in the world and have been nesting here for over sixty years. The colony has grown to over a thousand pairs, at a time when kittiwake populations worldwide are suffering a huge fall in numbers. They're only here for the breeding season; by late summer they'll be heading out into the Atlantic where they'll spend the winter. But despite all the possibilities of disruption to the birds and their breeding chances, plans are afoot to clean off the bridge and repaint it. Promises are being sought that this work will take place outside of the breeding season, but even if that's possible, disruption to the birds' habitat is inevitable. I clean the steam from the window again and wonder if, considering the great number of bridges that cross the River Tyne, it wouldn't be possible to accept that this one belongs to the kittiwakes, for civic bodies to embrace the rust rather than risk the possible loss of these beautiful, gentle birds for the sake of a coat of paint.

The window steams over again in seconds.

'I think we need to do something a bit more exciting with the day than sit and watch the rain on the window and eat more pie and mash. It's your birthday after all.'

'Can't believe I'm sixty-one.'

'Can't believe you've made it to sixty-one. Anyway, it's time for your special birthday treat, so let's go and get that vaccination. Then, if we really are finishing the Pennine Way, we'll have to buy some new rucksacks.' I walk out of the pub into the rain, imagining how I'd have felt when Moth was fifty-three and first diagnosed with CBD, if someone had told me that at sixty-one, he would have walked from Cape Wrath to Hadrian's Wall, with a little bit of cycling along the way. I'm sure I'd have been crying with relief, and yet here I still am eight years later, still seizing every extra step he's prepared to take, still pushing him to the next mile as if it's his last. But if I hadn't pushed, would he already have taken that last step? We're caught in an endless cycle of 'what if', where all we can do is take the next step and see where that leads.

The streets are full of revellers. England's playing Italy in the Euro finals, Newcastle seems united in song, and 'football's coming home'. Or at least until the final penalty kick. The city holds its breath, Gary Lineker can barely speak, but whispers out – 'so it comes to this', the ball misses the net, Newcastle exhales, then falls quiet. For at least thirty minutes.

The next morning, for a few who still kick their way through the debris of the night before, England flags draped around their shoulders, football's still coming home. But not for the girl with brown hair. She's propped against the column staring vacantly at the street. I want to take her to the moors; I want her to stand in the wind with the sun on her face, under skies that bend into infinity, to lie under the stars and hear the call of the plover; I want her to know she's not alone. But she doesn't respond when I speak to her. We give her a coffee and she looks up momentarily, but we could be ghosts. It seems the streets have taken her and, without a safe space to call her own, that's where she'll stay.

The train pulls into Haltwistle and we head back to the wall, falling into a post-vaccination haze of headaches, body aches, walking and sleeping that seems to go on forever, where the only thing not aching is my shoulders. I couldn't resist a beautiful, simple canvas rucksack that had no bells and whistles, but was just really well made. I put it on and it felt like a second skin. But with a ten-litre smaller capacity than my old one I needed to reduce the contents to the bare minimum. By losing every spare ounce from my rucksack I also seemed to have lost the shoulder pain. I try to count how many hundreds of miles I've backpacked while moving the weight of my old pack from one shoulder to the other to relive the pain, unsure if I feel relieved or foolish.

Days pass as if in fog, where we barely notice the weather, less still the wealth of Roman history around us. It's late evening as we pass through Alston. The streets are silent, the Co-op's about to close and lights are coming on in the houses when we hear screeching. Swifts. Tens of them, gathering and swooping, so fast my eyes can't follow. They rise over the roof tops, screech down into the streets, then up and away, only to appear at the other end of the road and repeat, and repeat. I'm mesmerized by their sleek black arched wings, their unison, their powerful calls. And suddenly I'm awake, as if by following the motion of the birds, the vaccine-fog has left me. We camp by the river, closing the tent against the large black Pennine midges with their very direct northern attitude.

25

Empty and neglected houses line the path as we get closer to Garrigill, a tiny village where the pub has closed down and the local shop has only a scattering of items on the shelves. I pick two cakes from the counter, the only food in the shop that doesn't need more cooking than we have gas for. The woman behind the counter serves me hurriedly and locks the door as I leave. We're eating the cakes on a bench under a tree when an old lady sits down next to us with her dog. We talk about the weather, how dry it is, how it hasn't rained here for weeks. But I have a burning question so have to ask it.

'Why are there so many empty houses around here?' She doesn't want to answer and fusses in her bag for a dog treat, but I press for an answer anyway.

'It's the incomers. They've bought up the village, pushed the prices so high no locals can afford to live here any more. Then Covid came and no one could travel to their second homes any more, so there's no money coming into the village to keep the pub or the shop going. Everything's shutting down, putting people out of work. And now there's nothing here any more the second-home owners are all saying "It's not the same as it was" and trying to sell their houses for the same price they paid for them before they ruined the place.'

She stops and takes a deep breath, but as she gets up to leave my thoughts are drawn back to Cornwall and how dark the villages are in the winter, how few houses have their lights on. We walk away up a stony track and I'm beginning to real-ize that there are villages like Garrigill all over Britain, where second-home ownership has pushed house prices out of the reach of locals, turning thriving local economies into little more than unsustainable leisure facilities. By the time we put the tent up I'm beginning to think we could possibly go a long way towards solving the housing crisis in this country if we first resolve what has evidently become a second-home crisis.

The moors of the Pennines from north to south and west into the mountains of the Lake District are silhouetted in deepening shades of blue against a sunset of deep gold and pink. Our bowls of rice and peas are glowing peach in the light, looking far more interesting than they are, when a man and his dog appear on the path behind us.

'I was hoping to get to the top of Cross Fell for the sunset, but I'm not going to make it now, I couldn't find anywhere to park my van. I pulled up in the village and some bloke came out of his house and told me to fuck off.'

'I shouldn't worry about it. I don't think you're the problem – they're just a bit edgy down there at the moment.'

He threads his way up the side of the hill until he disappears in the twilight. The light fades to darkest pink and blue, filling the sky, until the colours recede to a thin line on the far horizon. We zip the tent against the wind and listen to golden plovers calling across the peat.

We're close to Greg's Hut bothy the next morning when we pass the man and his dog on their way down.

'I didn't make it to the top, but I still caught the sunset. Did you see it? Just so beautiful! You know, I used to run marathons, keep to schedules, cycle long stages, but now, well, now I just think what's the point? Being out in the countryside isn't about all that, it's about this.' He gestures to the wide horizon, as if with one sweep of his hand he's painting a magnificent picture. 'I grew up in an Arabic country and we had a saying: *inshallah*. It means "if Allah wills it". But that's not how it was used. What we were really saying was: "Who knows? It will happen when it does." *Inshallah*, my friends, *inshallah*.' He disappears down the stony track and we head to the summit of Cross Fell.

Standing on the summit in a hot wind, under a hot sun, I turn in circles, marvelling at the 360-degree views of England shimmering in a heat haze. A couple are squatting in a tiny beach tent, coming out occasionally to reposition a twenty-metre-high aerial. We make tea by the summit cairn, wondering if they're spies, or alien spotters, as the sun gets hotter. Cross Fell has something that exists nowhere else in Britain: a named wind. I could create a lot of names for winds we've walked through on our way to this fell, but the Helm Wind is so far our only named wind: a north-easterly wind that blows down the south-westerly slope of the fell. It's often accompanied by a roll of cloud known as the Helm Bar that sits across the fell. Today's wind is hot and dry and there's not a cloud to be seen. We could stay here all day, basking in the wonder of the views – north into Scotland, south to Yorkshire, west into the Lake District – and the incredible luck to have hit the highest point on the Pennine Way on a clear day. But the heat is rising and I feel as if I might soon become as burnt and dusty as the boglands around us, so we head south across Little Dun Fell, Great Dun Fell and Knock Fell as the day gets hotter and our skin redder.

The path drops off Knock Fell down into the valley, but the moment we leave the high ground the wind disappears, and the heat increases still further. We cross broad riverbeds of rock and boulders, where at times water must cascade at force, but today they're dry. There's not a drop of water. No rivers, no streams, not even trickles of water. Nothing but boglands steaming as they dry, and crisp grasslands grazed to soil, carpeted in sheep droppings. We finally reach the valley floor in late evening. Moth's feet are so painful he can barely walk, his broken finger has swollen so much we've had to unbind it before the tape cuts off his circulation, the heat is making my head pound until it feels twice the size, and we've run out of water. Gasping with thirst and shivering with sunstroke, we finally get to Dufton.

It's still hot as we put the tent up in the light of the campsite floodlights and stand under cools showers, washing away the dust of Cross Fell.

The morning is hot even before the sun comes up, but it's cool under the trees. So we stay, hanging out in the café, swallowing paracetamol and drinking tea, while Moth props his feet on a chair and hopes that a day of not walking will be enough for them to recover. A day off won't help his finger though; even when the café owner gives him a bowl of iced water to soak it in the swelling doesn't go down – it still hangs over his ring by half a centimetre.

'Told you to take it off.'

'I know, I know.'

The climb out of Dufton is hot, dusty and full of sheep. Fields crowded with sheep. Sheep on the paths, sheep stuck in hedges, sheep in gardens. The air is thick with the smell of sheep, only clearing as we reach the high ground and a gentle breeze blowing out of the U-shaped valley below. This is a place of geologists' dreams. The outcrop of rock beneath our feet is the edge of the Whin Sill, a layer of dark, volcanic, crystalline dolerite rock that forms the bedrock of Lindisfarne Castle, crops up as the escarpment beneath Hadrian's Wall and again here, at the head of High Cup Gill, where the high-altitude waterfall of High Cup Nick falls over the edge of rock and down into the gill. Gill is an old Norse word for a narrow valley, but this is far more dramatic than just a valley. Moth poses for a photo at the edge of the U-shaped glacial landscape, where each side of the U is topped by crenellations of dolerite crags. It's so perfectly proportioned that I feel slightly dizzy looking at the vast half-pipe shape of this completely natural phenomenon. It could be the view making me dizzy, or possibly Moth's shirt, a bright blue Hawaiian design of leaves and parrots that he found in a charity shop in Newcastle and he now seems inseparable from.

We sit down to eat the sandwiches prepared by the ladies in the café, not noticing the couple sitting nearby.

'That's a great shirt.'

I roll my eyes. *Oh no, don't encourage him or he'll never take it off.*

'Oh, thanks.'

'Are you walking the Way?'

'Yeah, heading south. Are you?' I glance at their rucksacks as Moth asks, but they're not big enough for the whole trail.

'No, well, yes, but just in stages. My dad wanted to walk the Pennines, but he never had the chance, so we're doing it with him.' I look around for his father, but don't see anyone else. 'I promised him I'd bring him here. My family didn't want it, so I had no choice but to take some of his ashes and bring him. I had to, I promised him I would.'

I feel tears choke my throat as the man tells the story of his father. Of a life lived without achieving his aims, without doing the things he wanted to do; of wishes and hopes that became nothing but regrets in the end. We turn away, wishing them well, passing through a herd of ponies out on to open moorland. It's so easy to put life off, put dreams on the top shelf where you can no longer see them, so never have to acknowledge that they're unfulfilled. Too easy for it all to end without ever having breathed life into hopes, never having given them a chance to fly. Better to spare the money, the time, the effort, walk that path, wear that parrot shirt, or whatever it takes to fulfil that dream, than to reach the end filled with regret.

'Great shirt, Moth.'

'Yeah, I know.'

The moor is part of a scheme to protect ground-nesting birds, and for the first time for days I can't see any sheep. I can't see any birds either, but maybe they're on the ground. It's late in the day as we reach the edge of a reservoir, where water escapes beneath the concrete of Cow Green Dam, falls down the Cauldron Snout waterfall and becomes the River Tees in the valley below. We scramble down, following the water and pitch the tent. Despite the horseflies being joined by oversized midges, I can see why the man in the blue waterproof said that this section, from Dufton to Middleton-in-Tees, was the best. Even with painful feet and a swollen finger Moth is transfixed, watching the waterfall through the midge net of the tent door until darkness, when the water takes the shape of sound.

Dippers are scattered along the edge of the river, small black birds with white heads that jump in and out of the water, showering themselves with droplets of reflected light. The narrow valley finally breaks out into open farmland: swallows high in the air, a herd of Belted Galloways and lapwings, so many lapwings. The 'peewit' call of these birds was the background noise of my childhood. It was hard to walk through fields in the spring without coming across their nests; watching the parents running over short grass with their tiny chicks was a common sight. But no longer. Now they're another bird on the Conservation Red List, their chicks a rarity, their call soon to be forgotten. But here they fly over the farmland in a flock of maybe thirty birds, so there's hope, if only in tiny pockets of the country. We walk on as I wonder why they're here, not anywhere else. Then we turn into the main Tees valley and I can see why. The wide river valley is a mass of wild flowers. Lady's bedstraw, foxgloves, thyme, meadowsweet, orchids, burnet and cow parsley line broad stretches of riverbank; the whole area hums with insect life. On the other side of the river the farmer is making hay, but he's mown around the wild flowers and they still stand, alive with bees and hoverflies. It makes me think of the decimation of the silage fields near Lancaster and it really isn't hard to see why biodiversity is thriving here but perishing elsewhere.

The air isn't just full of bees and hoverflies; the horseflies are here in clouds too. We dump our rucksacks and jump into the peaty water of the Tees to soothe the bites, washing away dust and sweat and anything else that might attract the biting beasts. I'm beginning to think the horsefly should be the symbol of the Pennine Way.

We dress, reluctantly, leaving the trees and heading back into the heat. A grove of low-growing junipers cloak a hill where we stop for a moment, making the most of a faint breeze. We hear them long before we see them. The gasping sound of people struggling for breath as they climb the hill up to the trees. When they do appear they're two small, delicate, but incredibly tough women, with rucksacks that are almost two-thirds their size. They stop, trying to catch their breath.

'You walking the Pennine Way too?' The older woman has such a broad smile it seems to stretch from ear to ear.

'Yes, we're heading south, and you?'

'Oh yes, very much yes.'

'You won't tell anyone you've seen us, will you?' The younger woman with the bigger rucksack seems very nervous.

'No, we won't, but why?' My imagination is running away with me. Are they hiding from something, are their packs full of all their worldly possessions, are they trafficked, or part of a trail-long game of hide and seek?

'I've wanted to walk the Pennine Way all my life. I live in Thailand but read of an amazing path up the spine of England when I was a little girl, big moors and big sky, and I said: "One day I'll walk that." My husband, he says: "No, you stay here, you cook dinners and wash clothes, you don't leave the country." But I did, I did. And now I'm here with my daughter and walking and so very, very happy.' The older woman glows with the joy of her escape, her happiness almost forming an aura around her.

'But that's why you must not tell anyone.' The younger woman is still fidgety. 'My father says he's coming to Britain, and he will find her, he'll take her home. She can't go home yet; first she must finish walking this path.'

The older woman is laughing. 'He's a stupid man. What does

he think, he'll just come here and find me? He doesn't know the Pennine Way, and he doesn't know me. We must go, long way to go yet.'

They walk down the other side of the hill, the old woman's laughter carrying up through the junipers.

We follow the river, as so many have before, along a path worn into the ground by thousands of feet, carrying thousands of hopes and dreams across this same piece of land. My feet join theirs, connecting me to each person that has trodden this ground, each life that has gone before, each story that has yet to come. Our energy beaten into the ground, until part of us has become this ground.

We eat chips outside the chippy in Middleton-in-Teesdale and listen to the conversations of the locals around us. Their voices seem to tell us this is a small town that guards itself against the incomer but is greatly loved by its inhabitants, from the ladies gossiping on the corner, to the army of people litter-picking in the street, to the café owner teaching her very young staff how to deal with customers. This feels like a community that will close its gates on the world if it has to and be content to do that.

A taxi driver from Barnard Castle sits on the table next to us, eating a plate of pie and chips before his next pick-up.

'Glad to be out of Barnie, it's heaving right now, can barely drive down the streets, there's so many tourists.'

'Why, is there an event?' Moth shakes some more vinegar over his chips.

'No, since the whole Dominic Cummings business, tourism there's gone mad. Good thing though – the town needs the money. They spent a huge amount, two million I heard, on a massive new building at the pharmaceutical factory, but it sat there unused for years. Now they say they're going to make Covid vaccines there. No jobs in it for the locals though. No, nothing for us, but it's obvious what's happening, anyone who can't see what's really going on there needs their eyes testing. Anyway, got to be going.' He drops his chip carton in the bin, gets back in his taxi and drives away.

'What did he mean?' I pick up my rucksack and get ready to leave.

'I'm not sure, but you know taxi drivers, they hear everything.'

26

Fog descends, covering the Pennines in thick, wet air that stays for days. Hanging moisture wrapping clothes and skin until everything's wet. Too hot for waterproofs, too wet without them. Bogs, dales, paths: they all look the same. All we can do is focus on our feet and not lose sight of the trail. After a day of relentless walking up what feels like a hill, even though we can't see one, we're beginning to despair of ever reaching the top. This never-ending, bleak, dark moor hides its history in the fog-shrouded bogland. It was here, somewhere on this dank hillside, that Eric Bloodaxe was killed. The Viking King of York, who claimed the whole of Northumbria as his, lost his final fight here. As Northumbria fell to the King of Wessex, the north lost its independence forever. But I'm sure I can still hear the cries of Vikings in this place that even now feels like a world apart.

We finally see a light through the mist and as we get closer we find cars are gathered at the side of the road. The Tan Hill Inn. In the clag of the Yorkshire Dales what is apparently the highest pub in Britain is gearing up for a mini festival, expecting 450 guests the next day. We've come out of the fog straight into party central.

'The Covid numbers are skyrocketing again, but the government says we've got to live with it. So this is living with it: we're just going back to normal. Good job you're here tonight, no chance of finding anywhere to camp tomorrow. Anyway, you can camp outside if you eat something, so what you having?' The barman is as direct and to the point as everyone else we've met in this area. This is Yorkshire, where people say what they think, when they think it. Maybe I've got soft with spending too much time in the south, or among the glens of Scotland, but for days I've been thinking people here are just plain rude. Then I remembered my dad – not from Yorkshire, south of there, but still with that same directness, that sense of 'a spade's a spade so why call it anything else', and realized it's not rude at all. After all, why waste words on couching what you're saying in niceties? I can almost hear my dad: 'If you've got something to say, girl, just say it'.

'I'll have pie and chips and a tea.'

'Not a beer?'

'No, a tea.'

'Perfect, I'll get you that now then.' Not rude at all, just to the point.

I look through the news on my phone while eating the pie. On last night's edition of *Newsnight* Emily Maitlis announced that the Amazon rainforest is now emitting more CO_2 than it absorbs. I think about all the miles of exposed blanket bog, the glens with no trees, the decimation of ecosystems for housing, and as we sit in the pub in the fog it feels as if there's no way back, we're standing on the brink. We eat chips, while the Tan Hill parties, and the world burns.

A day of heat, sheep and flies leads us through the hot little hamlet of Keld, where everything is closed. The Coast to Coast Walk intersects the Pennine Way here; if we turn east or west within a week we'll be on the coast. We sit in the shade for a moment and consider the option, but choose to stay on the Way and head on to the top of Great Shunner Fell. In his guidebook Paddy warns us that up here we'll be walking through a squelchy bog, but all we find is heat, peat, dust and no water. Of all the things I thought the Pennines would be, a desert of peat wasn't one of them. There's not a tree to be seen on this broad open fell, the only shade of any form is from the drystone walls, and as the sun reaches its highest point in the sky even they offer no protection. A dead rabbit lies on the side of the path, stiff and covered in flies. I pull my hat even lower over my head and cover all the bare skin I can, but I'm still burning through my clothes. I'm putting the sunscreen away when I see something coming towards us through the heat haze. As it gets closer I see it's a man weaving his way along the path. No, not weaving, staggering. Maybe he's drunk. Maybe these endless moors are enough to drive you to drink. He gets closer and I think he's wearing pink, but as we reach him we realize it's not pink clothing, it's pink skin. He's covered in second-degree burns; his face, neck, arms and legs aren't just burnt, they're scorched by the sun.

'I put sunscreen on but it wasn't enough.' He's not joking. Skin has peeled away, leaving raw, red new skin underneath, with huge watery blisters hanging from his knees. 'I've been sick for two days and I still feel weird.'

This man should be in hospital. Why doesn't he stop and get help, or go home?

'I only got enough time off work to walk the Way because I said I needed time for my mental health. So I can't just go back.'

I wonder if being in what must be extreme pain is actually good for his mental health; it looks more like self-harm than self-care.

'Work's a mess, no one can solve it but me – there are so many problems and I have to sort them. I just need a few days to myself first.'

This man doesn't need to be walking; he needs to be getting his burns treated in A & E, then talking to someone about his work issues. We try to persuade him to go back down into Hawes and get help, but he won't, and staggers away into the heat haze. Walking can't solve everything. It can give you time to work through issues or put them out of your mind for a while, it can give perspective and space, but some things need to be faced before they can be resolved. Half a mile further on and we've become so worried about him that we backtrack and hope to catch up with him, to make sure he gets help, but we can't find him. He's disappeared.

Across the fell, past more and more dead rabbits, two stiles in the wrong direction and we find ourselves in the grounds of Simonstone Hall. From the heat of the fell top we've stumbled into the gardens of a stone manor house and a scene that seems completely surreal. Dusty, stinking and dehydrated, we walk through a crowd of beautiful clothes, fanning peacocks and trays of drinks. It feels like we've wandered on to a film set. A man stops us. It's not a film, it's a wedding, and he seems to be the groom.

'Can I help, are you lost, do you want a drink? God, I'm terrified.'

'It'll be fine; you'll have a wonderful day. Yes, we're slightly lost and I'd love some water and a tea.'

We drink tea under a marquee as family members fuss and the groom is finally driven away to meet his fate at the church in the village. Later, as we walk into Hawes, the wedding is just leaving the church in a cloud of confetti, all fears forgotten.

Hawes is heaving with tourists and motorbikes, so we stock up on food and head back on to the moors. We're camped on the side of Dod Fell when we finally get the guidebook out and realize we've walked over twenty miles through one of the hottest days Yorkshire has known. I thumb back through the pages of the guidebook, but there's no doubting it, the miles have been covered.

'Better be careful – before you know it, you'll start recording distance and time.'

'I might just do that.' Moth lies on his airbed in the cool of the evening, his head propped against his rucksack as the sun sets turning the three peaks of the Pennines into giant silhouettes, through a thicket of tall thistles and bracken.

Moth's sitting up in the early dawn light, trying to twist the ring on his swollen finger.

'I'm going to have to do something about this. I can't move the ring any more. What if it's cutting the circulation off completely?'

I look at the finger; it's undoubtedly getting bigger by the day. 'Well, what can we do?'

'I'll have to get the ring off, so find a hospital, I suppose, or someone with a file and some pliers.'

'Well, I know where we can go for either, or both, but I've got to say it – again. I told you so.'

'Okay, okay, just make the tea, will you?'

We pack up early and are walking by six, hoping to get down to Horton in Ribblesdale before it gets too hot. But the day warms quickly and we're soon crossing dusty, sheep-covered moors and dried-up riverbeds in the heat. More dead rabbits, and behind a wall a dead sheep. The further we go, the more dead animals appear, until every few hundred yards there's another dead ewe. The track becomes stony and we're about to branch off towards Pen-y-ghent when we pass a ewe that doesn't move, but just stands swaying next to us. There are no obvious signs of what's wrong with her, but it's late July and she still has her fleece on. I look around and many of the sheep haven't been shorn and are out on the moor in the burning sun, with no shade and no obvious source of water. Without both, and probably a vet, she'll die, but we're a long way from either of those, so we guide her across to the shade of a wall, where we can do nothing more than leave her and hope.

We're on the side of Pen-y-ghent by late morning and the heat is extreme. We're wearing shirts to protect our skin, but they're hanging wet with sweat.

'What the hell are we doing up here? We should have gone straight down to the village.' Moth's looking at the guidebook and the mile left to go to the summit.

'It made sense to follow the high path while we were up here, rather than climb back up tomorrow, but this is intense.'

We reach the summit, but the view is lost in a heat haze and our thoughts are only of getting down and finding shade. Paddy Dillon promised we'd find many things on the Pennine Way, mainly rain, wind and snow, but he absolutely didn't mention heatstroke, dehydration and dead animals. Or that the path down from the summit of Pen-y-ghent, which he merely describes as 'rugged', is really a near vertical scramble over boulders, that at any minute could become a very long scree run to near certain fatality.

27

Lancaster hospital has a nurse who's a ring-removal expert. With some ice, a tube of lubricant and a lot of effort, she squeezes Moth's finger through the ring without needing to cut it off.

'That's incredible, I've been trying for weeks and couldn't budge it.'

'Why on earth didn't you take it off straight away? And how did you let me do that, most people would be screaming in pain?'

'I could feel some tugging, but it didn't really hurt.'

'Strange man. Okay, let's get you X-rayed.'

Hours later, his fractured finger professionally rebound, we're getting out of a taxi and knocking on a familiar door.

'Bloody hell, leave you alone for a few days and look at the state of you. Broken finger and you look like you've been under a blow torch.' Dave carries our rucksacks into the house.

'Yeah, it's been a bit hot. Thought you said it's always wet in the north.' I collapse on to the sofa in the cool of the old cottage.

'No, always sunny in the north, you'll have to go back to Cornwall if you want rain.'

We soak in the bath, rest a broken finger and sleep for two days, before getting back on the train to Horton in Ribblesdale. The train is packed; I doubt if another person could squeeze on and we're in the middle of a hen-do heading away for the weekend.

'We're going to York, but we've all had too many gins already and I think we're on the wrong train. Got any tonics left, Suzi?'

Suzi looks in her bag. 'Nearly all gone, I've got an elderflower left.'

'What's elderflower?'

'Not sure, I think it's a weed.'

'What? Fuck that, I'm not putting a weed in my gin, I'll drink it neat.'

There's something incredibly infectious about laughter, wherever it comes from.

There's no doubt, you should always be careful what you wish for. When rain starts to fall on the Pennines – I mean really fall, not gentle horizontal driving rain, but rain that comes at you like a pressure washer cleaning the patio – it can go on for days. We're on the side of Fountains Fell when it starts, too far from Horton to go back, too far from Malham to reach it. We're dripping in minutes, so it's pointless taking shelter. There is none anyway, other than the tent which will be soaked before we can get it up. There seems to be little else to do, other than walk.

The path stays above the cloud line and we walk in an unknown world of water. Water drives under hoods, through leggings, into boots, until we're so saturated we stop thinking about being wet and simply become the water. Two-foot-high waves blow across Malham Tarn, lapping on to the path and into boots already brimful with peat water. Driven by the wind, it acts like an incoming tide. The wind's picking the water up on the western side of the tarn and propelling it east until the waves break on the shore by our feet. When the wind acts as it is now, forcing the water into waves, the distance the wind blows over the water is known as the fetch. We were on the South West Coast Path when a surfer compared Moth's life to a fetch: the harder the wind blows, the longer it blows, the greater the fetch. I watch Moth wading along the path, head down against the weather, ankle-deep in water. If the surfer had been here now he'd be saying, 'I told you so. It's all about the wind; if you can ride the wind then you're surfing, man, you're riding the fetch that never ends.' Moth begins to disappear into the cloud, so I follow him. A broken finger, some sort of peripheral nerve damage in his feet, but in so many other ways more focused and stronger than he's been for months. Surfing his fetch, riding the wind. We pitch the tent behind a stone wall, pour the water from our boots, and try to sleep in our damp sleeping bags. Alone on the moors, where we haven't seen a single walker all day.

The morning brings a change to the rain. Less pressure washer, more horizontal shower jet, driven by a wind that makes us lean over like cartoon backpackers from 1970s postcards with an inscription underneath the picture that reads 'If you don't like the weather, wait five minutes'. We wait for ten behind a stone wall, but the weather doesn't change, so we carry on, heads down into the wind towards Malham Cove. The flat plateau of limestone pavement above the cove is a crazy paving of fissures, cracks and crevices where the water disappears, leaving a surface that resembles a tray-baked brownie that's cooled too quickly. Our feet slip and slide on the wet surface: porous stone worn glass-smooth by millennia of storms like this. The cove itself, a sheer curved seventy-metre-high amphitheatre of limestone, was apparently formed by an ice-age river carrying glacial meltwater over the rock lip. There's been no waterfall here for nearly two hundred years, except for one afternoon in 2015 after a storm like this one. We walk quickly on, hoping today isn't the day of the next flash waterfall.

We take shelter in Malham, behind a steamy café window, looking out on to a village that's keeping its doors closed and its streets empty. We would have found somewhere to stay – if every bed in the district hadn't already been taken. Instead we drink tea, then carry on walking. Torrential downpour finally gives way to grey steady rain over muddy, slippery farmland. The rain and the farmland go on for days. Days that blur, one into the other. Days of fields and walls and sheep huddled with their backs to the wind, of rain-sodden, bog-covered Ickorn-shaw Moor, where there are endless grouse butts, but no grouse. Days of little conversation, no wildlife, no people, just water. Days punctuated only by the occasional moment in a tea room, sheltering from the very worst of it. We now have all the things Paddy promised. Maybe I cursed us by thinking the Pennines was in the middle of a drought.

Finally, as we head down a deviation through the Golden Clough valley towards Hebden Bridge, the rain stops, the clouds lift and for fleeting seconds, we see the sun. I'm not sure if I was looking at my feet, or I blinked, or he beamed in from another dimension, but a man suddenly appears next to us, walking alongside as if he's been there all the time. It's only when I'm wondering why I'm so surprised by him that I realize that's it's actually been days since we saw another walker, but this lull in the rain has brought him and others out immediately. Faisal loves the Pennine Way with a passion. He also really loves talking about it.

'Are you walking the Pennine Way, all of it?'

'Yes, heading south.'

'I want to do that. One day I'll leave the taxi on the drive and my wife will say, "Why aren't you working?" And I'll say, "Because I'm going to walk the Pennine Way, all of it." I walk on the path every weekend; it's changed my life. I've driven that taxi for fifteen years, I was a young man with a young man's body when I started, but every year I just got fatter and fatter. Then I had a back problem and was off work for weeks and I felt terrible. But one day I thought, today I'm going to go for a walk.'

'And did it help?' Moth's waiting to hear the rest of the story.

'Oh yes. I started walking a short way, then a bit more, then in eight weeks I'd lost four stone and my back was completely better. I felt lighter, all over, but in my head too. Then the sick pay ran out and I had to go back to work. But I still walk at least thirty miles every time I have two days off. Sometimes I even walk at night.'

'That's remarkable.'

'I love the Pennines. I'm so very proud to call them my home. I know the area now as I never have before, I meet wonderful people like yourselves, I even walk with my brothers now and sometimes my cousins, but they aren't very good to walk with because they can't keep up. I think I'll never stop walking the moors, I love them so very much.'

'What a great thing.'

'Yes, my life is changed. Praise be to Allah, but also very much praise be to walking.'

Faisal disappears as suddenly as he had appeared and we realize we've walked straight past the Lumb Bank writers' centre, missed Sylvia Plath's grave and are almost in Hebden Bridge.

28

There's a greyness hanging over Hebden Bridge. The walls of the stone buildings shine wet in the low light, the streets run with rivers of water and the few pedestrians rush by with their coat hoods pulled close over their heads. At the lower end of the town the river roars between trees and under a stone bridge, leaving piles of broken wood, plastic bottles and paper cups on its banks. The town feels at maximum hydration. But this town grew around the power of the water, driving the mills, turning wool from the thousands of sheep on the moors into cloth. So much clothing was manufactured here that at one point Hebden Bridge was known as Trouser Town. Things are different now. According to *High Life*, the British Airways in-flight magazine, this is the fourth funkiest town in the world, maybe thanks to the amazing array of unusual shops and micro-pubs, or possibly because this is now also known as the lesbian capital of the UK.

I'm tired of being wet, tired of the smell of wet clothes, tired of eating damp cereal bars and above all else, just muscle-cramping, head-numbing, bone-achingly tired. We eat soup and drink endless tea in a pub while the staff decide if they have a room that's sufficiently in need of a revamp that they can risk housing two dripping-wet, mud-covered tramps. I think the rain has finally got into my bones; all I can think of is the feel of hot sand beneath my feet and the smell of salt air. I'm not sure if I'm feeling homesick or bogsick. And I have a Zoom event in an hour. Moth's exhausted and I'm fairly desperate, so it's beyond a relief to find they actually have a room, with a bath, and I haven't got to focus on my phone screen while covered in mud with bits of birch twig stuck in my hair as hundreds of Americans watch on.

We sit on the end of the bed comparing our feet. Mine are white and wrinkled from days in boots full of water; the skin on my toes is swollen and seems to be lifting away from the nails – in fact I think I've probably got trench foot. Moth's are damp and a bit red in places from rubbing against damp socks, but the pain in them is almost more than he can bear. He takes a double dose of painkillers. Swamped with guilt again, I stop whinging and get in the bath. Wrapped in the heat of the water, the days of bogs and peat begin to fade away. But our sodden, steaming belongings and my boots, upturned in the sink, are literally oozing water, filling the room with a distinctly wet-dog smell.

'There's no way our things will dry tonight.' Moth's laying out the wet socks on the radiator, but the heating isn't switched on. 'Shame, I'd love to put some dry socks on.'

'I could dry them with the hairdryer, I suppose, but it might take hours.'

'Shall we go to that little shop we saw, and buy some new ones on the way out tomorrow?'

'But we're only days from the end of the Pennines – is it worth it?'

'Ray, my feet are killing me. I could just stop now and get on the train, but I have to finish this path. It's just a fucking pair of socks.'

How bad have his feet been to make this calm man so angry, or is he bogsick too? I sink into the now lukewarm water. Guilt, always more guilt.

'I didn't mean you shouldn't buy a pair of socks.'

'Good.'

The outdoor shop has a dusty, slightly old-fashioned feel. Moth finds a couple of pairs of socks in his extra-large size, but there aren't any in a standard size.

'Oh no, I don't have a medium, that's the size everyone wants.' The woman stands by a rack of socks shaking her head as if I've asked for the latest iPhone and there's a queue around the block. I only want a pair of socks. I don't bother to ask why she doesn't have the most popular size; I already know the answer.

I'm picking up my rucksack and about to leave the shop when a woman holds out a walking boot and I see the shop owner's shoulders sag.

'Do you have these in a size six?'

'No, madam, but I have got them in a size eight if you'd like to try those.'

Even if you live in the fourth funkiest place in the world, it would still be hard not to despair if your business is suffering for reasons beyond your control, and it never stops raining.

Stoodley Pike monument was originally erected to commemorate the defeat of Napoleon in 1815, but it fell down after a few decades of Pennine weather, so was replaced in 1854 with a 120-foot-high monument that's visible from miles around. Normally. But we're back in the clouds, on the edge of another moor and I'm becoming convinced that the Pennines may never end. Just a few miles into the day and it already doesn't matter if my socks started out as old or new, wet or dry, they're soaking again.

'My feet are so wet, every step feels like I'm squelching in mud. How are yours?'

'Yeah, good, they're still dry.' I look down at my feet, at the water oozing out of the leather with every step, and finally have to admit my old boots have come to the end of their days.

The cloud lifts slightly, leaving rain-heavy cumuli rushing east on a high wind. Finally it's dry enough to sit down. We hang our feet over the edge of a bleak outcrop of rocks on Blackstone Edge, our clothes drying in the wind. To the south, a stream of traffic heads east and west along the snake of the M62, and beyond that to the south-west, appearing like a small hamlet in the far distance, is Manchester. The faintest break in the clouds allows low beams of sunlight to cross the landscape, lighting the bogs and streams in a shimmer of silver. For a moment our spirits lift with the chance of daylight, but just as quickly as it came the light goes and the dark austere Pennine landscape of bog and stone returns. I close my eyes against the wind, and for a moment I'm turning a 360-circle on Cross Fell, marvelling at the endless expanse of never-ending sky, moor and light, our skin burnt by the sun. It feels like a lifetime ago, as if this dark world of bog has sucked me in and I may never escape. We might be found, thousands of years from now, preserved by the peat, dug up and put on display as bog people. Scientists will marvel at the grave treasures they find with these tribesmen of the boglands, treasures of titanium pots and tent pegs. Items to prove what a primitive era we came from. Or we could just keep moving, in the hope that one day we might be back on dry ground.

Paddy Dillon tells me that this section of the M62 was built six years after the opening of the Pennine Way. A footbridge was erected at the same time, to allow walkers to safely cross the motorway, and possibly to stop and watch the traffic passing beneath, and maybe wonder 'what's the rush'. On a sunny day in 1971, it might have felt safe to watch a few cars pass beneath a newly built bridge. But on a late afternoon in early August of 2021, when the traffic roars beneath a bridge that has seen better days and bounces with every step, in a wind that's almost blowing us off our feet, it's not somewhere I want to linger. Today, Paddy, there is a rush, but only to get off the bridge.

The moors roll on, flat, black, brown, dark, until a moment in early evening when the light breaks through. Dense, impenetrable clouds begin to part, wisping down to earth in squalls of rain, racing by on high winds, dissipated by the speed. From an outcrop of broken rock, the landscape transforms in dark and light, silver and green, as clouds stretch and separate like trailing fingers of lovers' hands going their separate ways through the sky. Tomorrow we have options. We can hurry on by, heading south as quickly as we can, or we can take a detour of a few miles into the village where the Poet Laureate was born. We're looking down the valley of trees and rock that bends away towards Marsden, when a large grey bird appears. A peregrine falcon has lifted from a rock ledge just metres away, holding for a moment in the high wind, as if unable to go forwards, then dropping back to the ledge. Moments later he rises again, but not alone; two of them take off, hold, then plummet back down, before coming up again. As we watch, it's as if they're testing the air, waiting for a slight lull in the wind, a moment when the air pressure shifts and there's space between currents, allowing them to slip through. The wind pushes at my face, rattles my clothing, finds unprotected spots and chills them to the bone. I think of shelter and protection. The peregrines hang on the wind. Their experience of the air is as different to mine as my understanding of water is to that of a fish. Other dimensions exist all around us, not as a parallel universe, but in how we experience this one. Those birds feel the air in ways I never will; I feel the earth in ways impossible to them, as fish know the water in ways we cannot. The peregrines hover in the air, one behind the other; then, as if they're feeling it with the same sense of knowledge we take from sight, they find their moment, ride the opening within the air and are gone. They leave a gap in the mist, a place that fills with an understanding of the way another life form inhabits this earth, a space where I can only wonder at the arrogance of humanity when we assume the right to destroy this world, as if it's something we own, as if we have the right to make that choice.

The cloud re-forms and drops and within minutes we're enclosed in the wet air. The view down the valley disappears, the edge of the rock vanishes, we're back in a bubble of bog and water and it's almost dark. We put the tent on bog-grass and hope the ground sheet has no holes.

★

I've never met Simon Armitage. He followed in our footsteps on the South West Coast Path, often days, sometimes only hours behind. For miles of the path people were waiting for a famous poet to pass their house, many of them with no idea what he looked like, just knowing he was a middle-aged man with a rucksack heading west. But in preparation for this stranger, they had made tea and cakes and all manner of baked goods to offer to the wandering wordsmith as he passed. Moth looks nothing like Simon Armitage, but as he went by, middle-aged, with a rucksack, heading west, they came out of their houses with their offerings. We were hungry, sometimes possibly starving, and they'd put so much care into their baking, it would have been rude not to accept. So to find ourselves here, in the birth-place of the great man, there really is no choice. We follow the detour.

Since not-meeting Simon, I've read quite a few of his poems, trying to get a feel for who the man is that inspired so much effort. But somehow, even in his words, I've never quite found him – until today. The path leads downhill, and down and down, through clinging wet air, which starts as cloud and ends as straight-down rain. Not hard rain, or soft rain, but straight down, straight to the point, no messing Yorkshire rain. And here he is, the essence of the man is in this place from where his words emanate. Among the dark, austere stone houses, on streets that thread down the hillside, I can see the boy who, as he writes in his poems, 'spied [his] mother down in the village / crossing the street' and reached 'towards a hatch on an endless sky / to fall or fly'. His words echo these streets; they echo him. Suddenly, I have more of an understanding of the man who maybe hasn't 'padded barefoot through the Taj Mahal', but 'skimmed flat stones across Black Moss on a day / so still [he] could hear each set of ripples / as they crossed'. A man whose adult words are formed from his boyhood connection to this place, this town, this land.

We thought we'd eat cake to commemorate the moment, but

we're early and the only places open are the Co-op and the Homemade Kitchen café. We choose the café. It's tiny, with makeshift Covid-proof barriers between the tables that take up a lot of what room there is, so we half expect to be turned away. Instead we're welcomed into the hot, homely space, squeeze our dripping rucksacks in the corner and peel off layers of wet clothing. I turn my boots upside down, hang my socks to drip from the chair, and watch water forming a stream running towards the door.

'What on earth are we doing?' I sit back in the chair as a wave of exhaustion washes over me.

'Ordering breakfast.' Moth's scouring the menu.

'No, keeping going in this hideous weather.'

'You're surely not suggesting we go home? It's only two days to Edale, then it's over.' He looks back at the menu. 'You know, the first time I ever thought about a long-distance path it was the Pennine Way. I'd actually given up hope of ever walking it.'

I watch Moth as I eat the biggest, best breakfast I've ever eaten – a mountain of potatoes, eggs, squash, leeks and peppers. He's eating as if he hasn't eaten in a month, his fork going to his mouth with barely a tremor, while studying the map that came with Paddy's guidebook.

'I think we should try to camp on Black Hill tonight, see where we get to tomorrow, then Edale the day after. And that's it, done. If we want it to be done.' He puts the map book away.

'Do we want it to be done?'

'Might order some more tea before we go.'

29

Despite all the rain, the reservoirs above Marsden still aren't full, but as we pass them the rain stops falling, the cloud lifts and the moors reappear. It's early evening as we climb to the summit of Black Hill. People are heading down, back to their cars, so we wait at the bottom of some narrow steps as a tall man wearing a brown Pakol walks down towards us.

'It's very late to be heading on to the hill, where are you going?'

'Just heading up. We'll camp somewhere up there tonight.'

'I can see you're walking the whole of the Way – you look as if you have many miles in your boots.' He's a very polite man. 'And how are you finding my hills?'

'Your hills?'

'I know what you're thinking, how can a man whose roots are obviously elsewhere be calling the moors *his* hills? It's because I love this land with a passion. I walk up here all the time. I came to this country when I was young; now I'm not so young. Even when I barely spoke the language and felt like an outsider, the hills welcomed me, they took me in and they became my friends. I know them so well, from Edale to Hebden Bridge, these hills are my home. Even now, when I am part of the community, when my family are born here and their lives are here, I never forget where I really belong. Here among my old friends the hills.'

I watch the gentle, calm man walk away towards his car parked on the road and feel a lump in my throat. I've heard more passion and love for these hills among people who have come to them from other countries than from the many home-grown yompers rushing by, counting miles and time. Theirs has been a connection to the land that can't be found by counting steps. Maybe we all need to slow down, to look at our world with fresh eyes and remind ourselves of the wonder of this landscape, before we let what we have slip through our fingers.

There's nowhere to put the tent on the summit of Black Hill, so we forgo the limitless views and follow the flagstone path through deep peat boglands on the south side of the hill. It's virtually dark when we find a slightly drier hummock just off the path and pitch the tent among rustling bog-grass. After days of hearing virtually no wildlife, we stay awake listening to the calls of a golden plover, and when we open the tent flaps to the daylight, the swift, air-splitting blackness of a sparrowhawk flashes by, so close I can feel the air move in its wake.

The path follows a line, where a stream and thousands of human feet have gouged deep scars into the peat. Wide, dark highways of exposed carbon. When we finally climb uphill to a narrow path along a rocky edge, the last miles of the Pennine Way stretch into the distance. There's a rising excitement in the air between us. Not just because this long, tough path is coming to an end, but because we're walking into our own history. Ahead of us lies Bleaklow and Kinder Scout, two monsters of the Dark Peak. A world of peat hags, boglands, big skies and escarpments that hold views into the English heartlands. These are the hills of our early days together. Days of sun and wind and cloud-strewn skies, where we ran free between the high moors to the north and the gritstone escarpments further south. Forming connections to this land and to each other, bonds that have never been broken. Each step draws us closer to this place, to a familiarity I didn't realize I was craving until I could smell it in the wind. That deep, rich, acidic peat and dry limestone smell. Where the air is filled with the calls of kestrels, where the wind always blows over the edge with the promise of something new not far behind, where you can smell the rain as it falls across the flat lands to the south in curtains of grey obscuring the landscape. The place where I can feel Moth's twenty-one-year-old hand in mine, and a lifetime of possibility stretching ahead.

We've crossed over the Trans-Pennine cycle route that runs west to east across the moors and are sitting on a rock in the heather, looking back to Black Hill. The distance we've covered spreads out north and north and north, a vast unknown expanse now filled with knowledge and understanding, as if at last the complexity of this country has started to unfold. From nowhere, a couple flop down in the heather next to us.

'Well, hello there. We're walking the Pennine Way, going north just a few days at a time. But you, I know you've walked a long way.'

I look down at my clothes, muddy, ripped, smelling of dried bog-water. 'I know, we do look a bit of a mess.'

'No, you can't get away with it like that. I know who you are. Your book changed our lives – it changed the way we live our lives. We would never have given ourselves the time to just walk, not before we read your book.'

I look at the couple, heading towards middle age, but glowing from the wind, sun and enthusiasm. 'The book might have given you an idea, but it didn't change your lives.'

'How do you know that?'

'Because books don't change lives. They can change how you think, but it's you that changed your life. You allowed the book to influence you, then you chose to change how you live. The power was always in you, the book just opened the door.'

'Ooh, you make me feel quite powerful, quite in control.'

'I think we all are, if we allow ourselves to be. Do you want a jelly baby?'

We eat jelly babies and compare walking stories until the light begins to fade and we need to find somewhere to camp.

The tent sits on heather that bounces like a waterbed when we lie on it. The sun's setting over Manchester, lighting the city like a white citadel in the far distance, as grouse jump and cackle in the undergrowth. A deep rich smudge of colour spreads across the western horizon, behind the glow of city lights. An owl criss-crosses the heather in search of rodents, flying by again and again as the midges start to rise.

'I don't remember there being midges when we came up here in the past, but I suppose it was nearly forty years ago.' I'm fanning my face with the guidebook to keep them away.

'There weren't any, that's why. They're moving south, in the same way the cuckoos are moving north. It's climate change happening right under our noses, but people just don't seem able to see it. But then I think you have to really look at wildlife before you can see it change.'

'Oh, you mean like that time when I cut my hair off and it was two weeks before you noticed, because you were so busy finishing your dissertation for uni?'

'Yeah, something like that, but will you never let that go?'

'Probably not.' I pass him the guidebook and he fans himself to drive the midges away.

From the side of Bleaklow we cross the Snake Pass on to the northern edge of Kinder Scout, and suddenly life changes. The scarred, worn peat cloughs of the day before are behind us, and ahead lie mile after mile of flagstone pavers. This part of the moor has been saved from the desperate state of erosion of what a sign says is a 'seven-thousand-year-old blanket bog'. No twenty-metre-wide scars of exposed peat here. Here the bog-grasses and heather have regrown, covering the peat right to the edge of the flagstones, keeping vast amounts of carbon locked safely in the bog. We stick to the stones, stepping from one to the other, as does everyone else drawn along this thread of stone through the boglands. Isn't this the way humanity should approach everything we do on this precious planet? Keeping ourselves to a narrow corridor of use, treading on this one earth lightly and with care.

Back on the familiar rocky outcrops there's a sense of a

homecoming that I hadn't expected, a feeling of warmth, of being full to the brim. We'd sat on these very rocks as youthful dreamers, looking at this same view, imagining our lives ahead. We took a road where we gained and then lost all the material things society says we should aim for, a road that has led us to today. To two considerably older, slightly wiser dreamers, sitting on a rock, imagining a new road, with hardly any food left in the ration bag.

'There's that bag of dried potato powder. I think I might have been carrying it since Edinburgh.' I shake the bag out. 'And a sachet of tuna in lemon oil.'

'I really haven't fancied eating that potato, but it looks like there's no choice.'

I stir the tuna into the rehydrated potato and we start to eat it while watching a queue of people waiting to cross some stepping stones over the river, where the Kinder Downfall waterfall drops over a rocky lip. Moth looks at his fork, then at me, and raises his eyebrows.

'Why haven't we eaten this before? It's actually really good. Wow, when I think of all the noodles we've eaten, then we discover this on the last day.' He looks at the horizon, then back at me. A long look that has nothing to do with potatoes.

The top of Jacob's Ladder is crowded with a school trip from Manchester – excited teenagers clambering over rocks and laughing – a large family playing hide and seek in the boulders, and two elderly men sitting on the ground catching their breath after climbing to the top of the Ladder. As we wait for a group of young women to reach the top of the path, the old men tell us they came from India to start a new life in the Peak District when they were in their twenties. They're nearly seventy now, but still come to these hills every other weekend.

'We love it here – the moors are in our bones. Up here we're all the same, on the same hill, under the same sun.'

We head downhill with a warm sense that we belong on

this moor top, as does everyone – on the same hill, under the same sun.

Jacob's Ladder isn't really a ladder, just the start of a steep descent into Edale, a small village with a couple of pubs that marks the end of the Pennine Way. We walk into the village hand in hand. Two hundred and sixty-eight miles of sun, rain and bogland between us and Kirk Yetholm. Seven hundred miles of wilderness, wildlife, towpaths, coastline and moorland between here and Sheigra beach. Months of trails, paths and ways, drovers' roads and military roads. Nearly three months of following the lines that weave through the land, connecting the people to each other, connecting the people to the land.

We're taking photos of the post that marks the start of the Pennine Way, choking on tears of disbelief, when a large family offer to take our photo together.

'Have you walked the whole Pennine Way?'

'Yeah, we have.' They're cheering and clapping, and it feels like a welcoming committee.

We sit in the pub with a huge jug of iced water, a pot of tea and a lot of food.

'Can't believe it's over, can't believe we've walked so far. And look at you. Would you have imagined this possible that day when you fell in the orchard?'

Moth's smiling through a mouthful of pie. 'I thought I was done that day. I thought there was no way back.' He puts his fork down, covering my hand with his. 'It's hard to describe how it feels when your body's letting you down, but then it starts to respond again. It's almost impossible, it's almost like rewinding time, as if I have my life back. So I've got an idea, I don't know what you think, but—'

I don't let him finish the sentence. I saw his face as we ate mashed potato on the hill: I know exactly what he's going to say. The sun and wind have turned his face the deep colour of aged rust, highlighted by the silver-white hair that stands vertical no matter how long he wears his hat. His arms have lost every ounce of spare flesh despite the vast quantities of chips and noodles he's eaten, exposing the muscle moving just beneath the skin. Not the powerful arms he had in his forties, but still there, still strong. But more than that, there's a light in his face that was lost in the dark fog of this encroaching illness. It's the light of hope, of possibility, of the desire to keep trying. He wants this and I know I'll follow him. I've followed his wild enthusiasm for all of my adult life, followed it like a beacon through every twist and turn, in every hidden corner and exposed headland. But can *I* do it now, do *I* still have the strength? Sharing the roller coaster of life with just one person, I haven't seen the years pass, haven't marked my age and the passing of time, but today those years are weighing heavy. The hands on the table aren't those of a young woman, the skin has wrinkled and sagged, brown spots appearing where they don't belong. There's a problem with a vein in my leg that's getting worse with every mile, causing pain that keeps me awake at night, and my feet haven't really recovered from the torturous black boots of the Cape Wrath. But as I watch him scoop the peas off his plate and they stay on the fork until they reach his mouth, I know I'll follow the light of this man, no matter where it leads.

'Yes, okay, yes, let's do it.'

'You don't know what I'm going to say. You might not say yes if you know.'

'You're going to say let's walk home.'

He doesn't answer, just stuffs another forkful of pie in his mouth, but the raised eyebrows tell me we're heading south.

PART FOUR

Heartlands

A sense of falling, like an arrow-shower
Sent out of sight, somewhere becoming rain.

'The Whitsun Weddings', Philip Larkin

Paths, Towpaths and Offa's Dyke Path

Edale to Chepstow

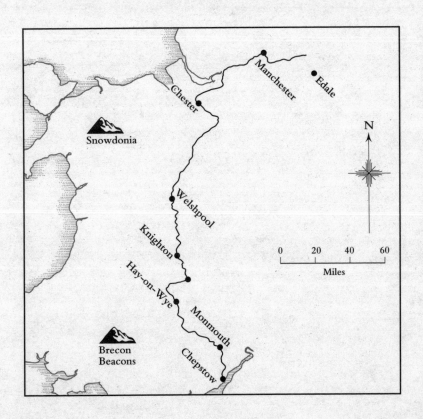

30

'That's brilliant, thanks, that made such a difference.'

'No problem, have a good one.'

The man we met outside the shop drives away, and we head west along the Trans Pennine Trail, the shining citadel we'd seen from the side of Bleaklow lying ahead. We know Manchester. It's many things: a centre of musical history, universities, football and northern determination; but it's definitely not a shining citadel. It's a wet, dark city in torrential rain, a hub of life, traced through with the record of the movement of goods and commerce in the past and the present, on roads and canals, railway lines and runways.

We find a hotel, book in for two nights, peel off socks that are fusing to skin, wash our clothes in the sink, empty our rucksacks, eat all the free biscuits and sleep for twelve hours. The next morning we head into the centre in search of new walking boots. Moth needs something that absorbs some of the shock of each foot strike, something to ease a little of his foot pain. I need boots that keep out more rain than they let in and allow the trench foot to heal. But the basements of the outdoor shops are flooded. Too tired to wander around the city, we drink endless tea while they pump the water out. Late afternoon, when they finally reopen, it seems the water isn't their only problem. Like everywhere else in the north, their stocks are low; they think it might be something to do with the queues at the border. Moth chooses the only pair they have in his size, a pair of black fabric boots that look as if he's walking on huge black doughnuts. They don't have anything in my size, so I take a pair that are a size too big, buy some extra socks and hope for the best. On the way back to the hotel we stock up on painkillers and blister plasters. While I'm standing in a queue for the counter I see a tubular foot bandage; I'm not sure why, but I'm strangely drawn to it. As the queue gets shorter, the bandage gets closer. I try not to look at it, but by the time I'm paying I can't resist it any more and it goes into the bag. Maybe we've been walking too long, maybe it's rained so much I have some kind of bog-fever, or maybe I just need more sleep.

We head back towards the hotel, past homeless people in every doorway, past posters saying Manchester is tackling its homeless problem, past people begging for food and help. Manchester is doing more than most cities to resolve its homeless problem, but, as with everywhere else in the UK, the 'Everyone In' campaign that put homeless people into empty hotels during the pandemic has come to an end. Now it seems everyone's back out. The scheme did amazing things, showing how the homeless problem can be solved if there's the will to make it happen. But while we've been walking, life on the streets has returned to normal. The pre-pandemic strategy aimed to cut rough sleeping by half by 2022, but walking through these streets I think I agree with some indications that suggest it could take another decade, or even longer, to achieve. The new policy on homelessness appears, in many places, to be a return to the old normal.

It finally stops raining and we sit at a café by the canal. We've spent most of the day sitting in bookshops, looking at maps of the area, trying to work out what path we could pick up to head south, but can't seem to find anything that works.

'Probably shouldn't have come into Manchester, we could have gone south on the Limestone Way.' Moth's looking through the folds of a map he bought, but it seems to be all roads and canals, no paths. He looks at the map again, opens it fully out on the table, then looks up at me as if someone's just told him he's won the lottery.

'What?'

'Where are we?' He has his finger on the map, but I can't see what he's pointing at.

'What do you mean? We're in Manchester.'

'No, but where?'

'In a café.' I'm starting to feel a bit concerned now. Have we walked too far? Is it really time to stop walking and just get on the train?

He's shaking his head. 'But where's the café?'

I look around at the brick buildings that sit back from the road, at the edge of the canal. 'Oh, now I get it. On the canal.'

He folds the map up and eats yet another pie. Of course, the canals.

The Bridgewater Canal leads out of the city, past its built-up, run-down, industrial outer edges, until grey sprawl eventually gives way to green. As rain clouds finally break into cumuli racing through patchy blue skies, we realize we're no longer on the side of the Bridgewater but somewhere alongside the Manchester Ship Canal. This wide, deep industrial canal won't take us where we need to go; if we follow it much further we'll be heading towards the Irish Sea. We take the first road south into some kind of transitional edgeland, weaving our way through scrubby hedges and small roads until it's nearly dark. Moth stops with his hands on his knees, taking the weight of his rucksack off his shoulders.

'I'm completely done. I don't know if I can go any further.' He puts his rucksack down and sits on it. 'Have a look in that field, see what you think – can we put the tent in there?'

We're close to houses and cars pass regularly, but the only thing in the field is an old donkey with half its hair missing and a wire feed container, standing in a patch of mud in the corner.

Inside the tent, Moth snores through the night, and outside the donkey grinds its teeth and sniffs as car headlights shine through the hedge, passing arcs of light over the tent. It's hard to understand why we're here, lost in the north Cheshire lanes, when we could have caught a train and been in our bed in Cornwall by now, with Monty happily asleep under the table. But for the first time since getting in the van to head north, I feel no guilt. We're here because Moth thinks he has further to walk, and that's reason enough.

Endless lanes and footpaths through monocultures of arable land and weedless grass eventually lead to the Shropshire Union Canal. We step on to its towpath with a sense of having come out of a desert into a garden of Eden. The hedgerows bordering the canal are filled with wild carrot and the air is thick with insect life. There's a hazy mist hanging over the flat water, but the call of waterfowl breaks through, ducks and moorhens appear and disappear into the reeds, swallows swoop low, feasting on the insects. This is a world apart. For a moment it feels like déjà vu. For a moment I'm reminded of the South West Coast Path, where we witnessed the same phenomenon. On the land side of the coast path, monocultures of grain stretched on for field after silent field. Acres of wheat, oats and kale, where little moved other than a few crows. Yet the path itself held an astounding density of wildlife and biodiversity. This feels the same, like a haven. Looking through the hedges at the green weedless fields beyond the canal, I can see why. It's easy to forget when we look at lush fields of green grass that so much of pastoral England is doused with herbicides, ridding our fields of sorrel, thistles, nettles and all manner of other plants we consider to be weeds. What's left is smooth and green and to the glancing eye still perfect rural England, as it has always been. But the habitats necessary for so much of our insect life are gone. I know only too well that when your home and food source has gone, it can be really difficult to survive.

After the surfaces we've walked on, the towpath feels like a moving pedestrian walkway. Flat easy ground, springy new boots and legs that have crossed bealachs and bogs allow us to fly down the towpath as if we're in a world without gravity. Until, seemingly without effort, the Roman walls of Chester appear ahead. We're almost out of food and it's still early: plenty of time to find somewhere to sleep later, so we step into a pizza restaurant. It's a large space, with many tables, but only one taken by a family sitting in the window. I see the waitress look us up and down and put down the paper menus she's holding.

'I'm sorry, but we don't have any tables free.'

I look around, there must be twenty empty tables. 'But there's no one here.'

'Yes, but the tables are all booked, people will be here very soon.'

I look at Moth and he shrugs his shoulders. We both know what's going on; it's such a familiar experience. I can't stop myself, but take off my rucksack and prop it by the door. Rejections like this were such an everyday part of our homeless experience, she's touched the nerve and I'm surprised how raw it still is.

'Now, let's pretend you haven't seen my rucksack. What will you say now?'

'But I have seen your rucksack.'

'Just go with it for a moment and imagine you haven't.'

She looks around for guidance but there's no one to help, so she steels herself to reply.

'Would you like to take a seat?'

'I thought so, and no, actually, I'm not hungry any more.'

31

We slip through Chester in the early light. The streets are quiet, no people or cars, just a few seagulls pulling wrappers out of the bins. Walking within the city walls while they're empty of people is like being in a multi-time capsule, like slicing through a layer cake of Chester's existence. From its Roman origins, through the medieval, Georgian and Victorian periods, to the present day as the bakery opens its doors to the two builders waiting outside. We turn on to the towpath, leaving the waking city behind, disappearing into the silence of the canal.

Miles pass; miles of just us, the water and the wildlife. Even as the day warms up there are few people about. The towpath along the Shropshire Union canal seems to belong only to the dog walkers, cyclists and wildlife. Families of ducks bob on the water: mothers with almost fully grown young, others with late hatchings of ducklings, all weaving through the reeds at the edge of the canal. A sense of calm hangs over the still water, a wildlife corridor between tall overgrown hedges and mature trees. We walk for hours, along paths that have been trodden for generations. Where horses pulled narrowboats loaded with cargo down waterways that were once major transport links. Now, these are places of leisure – no more cargo, just the slow transit of people enjoying the quiet water in a place where time is slow.

Days spent in urban areas have built up inside me, like an internal head of pressure growing with every hour, but finally in this still place a profound sense of relief washes in, like the wake of a slow-moving boat. I'm coming to realize that the intense sense of claustrophobia I feel in populated areas has little to do with the people there, and everything to do with me. We've walked and cycled for three months. Shrugged off water with the deer in Loch an Nid, flown free with the eagles in the glens, become one with the weather on the wild moorland tops, and, without realizing it was happening, we've stepped away from the normal life we'd worked so hard to refind after our months on the headlands of the coast path. Normality has slipped from us as surely as butter from a hot knife. We haven't counted hours or days but have simply fallen into a state of being, a place that exists when our ordinary civilized world loosens its grip and our wild state creeps in.

Maybe it's caused by the flat straightness of the canal, its unchanging dimensions, or some other point of physics that I don't understand, but there's a strange sense of parallax on a towpath. We're walking at a pace, being passed by narrowboats that are moving only slightly faster but in the opposite direction, and it begins to feel as if we aren't moving at all. As if we are actually standing still and all of life is moving past. After a day of surreal calmness, we camp in scrubby undergrowth behind the canal hedge. We boil eggs that we dared to buy, knowing the path would be flat and the chance of breakages lower, and eat pastries from the bakery, squashed flat and leathery in the rucksack by the weight of the eggs on top. Time has stopped here. Boiling water by the tent, listening to moorhens in the reeds, the same as anyone moving down this waterway throughout the centuries would have done. When life is pared back to necessity, time dissolves. We eat the eggs, watching a vole in the undergrowth. This could be any year, any time.

It could be, until I flick through the day's news on my phone as we make the final cup of tea of the day, and I spot something that makes me take the water off the gas so I can read it in full. The UN climate report has been published. They're calling it 'code red for humanity'. It seems the world will reach the global warming tipping point of 1.5 °C by 2040. The point of no return within the lifetime of many of us. A death knell is sounding across these fields, whose only purpose is to feed the exponential growth of humans. And yet we just watch, and eat, and reproduce, as if we're outside any catastrophe that might await this earth. Onlookers at the show.

I'm still shocked by the report as we wake up among the dry seed heads of grass and cow parsley. But despite that the sky brightens into the pale yellow of an early-summer morning and we head back on to the towpath.

Slipping south-west off the Shropshire Union and on to the Llangollen Canal the vegetation becomes so dense it's hard to see the path between the canal-side festooned with reeds, yellow iris and knapweed and the overhanging hedgerows. The air's alive with the sound of insects, bees lazily hovering from flower to flower, electric blue damsel flies, water skaters and huge horseflies with a bite worse than the Pennine version. But just as the coastline is in places becoming a last stronghold for our wildlife, so it is here. These ribbons of life are becoming, for much of our biodiversity, the last hope.

A couple pass in their boat, shouting good morning and waving as they heave their way through a lock. They pass us again later, after the lock, shouting as they go.

'Bet you'd like a cup of tea?'

'We'd love a cup of tea.' They chug on, laughing at us as they go.

Arched Victorian brick bridges cross the canal, each one numbered and preserved. We're falling into a rhythm of counting bridges and the number of paces between them. But we start to miscount when moored narrowboats begin to appear on the opposite side of the canal. At first they are in ones and twos, obviously permanently moored as they've created gardens on the canal bank – haphazard gardens, designed gardens, gardens with decking, sheds and pot plants, gardens with sitting areas and storage. Then suddenly there are no spaces between the boats; they're end to end as if they're in a canal traffic jam. A man shouts across the canal from an empty boat with no garden.

'Good morning! Wonderful day for a walk – where are you heading?'

'South. Yes, it's a beautiful day. What are all these boats doing here? It seems such an out-of-the-way spot for so many boats?' Moth seems to have become more and more direct with every mile we've walked, but the man seems unfazed.

'There's a stretch of canal-side that no one owns, it's quite long, probably between your last bridge and maybe one or two that way.' He points west along the towpath. 'I'm dead lucky to have found a spot just when I bought my boat.' The boat has obviously seen much better days, it's brown with rust and peeling paint, but the man has an energy and enthusiasm that's infectious. 'I've given up work and I'm going to do her up, make it cosy, get a stove, and live the canal life. No bills, no responsibilities. I can't tell you how happy I am.'

We wave and keep walking, passing at least a hundred boats, their cheerful owners and vast arrays of pot plants. The boats finally end and the canal is quiet again, until up ahead we can see a boat moored on our side of the canal. As we get closer we find there are two deckchairs blocking the towpath. We reach the chairs and it's the couple from the lock.

'Oh, you made it. Sit down, take the weight off, do you take sugar in your tea?' Like everyone else we've met on the canals, this couple seem alight with life. Happy with their lot and happy to share it.

'That's so kind of you. I could kill a cup of tea.'

We sit in the chairs as they feed us tea and chocolate bars. They retired from busy lives to live on their boat, but can't quite afford it, so have gone back to work part time. They moor up during the week and travel out when they're not working.

'Yeah, I had a good job, worked for the council for most of my life, but I drive a taxi two days a week now and I've never been happier. My wife, she's an end-of-life carer. Sits with people as they die during the week, polishes the boat and opens locks at the weekend.'

His wife comes back out of the boat with more biscuits. 'Yeah, it's calming out here, a good life. Well, it's all about

getting the balance right, isn't it? I think we've done that now.'
She opens the side door of the boat and two large Labradors
jump out and race down the path. Looks pretty balanced to me.

The air becomes damp with rising dew as the sun disappears
and the sky turns a deeper blue. We sit on a bench by another
lock, looking at the map, trying to decide where to spend the
night, when a boat pulls into the bank, waiting its turn, as
another boat leaves the lock.

'Are you lost?'

'No, just trying to work out where we can camp tonight.'

The two elderly men are fussing around their boat, obviously
enjoying every moment of the rituals of mooring and preparing
for the lock.

'Just making tea, do you two want one?' The younger of the
two has a teapot in his hand.

'I never say no to a cup of tea.' I look at Moth as he speaks.
There's something in the way he said it, something in his face,
something beneath the surface of exhaustion. I can't quite read
it, but it could almost be contentment. The man comes back out
with mugs of tea and a plate of biscuits. The older man tells us
he's been on and around boats all his life, until he gave up work
to care for his wife as she died. Now the two men own a share of
this boat and take it out for weeks at a time.

'I'm so sorry about your wife.' It seems hollow but I don't
know what else to say.

'I'm not – it was the best thing. I couldn't cope any more and
I couldn't put her in a home, so the best thing.'

We watch them go through the lock, and I wonder aloud
how it's possible to be so practical about the death of someone
you've shared your life with. Maybe I'm approaching Moth's
illness with a selfish sort of weakness. Maybe I just need to be
stronger and start to detach.

'Don't talk like that.' Moth's shaking his head and looking at
me as if there's something I just don't understand.

'I'm trying to explain how I feel.'

'No, don't wave your hands around when you're talking, you're going to drop the last biscuit.' I look at the shortbread biscuit in my hand as he snatches it from my fingers and eats it.

We wander down a lane away from the canal in the hope of finding a field to camp in, but the roads are lined with arable fields, no grass anywhere. It's twilight when we stop looking and climb over a fence into a field of maize. There's nothing in this field *except* for maize. No weeds underneath, no insects above, just maize running in lines that disappear into the dusk. But somewhere in the distance I can hear a blackbird singing. Walking through the middle of a monoculture as the light fades, I can't help but think again of the thousands of other fields of maize, grain and sugar beet that blanket rural Britain. All sprayed with a plethora of pesticides and herbicides to maximize production, leaving nowhere for wildlife to survive, creating an equation that doesn't balance. Our wildlife is slowly disappearing as it becomes stranded in pockets, left on small islands between monocultural deserts, but there are too many humans for us to survive without planting vast areas with crops. And taking hundreds of thousands of hectares of prime agricultural land out of production and rewilding them, as has been proposed, won't keep us fed. Food security is the crisis waiting in the wings, the thing the West has chosen not to talk about. But as populations rise, producing enough food to feed ourselves is becoming an increasingly big issue, even here. Britain only produces 60 per cent of the food we eat, leaving us vulnerable to climate and political changes elsewhere in the world, so our own food production is essential. But at what cost? With the new freedom afforded by Brexit, the government have recently reintroduced the use of an EU-banned neonicotinoid pesticide that prevents a disease in sugar beet, but kills bees as a side effect. It doesn't matter how many bug houses we buy from the garden centre if on the other side of the fence the farmer is spraying neonicotinoids on his crops. We have to find a balance. We can all survive without that extra spoon of sugar in our tea, but many of us won't survive if we lose our pollinators.

We follow a gap between the maize stalks and pitch the tent in a clearing where the maize hasn't grown. The darkness becomes absolute as the wind clatters the stalks overhead. The gusts grow stronger, the noise of the maize louder and there's no chance of sleep. Then the storm really hits, huge hailstones pounding the tent as we cower inside, expecting them to burst through the weathered flysheet.

At first light we open the door flap and push aside piles of hailstones the size of marbles. The flysheet has split along the pole lines and is only holding on in parts. We hang out in the middle of the maize field trying to repair it with half a roll of duct tape, but as soon as we shake it the tape falls away and the poles slip out. The tent's days are over. My throat tightens and tears stream down my face. I look away, hoping Moth can't see, but there's no hiding it and I sit in the wet mud, sobbing. This tent kept us safe and protected across the wild headlands of the South West Coast Path, it's been our shelter, our salvation, through some of the harshest moments in life. It's not just a tent. It's been battered by storms, had the poles and the pegs replaced, but the shell of this old Vango tent was home, when this was the only home we had. The thought of going on without it seems hopeless, as if an old friend who has held us tight through life's difficulties has just let us go. I wipe snot and tears from my face as Moth packs it away and books a bed for the night in Welshpool. Somewhere in the distance a blackbird is singing as if nothing has changed.

The Montgomery Canal is known for the water plants that line its edges. Thick and abundant, they billow across the path and hum with insect life. The sky's cleared and the mid-August hailstorm is just a memory. There are many miles to cover, but it's early, there's time. We fall into a metronome of walking, miles passing with little conversation. But as I follow Moth's feet I become transfixed by his black doughnut boots. They're walking in a straight line, each boot hitting the ground with the same pressure, they're in sync, moving to the same beat. One-two, one-two, one-two, not one . . . twoo, one . . . twoo. I'm mesmerized. The hesitant gait that I've become so used to seeing has gone. I follow him in silence, a smile creeping back on to my face. *One-two, one-two, one-two*. It's late when we reach Welshpool, eat chips, find the hotel and stand under a hot shower washing maize dust out of our hair.

'I can't find another three-man, but there's a two-man version of the same tent. Just a bit smaller, what do you think?' Moth's sitting in the bed looking at his phone.

'What's the point? Where would we have it posted to?'

'The only hotel I can find with a vacancy is in Kington, but that's three days away.'

I look at him sitting in the bed, comparing the guidebook to the phone, focused on the problem. 'What do we do for three days without a tent?'

'We could use bivvy bags? They'd keep the sleeping bags dry, and the weather looks good anyway.' He's looking at the guidebook, has located a tent, checked the weather app and is about to book a hotel. I sit next to him, unsure what's going on. In the winter he would leave an email unanswered for a week, because to answer it seemed too complicated. How is this happening? I'm not convinced about the bivvy bags though; it's a long time since I've slept on a hillside in a plastic bag.

'So where are you sending the tent?'

'I'm just going to call the hotel and check it's okay to send it there before I order it.'

I watch him in awe as he speaks to the hotel, books a room, orders the tent and makes a cup of tea.

'Just thinking, we haven't got bivvy bags with us, we certainly won't get any from here, so shall we pick up some heavy-duty bin-bags in the morning, just in case?'

I drink my tea in amazement. 'Yeah, good idea.'

32

Debatable history suggests Offa, the English King of Mercia, decided to build a dyke in the late eighth century. Apparently, no one's completely sure if he was trying to keep the Welsh tribes out, stop the Mercians escaping into Wales, or he just liked a very definitive boundary, but for whatever reason the dyke was built. Offa instructed an army of men to begin digging a ditch, with all the removed earth being piled alongside to form a bank, until eventually the dyke formed a boundary from sea to sea, from Prestatyn in the north to Chepstow in the south. But if it was meant to be defensive, it really didn't work. The Welsh didn't agree with where he'd put it and the ditch became just another thing to argue about in a centuries-long dispute between the Welsh and English. All these very debatable historic stories have been ruined by science, as it's now proven that the dyke was begun in the fifth century, long before Offa. A national trail, Offa's Dyke Path, now follows the dyke as it weaves its way down the modern border between the two countries. We've intersected it close to the halfway point and head south into the Welsh Marches, the deep-country borderlands where Shropshire and Herefordshire meet Wales. I decide to ignore the science. The idea of walking the Sub-Roman Dyke just doesn't have the same romantic ring to it.

It's dusk when we find a copse of trees that seems sheltered enough to bivvy for the night. By the time we construct bivvy bags out of wheelie bin bags and duct tape, it's almost dark and we finish them by the light of the headtorches. The airbeds and sleeping bags fit into the plastic bag, but it's too short to cover the whole sleeping bag length, so we rip the bottom out of a second one and tape it to the first and we have a huge, super-lightweight, but not very durable, bivvy bag.

The night air is cool and damp on my face, I want to sleep but I'm aware of every sound, feeling every movement of the air. There's a small animal somewhere in the leaves nearby, a mouse or a vole, too small for a rabbit, I can hear it tracking backwards and forwards, the grass moving around its body. A tawny owl calls somewhere close by, then a sound like air brushing through the branches and scratching on bark. The rodent is silent. We're silent too, listening. But there's not a sound, just total damp darkness. Sleep is drifting in, then suddenly air movement, leaf scuffle, the faintest cry, then silence again. We lie in our plastic bags as wild survival plays out, for some if not for others.

Hills, hedgerows and scattered white cumuli roll on for miles with rarely a human in sight, and when we do see one they only grunt in acknowledgement of our passing. Until 1974 Radnorshire was a county in its own right, before being absorbed overnight into the newly formed county of Powys. But there's still something different about this place, still separate. It's a green land of farms and farmers, hedge layers and agricultural engineers, a place that has been overlooked by the speed of modern life. We pass through Knighton, one of its main towns and follow the dyke up to a dip on the side of Hawthorn Hill. The skies are dark, a deep black dark, littered with myriads of infinite stars, lit only by a crescent of new moon.

'I'm not really sure why I'm here, lying in a bin bag on the side of a hill, but I'm strangely glad that I am.' Moth's hand reaches out in the darkness and takes mine, wrapping it with his. The moon tracks across the sky as we drift in and out of sleep, but I don't care if I don't sleep at all. I stare at the sky until I feel as if I'm slipping into it, folded between the stars until they begin to fade and a pale light creeps across the blue, drying the morning dew from my face.

*

The single street of the tiny town of Kington has a relaxed air, with small shops selling everything from dreamcatchers to walking boots. We leave the following morning with the new tent and a huge bag of pastries from the café, then climb the steep hill out of town on to Hergest Ridge. The path follows mown strips of heather over a broad mound of moorland. For a moment it feels as if we're back on the Pennines. Exposed peat, tiny yellow potentilla, gorse, and skies that wrap from Powys in the north into Herefordshire in the west and south. Moth's striding out over the flat ridge top, his movements easy, even his dropped shoulder seems less pronounced. He stops to talk to a farmer who's trying to mend the mower on the back of his tractor.

'Got a problem, mate?'

'Yeah, this back plate came off and I can't get the bolt back in. I need another pair of hands. Fucking thing, I'll have to unhook the mower and go home to get someone.'

'I'll do it. Here, I'll lift this, you thread it back together.' Moth drops his rucksack and lifts the heavy piece of metal off the ground. I wander on, watching them from a distance. But my eyes are constantly drawn north, to the miles spreading out behind us. As if I can feel the way back to Sheigra and the climber standing in the sunset on the cliff edge saying, 'You're putting yourselves in the way of hope. Do that and anything can happen.'

Somewhere on the ridge England becomes Wales and we're back to being border runners, skimming between countries, between cultures. But just as in Scotland, the people who live on the borders aren't separated by them. They live in their own liminal space, a place where nationality is of less importance than whether they have to wear a mask to go into the Co-op on one side of the road, but not in the garage on the opposite side, or is it the other way around? We drop down into the village of Gladestry, along a narrow rocky path. I'm standing on a boulder, waiting for a group of horse riders to pass, feeling strong, content, as if I'm finding answers after a long time searching. Then I step off. By the time my foot hits the ground all I can feel is pain. Hot, searing, stinging pain. I hobble down into the village past an old lady shouting at a family of walkers heading uphill, who've taken the wrong gateway and ended up in her garden.

'Get away from the bees. They're my bees. Don't you dare damage my beehives. Look, you're making them angry.' The walkers turn around to head back the way they came, but the old woman stops them. 'Don't you dare go back through my garden, trampling on my plants.' The family stand by the beehives, trapped in the woman's enclave, as the child starts waving bees away and inevitably gets stung. I limp away. It seems whatever side of the border we're on, obsessive defence of our boundaries is the human condition. Does nationalism, separatism, devolution, or even the invasion of sovereign countries all come down to the same thing? We all live in the same garden, but rather than revel in that and share the beauty of it, all we can do is argue over who owns the bees.

I drag my foot over miles of farmland to a spot on Disgwylfa Hill, where we pitch the new tent among gorse bushes and a carpet of sheep droppings. We squeeze in side by side and it's shockingly small, the shape of a coffin for two.

'Well, I suppose it'll be warmer.' Moth shuffles to turn over, but there isn't room and we have to lie top to tail to make enough room for our shoulders. 'Are you going to look at your foot?'

'I can't, there isn't enough room to get to it, it can wait until morning.'

In the early light of morning I dig in the rucksack for the foot support I'd randomly bought in Manchester. Obviously a premonition, not bog-fever.

'It's a pity I didn't have a premonition about that boulder.'

'It wasn't the boulder that was the problem, it's your boots. You're wearing a size eight when you take a seven, your foot's slipping around.' I put the foot support on and my thickest pair of socks and the boot does feel a little more secure. I wonder how long these low levels of supply will go on for, or if this obsession with borders will mean that soon we'll all be wearing size eight boots? I take a double dose of painkillers and stand on the foot. It's bearable.

33

It isn't bearable for long: every downhill, in this borderland of hills, is agony. The pain in the front of my foot is intense with every downward pointing movement, forcing me to walk downhill sideways, through a morning that feels as if it will never end. Finally we hit the flat edge of the River Wye and follow it into Hay-on-Wye, the bookshop capital of Britain, a small town balanced precariously on the Welsh side of the border. In Wales, but only just.

A wedding party is billowing on to the street, trying to head into a hotel but repeatedly returning to the street for another photograph. We sit outside a café opposite, watching the hats and laughter in the early-afternoon sunshine. We've visited this same café for decades and as I sit in the sun with my boot off massaging my foot, there's a warm feeling of familiarity. Very little has changed in all those years. The town still has the same bookish, bohemian feel it ever had; even the castle that always seemed partly ruined is still partly ruined, with just a little pointing work having been done on the masonry. I put my boot back on and eat a huge bowl of green wonder, with not a noodle or pie in sight.

We hang out at the café for far too long, but my foot's so painful that I drag out every minute before I have to walk on it again. A waitress comes to the table, clearly wanting us to leave, so we order more tea and cake and make small talk.

'It seems very busy today.'

'It's been mad all summer – everyone's staying in-country for their holidays. We never have enough cake to go round. Where are you heading with those big bags?'

I think about it for a moment before I answer, wondering

what to say. The truth almost seems too fantastical to mention, but I try it anyway.

'We started out from the north-west of Scotland over three months ago, but we're just walking home now.'

'Oh, you live in the town then?'

'No, Cornwall.'

'What, you're walking to Cornwall?'

'Yes.'

'From Scotland.'

'Yes.'

She sits down on the spare chair. 'Wow, that's absolutely epic. But how have you done that, you know, at your age?'

That same old question, why do young people think adventures stop when you gather a few wrinkles? I don't have the answer, although I probably thought the same when the wrinkles weren't mine.

'You just keep putting one foot in front of the other. Well, you do if you haven't strained one of them.' I'm so annoyed about my foot, I can't believe I've hurt mine just as Moth's are feeling slightly better.

'Ooh, I did that a couple of weeks ago. Painful. I've got some cream in my bag that really helped. I'll go and get it.' She's gone before I can say no, but quickly reappears with a small colourful pot of something that smells like cheese that's been left in the sun. But we thank her all the same and start to leave.

'What you're doing, it's just incredible. I hope you make it home.'

It's late afternoon when we finally leave the town and begin the long walk uphill towards Hay Bluff hill on the edge of the Black Mountains. It takes miles of uphill trudging before we're far enough out of the valley to see the turbulent sky massing behind the hills and feel the strength of the wind rising from the west. Too far up to head back down. We climb across open moorland towards the lower slopes of the hill as wild ponies head down towards the treeline. There's something about being in pain that stops you retracing steps that you've fought so hard to take and we keep heading up, hoping to find a sheltered spot. We finally reach a hollow on the eastern flank and pitch the tent on uneven boggy ground. The wind rises, sending purple angry clouds scudding east, but breaking enough to allow late rays of light to pick out the city of Hereford to the south, before closing down and showing us why these mountains are known as Black.

At three in the morning the sound of the storm is deafening, but the wind is skidding over the rocks above us, driving the rain horizontally so it misses the tent, which stays still and dry. Moth's looking for the water bottle with his head torch, then turns and shines the light straight in my face.

'You know, until that waitress said the word epic I hadn't really thought of it that way. It's just been the next path, then the next trail. But when you join it all up, it is pretty epic.'

'Pretty epic for old people. Switch that light off, it's blinding.'

'No, I'm going to rub that cream on your foot.'

'At three in the morning?'

'Why not? Not as if we're going to sleep, is it?'

We finally fall into a fitful sleep, not disturbed by the wind, but by the overwhelming smell of rotting cheese in the tiny tent.

A faint grey light appears around the side of the mountain at eight in the morning. When we open the tent it's stopped raining, but we're in heavy cloud and the wind is ferocious. We close the zip on the mountain and the weather and go back to sleep until mid-morning.

The ridgeline is shrouded in dense cloud, like cold steam, driven by high winds that rattle our waterproofs and force us to walk bent against it, as if by simply straightening up we'll be blown off the hill. We follow a worn strip of peat, red sandstone and heather. A large dark form takes shape in the fog, then another and another until we're walking through a herd of ponies that stand motionless, watching us pass within touching distance. They know better than to run wildly into the mist; instead they just stand and watch. Finally, as the day stretches on, the cloud begins to break, showing glimpses of a patchwork of old field systems and small orchards. Until suddenly it lifts completely and Monmouthshire appears, spread out below us: west to the Brecon Beacons and Sugar Loaf mountain, south towards the Bristol Channel. We follow the stony path as it drops down for miles into Pandy and a scattering of trees, my foot screaming with every step.

We reach a campsite but can't find anyone to ask if we can camp. Looking around it seems it's quiz night in the campsite café and everyone's focused on trying to remember who won the FA Cup in 1976. Moth desperately wants to tell them it was Southampton, when they beat Manchester United 1–0, but I drag him away and we go to look for food to supplement our two bags of dried mashed potato and tin of tuna.

In a large square hotel at the other end of the village, a waitress brings a menu.

'Don't order anything with mushrooms in it, we're short of fish, low on chicken and almost out of vegetables.'

'A pretty tricky day for you then. What's going on?'

'Everything's stuck on the trucks at the port. We ran out of mushrooms days ago and now it seems it's all anyone wants.'

We eat soup and a bowl of chips in the bar, which is empty until two men and two boys sit at the table next to us and the waitress returns.

'Don't order mushrooms.'

They eat pie and chips, until one of the men can't contain his curiosity any longer.

'They're bloody big bags. Looks like you're out for more than a short trip.'

'Yeah, we've walked from the north-west of Scotland. Just walking home now.' Moth dips his chip in the soup with a look of satisfaction on his face.

'That's quite a long way. Where's home?'

'Cornwall.'

'Bloody hell, at your age?' I look at him and he almost is our age. 'We're just out for a few days on the mountain bikes with the boys and I'm knackered! How the hell do you keep going?'

'Well, some days it is pretty tough.'

'Have you read a book called *The Salt Path*? I tell you, you should read it. It'll change how you feel about walking. It's about this couple, they lose their house, he gets diagnosed with a brain tumour or something, then they walk the South West Coast Path. He dies at the end, but it's a bloody good book.'

I stick my fork in Moth's leg under the table and he carries on dipping his chips.

'Crikey, brain tumour, that's bad luck.'

An old man and his dog walk through the campsite, passing the tent as we're packing it away.

'Are you here on holiday? Me too, if you can call it a holiday – I just came back to have a look at the old place really. I grew up near here, used to be all farmland and woods. But then they cut all the trees down, widened the road. You might think it's beautiful now, but it's nothing like it used to be. I can't stand to see it, had to move away.'

The same story repeats again and again down the length of the country; surely there has to be some way of reversing this destruction?

Through rolling farmland, sheep, horseflies and kestrels, we reach the edge of a small village. Maybe it's the tiny white painted church of Llangattock Lingoed, or the graveyard full of wild flowers and grass heads, the swallows circling overhead, or just the sense of still calmness that hangs in the air, but this place seems almost out of time. Sitting on a bench at the edge of the churchyard, I try to put my finger on what the feeling is, but I can't. It's old, but very present, powerfully other. A woman and child move through the tall heads of wild flowers with a butter-fly net, catching insects and putting them in a jar. They walk over to a pub garden below the graveyard wall and sit on a bench talking about the insects in their glass cage, before letting them go and walking down the lane. I close my eyes in this place of complete stillness, where hours pass like a moment. A stillness that seeps into every corner of my being. If I had the slightest religious belief I'd tie the sensation to the church, or where it stands on an ancient burial site. Without that, this simply feels like stopping. Where the only sensation or sound is of the wind brushing my face and moving the seedheads.

We walk on, strangely calm and revitalized, as if we've come out of a deep meditation. Down lanes lined with blue scabious, through the first truly diverse farmland we've seen since the riverbank near Middleton-in-Tees, past empty houses and aban-doned farms, around the ruins of White Castle, beneath circling buzzards and red kites, across a land where time stands still, until finally we reach Monmouth.

Humans have settled here since Neolithic times, thousands of years of living and dying on the banks of the river. We take shel-ter too, drinking endless pots of tea in a café, watching the news on their TV. We've barely seen any news while we've walked and it hits us like an assault on our understanding of life. Shock-ing us out of the calmness of the lanes. Politicians are discussing the climate as if it's a commodity, and a desperate woman throws her child over a wire fence to waiting soldiers as the Taliban seize Afghanistan. There's no way back to the feeling of the graveyard after that. The café closes, we buy food from the supermarket and head south until the path dips down towards the River Wye, where we pitch the tent among the tall stems of Himalayan balsam.

I open the tent to a flash of electric blue, disappearing up the river. After all the lochs, rivers and canals we've followed, this is the first kingfisher we've seen. I close my eyes, trying to imprint the blue on my memory. It's a surprise to find, in the daylight, that we walked much further in the twilight than we thought and we're already near Bigsweir. Despite the heavy rain of two days ago, the river level is low, and flowing gently towards the sea. Cars pass along the road on the opposite side of the river, but I can't hear them. My head is full of thoughts of the sea getting closer and the sound of gulls in my imagination.

I'm not sure if it's the memory of the coast and salt-laden air calling us on, the strength of the Highlands in our legs, or Moth's feet, finally happy in their doughnut boots, but the flatlands at the river's edge disappear. Very soon we're climbing a steep hill, boiling water for tea and watching guinea fowl run and cackle in a field nearby. The Wye valley is steeply sided, deeply wooded and as soon as we leave the marker points of the river bends, it's hard to tell where on the path we are. We climb and climb, through dark, mature woodland. Centuries-old oak and beech line the path and we soon stop thinking about where we are, becoming lost in the different textures, shapes and feel of their bark. We're finally shaken out of the reverie when a noticeboard tells us not to enter this area; if we do we'll disturb the dormice that call this patch of woodland home. These tiny mice, with huge eyes and long tails, are under serious threat, their numbers dropping by half in the last two decades, partly because of habitat loss, partly because climate change is causing them to wake from hibernation before any food is available. We tiptoe back out of Lippets Grove Nature Reserve, trying not to disturb them, and realize that we've actually just walked straight through the dyke itself. We pass back through it, between two sides of the high bank of earth and stone, down into the ditch on the other side and back on to the path.

Tintern Abbey appears through gaps in the trees, a huge stone monastery built in the twelfth century for Cistercian monks. It's now just a ruin, a giant remnant of a time when belief and power moved vast wealth from the people into the coffers of the Church, until the Crown decided to change things and moved the money into their pockets instead. Meanwhile, the people continued to survive on turnips.

We walk on and on, through some of the biggest trees we've seen since Scotland, imagining a country where these rare and disparate stretches of ancient woodland are joined, interlinked, not left as lonely islands. A country where the mycorrhizal fungi in the tree roots can make connections across the land and in some way draw us into their connections, ground us in their earth. And almost without noticing the miles pass, Chepstow spreads out beneath us, stretching all the way to the Severn Estuary and the end of Offa's Dyke.

We hang out on the bridge in Chepstow, taking photos of the castle on the hill, before following the urban path as it winds its way on to Sedbury Cliffs and the end of Offa's Dyke Path, then down on to the salt marshes below. The tide is low and we can barely see the water, turning the broad width of the River Severn into a mile of mud and sand stretched out in the evening light. But on the other side is the south-west of England; all paths now are leading to Cornwall. All that stands between us and the south coast are the coastal Somerset levels and a few hills through Devon.

'I still can't believe we've walked so far. It's going to be a piece of cake from here to the Channel.' Moth's looking at the OS app on his phone again. Since he's been able to charge his phone regularly he can't stay off it, constantly checking in which direction the arrow is pointing.

'Yeah, it's going to be so easy, I can't wait to do this section now.'

Excitement builds as we look towards the last big land area still standing between us and the south coast. A sort of growing euphoria. We think we know what west Somerset holds; after all we've passed through so many times on the motorway and explored so much of east Somerset. The pull of the south coast is getting stronger and I can't wait to get going.

When will I ever learn to be careful what I wish for?

PART FIVE

To the South

There can be no happiness if the things
we believe in are different to the things we do.

'The Lycian Shore', Freya Stark

Highways and Byways

Chepstow to Plymouth

34

High above the vast border of mud channels and sand, the path at the side of the Severn Bridge vibrates beneath our feet, bouncing under the weight of four lanes of traffic speeding by. It's deafening, but at moments almost peaceful as herring gulls glide beneath us on a hot wind. Moth doesn't seem able to disconnect himself from the vibrations and leans against the barrier at the edge of the bridge, close to losing his cooked breakfast. After a brief stay with family in Chepstow and a lift through two miles of urban sprawl and traffic, our first few steps of the day have been straight on to the heights of the vibrating bridge.

'Do you think it's vertigo? If so, let's just get off here and you'll be fine.'

'I don't know what it is – maybe the vibrations after eating scrambled eggs.'

'Let's just get off the bridge and find some shade. It's so hot I can feel my skin frying.'

A man on a bike appears over the highest point of the bridge path. A small girl in a cycle helmet and summer dress rides ahead of him. It's a surreal sight and time seems to slow as the tiny child rides down the slope, glee on her face, her dress flying in the wind, beneath the towering sides of trucks roaring by on one side and the plunge down to the riverbed on the other.

On the OS map, the way south from the bridge appeared simple. No easily followed national trails or towpaths here, but paths and lanes all the same, hugging the coast all the way to the Avonmouth estuary. Or that would have been the case, had the way not been barred by heavy metal gates and 'Danger of death keep out' signs. On the map it looked as if we could bypass the miles of closures by going through a few fields and then back to the coast. But after two hours of brambles, nettles, barbed wire and footpath diversions we end up back exactly where we started, at the edge of the motorway.

We sit in a pub garden with a jug of iced water as two separate children's birthday parties in the same garden turn into mayhem. Moth spends an hour in the pub toilet, while the eggs, or something else, takes its toll. He's feeling weak, so we give up on the coast path and head inland on shady lanes and footpaths until we finally put the tent up in a copse of trees close to Bristol.

'I don't know if it was the eggs, it should have passed by now if it was, but I still feel grim.' He's sitting on a fallen tree trunk, his skin pale and waxy, dark rings growing around his eyes.

'Maybe you just need to sleep, I'm sure you'll be better tomorrow. At least we're near Bristol, so some chance of getting a bed for a night or two if not.'

'Or getting on a train and being back on the farm by tomorrow afternoon.'

'Would you do that now – just stop?' In Manchester he was so sure that he wanted to make it all the way to the coast, so strong as he walked down Offa's Dyke, it's hard to imagine how he would feel if he stopped now.

'Right this minute, yes, I would. But ask me again tomorrow.'

The next morning I ask him again.

'Shall we just stop and catch the train? You've done enough now.'

'No, I'll be okay, let's carry on.'

The nausea seems to have passed, so we carry on, but within a mile it's turned into diarrhoea and he's stopping every time there's enough undergrowth. Bristol can't come soon enough. We find a bed for the night and head across the city towards it, buying a large pack of Imodium along the way.

Homelessness has been a big problem in every city we've passed through, but here it's acute. Maybe hopelessness is more obvious in a small city, maybe homelessness was a big issue that's now even bigger, but there's need and suffering in so many doorways. Just like in Manchester, everyone who was in is now back out and the numbers seem even higher than before the pandemic. We sit for a moment while I search through the internet for reasons why the problem seems so obvious here. I already know the answers – Covid caused so many relationships to crack, so many families to fall apart, so many who were hanging by a thread to give up hope – but the statistics are shocking: as we began walking Bristol housing officials reported a 330 per cent increase in single homeless people in the city.

Shoppers in the street look at our rucksacks and eye us with suspicion. However many times I witness it, it still surprises me how having a rucksack on your back in an urban area changes how you're viewed. A group of homeless people stop talking and watch us pass, equally suspicious that we might be new to their patch. We stop and Moth tells them we're just passing through.

'That's good news, mate, good news. There's too many of us here. Too many and too little to go round. Where're you heading then? It's a strange place to be walking through.' A middle-aged man with greying wispy hair stands up and seems more talkative than the others, who stay seated on a patch of cardboard, bundled under duvets, even though it's a warm day.

'To Cornwall.'

'What, on the train?'

'No, we're walking. We've walked from Scotland.'

'Fuck me, that's a long way.' He turns back towards the others. 'We should do that, lads, just go for a walk, have ourselves a holiday.'

A younger man pushes his hood off his head and stands up. 'I've heard of that, of homeless people just walking. Why don't we do that? It's got to be better than just sitting here.'

'You should.' Moth hands them a pack of sandwiches he's just bought from a shop. 'Believe me, it can change your life.'

★

After a night where Moth spends more time in the bathroom than the bed, he's feeling a little better, so we leave the city, through the bohemian village feel of Clifton and over the heights of Clifton Suspension Bridge. But within half an hour his digestive system seems to have taken on a life of its own and he's repeatedly disappearing into the undergrowth. We try to keep going, passing houses of increasing size and obvious value. It's such a stark comparison, from extreme poverty to extreme wealth, within two miles. As we head away from the city through fields, woods and lanes we're surrounded by more and more affluence. The wealthier the area becomes, the more 'Private' and 'Keep out' signs we begin to see, as if with wealth comes the overwhelming desire to protect those assets. We pass along the outer edge of the grounds of a private school, where gates are barred, stiles are blocked with barbed wire, and warning signs are everywhere – danger from 'Guard dogs', 'Danger of pesticide poisoning', 'Danger of death'. We hurry by to a lane lined with even bigger houses and more and more signs – 'Beware – very dangerous dog', 'Beware – security patrols', 'Beware – vicious free-range chickens'.

We pitch the tent below the ramparts of a medieval fort and watch the headlight streams on the motorway below, and the lights coming on in Weston-super-Mare on the distant coastline. The tablets aren't working and Moth's in and out of the woods, squatting in the bracken, as I empty a sachet of tuna into a pan of rehydrated mash. We're finding safety and shelter here for the night in the very same way those ancient settlers would have. Food, safety, warmth, our basic human needs remain the same throughout time, although Moth would prefer to add flushing toilets to that list. I'm wondering what herbs medieval healers would have used instead of Imodium, but daren't research it in case I pick the wrong one and make things worse.

We cross a bridge over the M5, over six lanes of speed and noise, into ancient woodland that would once have surrounded the fort, but seems to have no place alongside the traffic and pollution of today. Or is that the other way around? Huge old oak and beech trees stand over a forest floor littered with dried leaves and squirrels and the first deer we've seen since the Pennine Way. The path winds down into Clevedon, a quiet seaside town, and suddenly we're in another era. The modern world has paused at the edge of the motorway; beyond that time has slowed and we're in the 1970s. In a world where holidaymakers return again and again. Return to a simpler time, return to their youth, return to play crazy golf and ride the mini-train in an endless circle.

Heading south along the coast towards Weston, the path runs out. We can see where we need to be on the map, but between us and there is a wide dyke full of water. Moth's sitting on his rucksack, exhausted, pale and wishing he'd caught the train, when a man in a rowing boat wearing a flat cap and rubber boots shouts across.

'Want a lift over?'

'What, you're offering us a lift?'

'Well, yeah, that's what I said.'

We scramble down and get into his boat.

'What are you doing here?' It seems such an unlikely place to be rowing a boat.

'Rowing. Why, what are you doing here?'

'Walking south, heading to Weston.'

He takes his cap off and starts to laugh. 'Well, good luck with that. You've got a surprise coming.' We're walking away when he shouts after us: 'Spend the night in Sand Bay, that way you can walk right through Weston tomorrow.'

We drop the rucksacks in the dunes behind a long sandy beach. The tide's high, leaving an arc of sand stretching south. It's late afternoon, but the sun's still hot in a bright blue sky, not even a haze over the sea to block the view across the Bristol Channel to the south-eastern edge of Wales. Herring gulls drift lazily by on slow thermals, still calling daytime calls. Moth boils water for tea, while I wander among the dunes, looking for somewhere to put the tent. There's a Second World War pillbox among the marram grass: maybe we could just unroll the sleeping bags in here? These concrete boxes would have held guns to guard the Bristol Channel, but now this one just holds pee, paper cups and condoms.

It's surprisingly quiet for an afternoon in August, just a few families further down the beach, so we swim out into a syrup-smooth sea in our underwear, the salt water washing away sweat and dust, soothing aching limbs and sore feet. The water isn't cold, more the temperature of the bath water when you wake up realizing you've been asleep for half an hour. Not unbearable, just not somewhere you would stay for too long.

We're drying and putting on jumpers when an old man with a Labrador walks out of the grass and on to the beach.

'Hi, beautiful day.'

'Yes, it is.' He lets the old dog off its lead. It walks slowly to the sea's edge and stands ankle-deep in the water watching it lap around its legs.

'What a lovely spot.'

'Yes, well, it was. It used to be perfect here, a hidden gem. But this summer, well, it's been found now. Very sad.' He walks along the shoreline with the dog, still ankle-deep, paddling behind.

A bright halo of artificial light hangs over Weston, only masked by the wooded hillside that separates us from the town. The sea catches the reflection of a large waning moon, but the manmade glow from the town is so bright its light is almost overshadowed. There's nowhere to hide the tent away from the houses that line the road beyond the dunes, so instead we lie in a sandy hollow between tufts of marram grass, inside our sleeping bags, inside our Radnorshire wheelie bin bags, and try to count stars until we fall asleep.

35

While Moth squats in the dunes, in the woods and behind a hedge I'm checking train and bus timetables, trying to plot the quickest route back to Cornwall.

'It's not as if I even feel ill any more, it's just like my body's lost control.'

'I'm sure it was the eggs in Chepstow. Maybe you need to see a doctor. Let's just catch a train and go and see the GP. You've done so much, walked so far, you don't have anything left to prove.'

He looks at me, a long look that makes me feel cold, even in the hot morning sun. 'You know it's not the eggs. This is another stage of CBD; this is the start of the part where I lose control completely.'

'What, the shit stage?' I try to make him laugh, but inside there's a strange sensation growing; it feels a bit like my heart shrinking. 'No, I'm sure it's the eggs. Do you remember that thing your brother had when he came back from Nepal and couldn't get off the toilet for two months? It might be that.'

'Let's get to Weston, at least there'll be more toilets there.'

The man in the rowing boat wasn't wrong. Weston-super-Mare is a hot, sweaty, loud shock to the system.

'We could walk across the town, get the train to Taunton then pick up the mainline train back to Cornwall.'

'Let's just get some food and water, then decide.'

The cafés are at bursting point, so we weave our way through overcrowded streets to find a Spar shop. The man behind the till looks exhausted as he puts bananas, bread and water into a bag.

'Is it always this busy?'

'August's always busy, but not like this. This summer has been almost unbearable and now the bank holiday weekend's coming. I know some shopkeepers who just can't take any more, too many people wanting goods we don't have because they're stuck on the trucks at the port. It's a nightmare, they're shutting for the weekend and getting out of town. I tell you, if I could I'd do the same.'

We walk back to the seafront, through streets crowded with people, on tarmac so hot it's beginning to melt, past cardboard boxes and broken glass, until we reach the wide concrete path at the sea's edge. The tide's out and even the seagulls seem to be keeping their distance.

'I don't want to walk through that mayhem again, even to find a train. Let's keep going for a bit, just see where we end up.' Moth walks away down the pavement, tired, pale, hunched. I want to scoop him up, put him back on the farm and say, enough, you've done enough, wrap him in cotton wool and let him sleep. I want him to be thirty with the wind in his hair and his mind free of even the knowledge of CBD. But instead I trudge after him, muttering.

'I still think it's the eggs.'

'Will you shut up about those fucking eggs.'

The sand is covered in parked cars, deckchairs, barbeques, screaming children and arguing parents. An animal truck is parked in the middle of the beach, a row of donkeys tied to the side of it in the burning sun. Further down the beach children are riding the donkeys, eating ice creams, distracted, uninterested, the exhausted animals dragging their hooves through the soft sand, their heads down, every ounce of their body language crying out to stop. A traditional British seaside sight.

A thin layer of high cloud turns a blue sky to pearl white as the air hangs still and hot. Turning down a cycle lane we leave Weston behind and walk for miles through flatlands of reeds and deep tidal mud channels, dodging cyclists and groups of volunteers clearing the path sides with strimmers and chainsaws.

Through the slatted sides of a bridge built for viewing birdlife without disturbing it, we watch white egrets feeding in the mud, and I'm struck with a sudden and unexpected pang of homesickness. It was early May when we left Cornwall; now it's almost the end of August: the whole summer has passed. Will there still be egrets on the mudflats of the river that runs past the farm? Will Monty remember who we are? The wind picks up in eddies of dry sand as we walk on through an unknown landscape, among strangers. The hard sand of the endless beach at Brean leads on to Burnham-on-Sea, we're inching further south, but right now all I want to do is get on the train with Moth and get into our own bed, while Monty sleeps at the end of it.

With no way over it, we follow a river inland until we finally find a bridge and turn back west towards the Bristol Channel, on a path along the top of a raised bank of tidal defence, the floodplain of the river beneath us on one side, fields of cattle beneath us on the other. On the opposite side of the river are wide salt marshes that border the Bridgwater Bay National Nature Reserve. Backing on to the marshes, home to so many of our precious wading birds, is the construction site of Hinkley Point C nuclear power station. And beyond that, the deepest, richest, darkest burnt rust and amber sunset, transforming the sea into molten lava and the hills into mountains of copper. It's almost dark when we put the tent above what we hope is the high-tide line, on a patch between the path and a field gate. The sky has turned to tones of bronze and darkest blues, lighting the deep tidal mud channel at the mouth of the River Parrett in streaks of gold.

We lie in the tent, curled like mice under open sleeping bags at the edge of the yawning channel of mud, listening to the night calls of wading birds. I can hear the tide coming in. Not the sound of water or lapping waves, just the deep low sound of heavy movement. Moth's breathing quietly: he seemed to be asleep within moments of putting his head on his jumper.

'I feel exhausted, as if every drop of energy has disappeared.'

'I thought you were asleep.'

'No, just so tired I can feel the weight of myself on the mat, but as if it's not really me.' He's half asleep and I don't know what he means. 'That's how my body's felt for the last few days, like I can feel it but it's not mine.' I pull his arm a little tighter around me and hold on to it. The same arm that has held me tight through my whole adult life. 'I feel as if I'm slipping – don't let me go.' I hold his hand and wipe the tears from my eyes.

'I'll never let you go.' Somewhere in the far distance a fox is calling.

I wake to the tent shaking with a rasping, snorting noise. I scramble out, expecting the source to be an angry person wanting us to leave. There's no one around, just a group of curious Charolais cows leaning over the field gate, licking the back of the tent. They move slowly away, disappearing into the mist. The mud channel has gone, and the sea and the fields. All that remains is the moisture-filled air that moves like mysterious hidden landscapes, hills and valleys of translucent white, silver and blue, which bend and sway in the breeze.

Moth wakes late and we eat cereal bars as the mist lifts and the power station construction site reappears. There's more birdlife here than we've seen since Scotland: herons, egrets and a couple of curlews wander along the mud line; two oystercatchers fly low through the channel and then out to sea. The birds are here, but not in the numbers you would expect to be attracted to such a wide expanse of mudflats.

'How much food do we have left?' It's mid-morning and Moth's still sitting in the doorway of the tent wrapped in his sleeping bag.

'Enough to get us to Bridgwater.'

'Can we stay here? I don't know if I've got the strength to go on.'

I look in the food bag; we have enough. 'Let's go back to

Burnham, we can catch the bus, then a train and you'll be in bed by tonight.'

He's crawled back into the tent and is lying down. 'I can't, I don't have the energy.'

The morning drags into afternoon as he sleeps. What if this walk has really been too far and it's used the very last of his strength? He chose to keep going when we were in Manchester, but he wouldn't have been here at all if I hadn't dragged him out in the spring. Guilt eats into the day, gnawing its way back into my bones like a grub through dead wood. I watch the tide come and go. It's like our life together, rich, full and heavy on a high tide, but now slippery, muddy and unstable as the tide slips away, exposing the vulnerability beneath.

Moth crawls out of the tent as the dipping sunlight catches the metalwork of the cranes towering over the steel framework of the power station, transforming its ugliness into a gleaming monument to human endeavour. Until the sun dips again, and the construction site returns to being what it really is, a vast area of steel, cranes and floodlights. A construction that began in 2018 and is said to be costing something close to £23 billion to build, £45.5 billion over its lifetime, that will leave French and Chinese energy companies with control of a sizeable chunk of our energy infrastructure. A very large amount of money for a project that will supply just six million homes, over a projected lifespan of only sixty years, but will offer the energy companies vast returns and guarantee escalating energy prices to consumers when it finally becomes operative in 2026. I wonder how many of the new homes built since 2018, and for many years to come, would be self-sufficient in green energy if only a small amount of investment had been directed that way? For a moment I'm back in the pub in Inverie, listening to the traders' conversation about how 'policy follows finance'.

Looking through the rising mist at the orange ball of light in the west, it seems to ask a big question: who's going to benefit the most from this monster on our shore? It certainly won't be the wildlife in Bridgwater Bay: fishermen are already reporting that fish stocks have dropped, and as the fish numbers drop, so do the bird numbers. And the power station isn't even operational yet.

The mist lifts on another morning. Moth's strong enough to walk and we're moving on.

'Are you sure you don't want to go back to Burnham? It's nearer.'

'No, let's take a slow day down to Bridgwater. It's easier to get a train from there, I don't fancy hours on a bus.'

We follow the raised walkway along deep tidal mud channels, until the call of Canada geese is drowned by distant screaming.

'What is that noise?' Moth's looking around trying to pinpoint the source.

'It sounds like pigs.' I grew up with the sound of pigs as part of everyday life. I know their contented grunts, their excited squeals, and this noise. A noise that's similar to a really strong, high-pitched scream. It's their call of distress. The path turns down past a huge corrugated agricultural building that's almost the size of a football pitch, one of a large group of buildings. Inside, the pigs are screaming. 'Maybe they're being moved.' Pigs don't like being moved and make that noise when they're transported from place to place. But the racket doesn't stop. These are the cries of over-crowded, unhappy pigs. We walk away, my head full of memories of the Large White sows and their piglets on the farm of my childhood, and the rising thought that I might already have eaten my last bacon sandwich.

A little further on is a high thick hedge, but through a tiny gap I catch sight of rows of poultry pens: sleeping huts with long wire outdoor runs. I can't tell what's in them, but my curiosity's spiked, so I force myself into the hedge and peer through. They're not full of hens as I first thought, these are pens of partridges. Pen after pen after pen of caged birds. They can only be in these cages for two reasons. Either they're being reared to be eaten, or they're being reared to be released, then shot, then eaten. Seeing the birds, I'm reminded that regulations are being drafted to prevent the release of pheasants and partridges within five hundred metres of a conservation area, because it's believed they endanger native wildlife. These beautiful birds have been in this country for around four hundred years – I wonder how long it takes for something to become indigenous? Maybe if we stop shooting them in the name of sport, they wouldn't be bred and released in such excessive numbers. Then these birds could roam free, their numbers regulated naturally by their wild existence. They remind me of the deer in the Highlands, and the cull numbers that each landed estate has to meet. Our wildlife needs balance, but left alone it will balance itself. Every species except one, one which doesn't see itself as part of the equation to be balanced, and spreads without control.

We're on the England Coast Path now, a new and as yet unfinished epic path that will, when it is finally complete, circumnavigate the whole of the English coast. But it seems as if no one really knows it's here yet, or maybe no one cares that it is. The path winds through piles of rubbish and nettle beds, under a collapsed zinc shed, eventually sending us into an industrial unit where it seems wheelie bins go to die, or maybe to be rebuilt – it's hard to say. There's no one here, so we sit on a concrete ramp and boil water. The River Parrett snakes past in an ox-bow, home to a group of Canada geese, the only things that move other than a wheelie bin rolling by in the wind.

Bridgwater arrives at the end of a hot, tiring day, a town with an extraordinary number of barbers, hairdressers and kebab shops. We're feeling flat and introspective as we drink a third mug of tea in a tiny café. We've walked through three countries, defied doctors and logic, weather, injury and illness and now we're about to give up and go back, just one county away from our goal. We sit in silence, our mood low, grey, and – although neither of us will say so, and despite everything we've done – defeated.

Moth rolls a teaspoon handle between his fingers while staring with a fixed gaze at a plastic gingham-checked tablecloth. 'Can't believe we're going to give up when we're so close to the end.'

'Me neither. I was really looking forward to following the coast up to Lynton and joining the Two Moors Way down to Plymouth. Never mind, another time, maybe.'

'I couldn't do the moors now. I'm so fucking annoyed with this bowel nonsense, I felt so strong when we finished Offa's Dyke, as if I could walk forever. Then it all turned to shit.' He puts the spoon down and pours more tea; despite it all, his hand is sure and steady on the teapot. We both stare out of the window, watching people come and go from the barber's.

'There is another option though.' There's a slight smile growing on his face as he stirs a spoon of sugar into his tea and I wait for the option that doesn't come.

'What? What option?'

'We could take a low-level route. Take the towpaths down towards Tiverton, then cut west through Devon and round the side of Dartmoor rather than over the top.'

'But you're exhausted – how can you do that?'

'Because I have to finish this. I have to make it to the coast.' He's drinking his tea, but the smile's growing.

36

I don't like cricket. I don't like cricket in the same way that I don't like strawberry jam. It's not that I detest it, like Marmite – it's that I can't see the point. Why would I eat strawberry jam when I'd rather eat strawberries? In the same way, why would I sit in a field watching men throw a ball and hit it, when I'd rather sit in a field and watch the sky? But all the same, we take a wrong turn heading into Taunton and pass the cricket grounds, and there's a match being played with only two hours of play left. Moth wants to go in, so I follow, thinking at least it's two hours of sitting down. We've walked over fourteen miles from near Bridgwater, down a towpath full of cyclists, dog walkers and picnickers swatting wasps, alongside a canal filled with ducks, moorhens and orange dragonflies, and I need to sit down.

Somerset are playing Nottinghamshire and it's hard to say who's winning. I doze in the plastic chair, watching white clouds overhead and listening to the crowd. There are two old men behind us; they've obviously been coming to watch the cricket for most of their lives. I slip in and out of their conversation, in and out of sleep.

'I asked Betty if Bill was losing his memory, but she said no.'

'Bet she'd say yes today, he didn't know who she was this morning.'

'Yeah, not the same without Bill here.'

'Look at that batsman, used to come in at three, he was good there.'

'Well, he's no good now.'

The clouds drift by and I put my jumper on in a chilly wind.

'He had seven overs, two maidens.'

'Well, he did then, but he's no good any more.'

I pull my socks higher and push my leggings down against the breeze.

'Why were you so late getting here then?'

'Went by Crewkerne.'

'Why'd you do that then?'

'Always go by Crewkerne.'

'Why?'

'Cos I know the way.'

'Why were you so long then?'

'Got lost, di'n' I, turned left not right.'

'Thought you knew the way.'

'I do, that's why I go that way.'

I put my hat on and watch a man and his son in front. The boy's trying to describe a school cricket match.

'I put my fingers like this and just bowled.'

'No, you should have put your fingers like this.'

'No, Dad, not like that, like this.'

'But it should have been like this, then you'd have done better. That's how I used to do it. Where'd the ball go anyway?'

'Through the wicket. I got him out.'

'Oh.'

I cross my legs to keep at least half of my legs warm. It seems even the old men behind are getting cold.

'It's a cold wind.'

'Well, it's autumn now.'

'It's not autumn 'til September.'

'That's only two days away.'

'Exactly, it's still summer then, i'n' it. Anyway, it's a chill wind and I need a coffee.'

'That's cos it's autumn.'

The day's play ends and I have no idea what's been happening on the pitch, but I think I can see why we humans rarely deal with the big stuff, why we get hung up over borders, will never face the climate crisis, or solve world hunger. However hard we try to hold our thoughts on what's happening in the game, our human brains will always want to scratch around in the small stuff. We'll always want to know what happened to Betty and Bill or see whose fingers make the right shape around the ball. We don't look up and see the swallows massing on the edge of the stadium, preparing to fly home early. We can't, we're too preoccupied by keeping our hands warm around the coffee cup, sheltering them from the chilly wind.

Devon folds out to the west in a patchwork of lanes and paths, through maize fields and cider farms, along rivers and roads. We're passing through a small village, between a huge old oak tree and a church when Moth spots people eating in a pub garden.

'Do we have much food left?'

'Couple of cereal bars and some dried potato.'

'Shall we go over and get some food?'

We find a seat in the garden, prop the rucksacks against it and go inside to see what food they have. It's full of people, eating, drinking, ordering food, but as we go through the door the room falls silent and all eyes turn towards us. For a moment I think I'm on the set of a Clint Eastwood movie – I'm half expecting tumbleweed to blow past the window. No one speaks, until a man seated by the window has the courage to open his mouth.

'Are you lost, or are you terrorists?'

I look around, thinking it's a joke, but the faces looking back are stony. I don't know what to say, but Moth finds a way to answer him.'

'Funnily enough, neither. We came in to order some food.'

'Too late for food.' The barman joins in, while his colleague takes a food order at the other end of the bar.

'But you're still taking orders.'

'No, you're too late for food.'

I can see Moth's back begin to stiffen, but hold his arm and we back out of the door, pick up the rucksacks and walk away as quickly as we can.

'Terrorists?' Moth's as confused as me. I suppose we're not what you would normally see in deepest Devon countryside. Scruffy, strangely dressed, looking as if we've walked the length of the country. And Moth is wearing those shorts.

'Maybe it's the camouflage shorts?'

He looks down at his legs. 'How many terrorists do you see wearing shorts and tights?'

Lockdown has made us all jumpy, slightly suspicious, wary. What we didn't know was that there'd recently been a mass shooting in Plymouth, just the other side of the county, making people doubly nervous. What they didn't know was that we'd walked almost nine hundred miles and just needed a bowl of chips.

The days and roads wind on. Days of tall hedges, tiny lanes and footpaths through farmland. Nights of stars and rain, camped behind hedges and in woods. Until the small Devon town of Okehampton appears, and at last we're on the edge of Dartmoor and just days from the coast. Moth's body has finally found some kind of normality; at last we can walk through a town without searching for public toilets. And we need to take our time here: there's something unexpected about this place – laid-back, relaxed, an almost Hay-on-Wye vibe, but without the books. Walkers pass through here on a daily basis, heading down from the moors or along the Two Moors Way, and it's a relief to be back where rucksacks are a normal sight, no one questions why we're here, and Moth's camouflage shorts don't even attract a second glance. Not even from the wedding party who cross the road in front of us: a family of fairies slipping out of the woods, a floating vision of sprites dressed in green and adorned with flower garlands. For a moment, we're caught in a scene from *A Midsummer Night's Dream*.

37

Beyond Oakhampton the landscape changes with every mile. The rolling hills of mid-Devon rise up to the western edge of dark green moorland. We skirt through the foothills of Dartmoor, but the rock, gorse and bracken of its higher flanks exert a magnetism, drawing our eyes constantly to its cloud-covered summits. Woods of ancient oaks and beech crowd around the Granite Way that runs down to Lydford Gorge, filling the air with the scent of damp undergrowth and birdsong. We sit in a pub on the edge of Devon, eating Cornish pasties and dodging the rain, before putting the tent up and lying under a canopy of creaking oak branches, as bats turn right angles between the trees.

The morning skies are clear, the air warm and the views stretch into the far western horizon. But it's always there, that green mound of moorland to our left, it never lets us out of its sight, overshadowing us, following us through the morning. We sit on a rock, looking up to the high moors, and I'm searching around inside myself, looking for that familiar feeling. The one that tells me I need to be on the summit, need to feel the wind, sense the extreme edge of life. I'm listening for the call of the moors, whispering that the top isn't far and the wilderness awaits, just a few more steps, just a little more effort and the wide expanse could be ours. I'm expecting it will come for one of us at any moment, and no matter how exhausted Moth might feel, we'll listen to that familiar whisper from the hillside, break away from the path and head upwards, not stopping until we're wrapped in wild, somewhere beyond the cloud line. Moth must see it in my face, because he holds my hand, his eyes finding the same spot on the green horizon.

'I never thought I'd say this . . .'

There's a long pause as I wait for him to say he wants to go up. Minutes pass; a kestrel hovers over a patch of thistles, before giving up and wheeling away west.

'Say it then.'

'We've walked further than I ever thought possible. Me and you, we just kept going.' He hesitates and for once I don't know what he's going to say next, don't know where his thoughts are taking him. 'I feel like we've climbed a mountain I didn't know was there, but I'm at the top now and I'll never come down.' He looks at me as if he expects me to understand. 'Don't you see? We're on the low-level path, but my head's on the highest peak, the view leaves me dizzy and there's no way down – I don't want there to be a way down.' He squeezes my hand and looks back to the moor as if he's explained everything, but he must catch the confusion on my face and tries again.

'I read something once, a philosophy, from Sufism I think. It's the idea that the action of walking for a long time allows the world to fall away; eventually the walker and the path become one, the walker reaches the wayless way.' He takes a long drink of water, then puts the bottle back in his rucksack. 'I'm so glad we didn't get the train, because I've walked all these miles, but it's only in the last few days, since I've felt so weak after being ill, that it's struck me.'

'What? What exactly has struck you?'

'That I don't have to go to the top of the moors to touch the wilderness. It's already here, imprinted on me, inside me.'

'Like you're no longer in the landscape, you're part of it, you are the landscape.'

'Yes. You know what I mean then?'

'Yes, I know it.'

We would have visited Lydford Gorge, but it's closed to visitors, so instead dodge cyclists on the NCN27 cycle route as the Granite Way becomes Drake's Trail, and keep walking, on and on through deeply wooded countryside. I drink a whole jug of water in a pub garden, while Moth goes in to use the toilet. It's only then I realize we haven't walked into another wedding party, but this gathering is a wake. The people are dressed in summer clothes, sitting in the garden in the sunshine. And laughter, so much laughter. Until one man stands up and everyone falls quiet.

'I think Mum would have loved today. It's been a celebration of life, not just sadness at its ending.'

Moth skirts behind the party and walks back to our table; we pick up the rucksacks and head south through the trees. Maybe this walk has become like a summer wake in a pub garden, a celebration of life, not in defiance of death, but despite it.

We walk until the light drops and a mist begins to rise in the valley bottom. It's completely dark when we camp at the very outer edge of a campsite, at the side of a river, and listen to the sound of water over rock through the night. Water falling from the high ground and heading inevitably, irresistibly towards the sea. As are we.

Tavistock is busy with early September tourists and weekend weddings. A huge froth of wedding dress billows in the wind outside the church as the bride enters, followed by the multi-coloured dresses of her many bridesmaids. Tavistock is a haven for artists, craftsmen and dreamers and feels like drinking an artisan craft cider after weeks of supermarket own brand. An eclectic mix of makers and bakers, and customers who insist that it's cream first on their scones. It's hard to tear ourselves away – we could stay here, sit in the sunshine and watch people going about their lives all afternoon. But the coast is calling: it's so close now.

Finally, after days of skirting the moor, the path rises over its southern end and we're high up in the hot sun among skylarks and waist-high bracken. The coast is only a day away; the south is finally here. Darkness comes earlier despite the clear skies, and we camp high on the side of the moor, on a dry patch of earth beneath an old twisted hawthorn, its branches heavy with red berries, and listen to owls as they cross the hillside.

It's dry when we wake and I make tea outside the tent before the dew rises. As the moisture of the morning begins to form the bracken around us is draped in light, the rising sun reflected from millions of water droplets hanging on a carpet of cobwebs, each tiny sphere of light reflecting this one perfect moment. Summer is over; the old man at the cricket match was right. The warm sun quickly dries the dew, but it leaves the soft promise of autumn in the air.

The cuttings of an old railway line take us down from the moors, down, down, down, through woodlands thick with squirrels, on a path strewn with hazelnuts and the first falling leaves. Between one side of the moor and the other a switch has been flicked on the seasons, summer has been switched off and a new season of copper and gold is waking up, throwing its first wash of autumn colour across the wooded hillsides.

The smell of cars creeps through the trees, pollution and urbanization tainting the path, but there's an excitement we can't suppress. Faintly in there, above the odour of exhaust fumes and tarmac, is a hint of salt. But we're not there yet. A tangle of roads and paths leads us into a new land, a land of concrete pillars and rubbish, beneath a concrete roof that carries speed and noise. But below it's eerily quiet. The A38 rushes over our heads in four lanes of destruction, yet down here a river passes beneath the noise, where a swan drifts between upturned shopping trolleys. The pillars are the canvas of graffiti artists, each smooth surface painted with names, slogans and comments. One stands out in large capital letters: 'ADAPT'. It feels as if it's been written here for us, nearing the end of this long, long walk. It describes our life. From learning to live without a home, to discovering how to live wild, to finding a way to live unwild; from learning to live with an illness, to learning how not to die from it. The last years have all been about adaptation. But we're all moving into a world where we need to adapt, in ways we can't imagine right now. Adapt to a new world, and a changing climate, like the cuckoos moving north and the midges moving south, adapt our lifestyles to slow that change, adapt our borders, adapt our thinking about why we choose to have borders, adapt to a new life, adapt to a way of living it. Adapt to survive.

Beyond the confines of the concrete, the river rushes out into the light, towards Plymouth and the inevitability of the sea. And so do we. Into a day of blue sky and a river filled with gulls, geese, swans, a myriad of birdlife crowded on to the water. Through the grounds of Saltram House, through woods, along the riverbank, past families, past bikes, past dogs and runners, we're walking faster and faster, we're so close now there's no stopping, as if we're hurtling downhill without brakes. And we're in Plymouth, through the industrial area, to the huge St Christopher on the wall, to the wide-open mouth of the harbour and the sea. Finally. The endless blue horizon of the sea.

PART SIX

A Dance of Light

Darkness cannot drive out darkness, only light can do that.

A Testament of Hope: The Essential Writings and Speeches,
Martin Luther King

South West Coast Path

Plymouth to Polruan

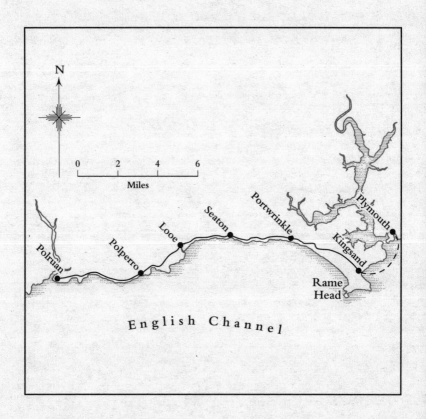

38

The light has changed. The green light of woods and moorlands has gone. We've walked into a blue world, where sunlight shimmers and reflects from the water into a silver haze. We sit under a canopy overlooking the harbour, squinting into the sun, eating chips. Maybe it's to do with the light, or a growing feeling that I'm almost afraid to acknowledge, but these are, undoubtedly, the very best chips we've eaten.

We catch the last ferry to Cawsand, a tiny village of stone houses, on the opposite side of the harbour. The sea has the still, treacle-heaviness of late summer, the air above it holding a thick ominous warmth. Beyond the headland the sky is changing colour again, the blue of late afternoon disappearing behind a bank of dark cloud. There's a purple frame to the wooded skyline, highlighting tree trunks with the last of the sun, as if they're lit from the inside. Late-afternoon swimmers float in the dense water, as the fast-moving storm skies of early autumn roll in around them.

The first raindrops begin to fall as we step off the ferry and on to the beach. They're pounding the ground between crashes of thunder by the time we take shelter in a pub intending to sit out the storm. But the rain keeps falling, pouring water through the pub garden canopy, finding its way past sandbags and into the bar. They have one room to spare, so we take it and spend the night listening to the roaring wind in the narrow streets and rain driving through the window frames.

We know we're back in Cornwall. It's not just the 'jam first' trinkets in the shops that tells us we've crossed into the final county, it's the weather. We leave the pub the next morning under calm blue skies filled with the calls of herring gulls, as if the storm didn't happen. This is it; this is the day. Moth holds my hand as we walk up the road and I can see in his face that the excitement is just as electric for him. The anticipation of reaching the coast is growing, but alongside that another unexpected but longed-for emotion is stretching the seams, ready to break free, finally, after so long.

The path over the headland leads through broken gates and collapsing walls, across fields of monoculture that stretch away into acres of green, past a field barn piled ten feet high with hundreds of empty herbicide containers. It's hard to understand how any wildlife can survive such an onslaught, but we know the answer, we're just metres away from it now. One last field, a scattered handful of chalets and we're here. I look down at my feet on the still damp dust and we're here; my feet have found it before I've seen it. A foot-wide strip of earth and stone. A thread of hope and familiarity and safety and knowing. The South West Coast Path is back beneath our feet. We're home. Back on the narrow margin of wilderness that surrounds the south-west, where the wildlife crowds into this last stronghold, this last strip of wild between the land and the sea. And beyond that, the wide expanse of Whitsand Bay and the coastline disappearing into the west, the final miles at the end of a thousand miles. We're home.

Finally, I allow the emotion of a homecoming to rise to the surface and I feel as if I could explode with the joy of it. This path has changed our lives, saved our lives, held us in a time of need and given us back hope when all was lost. But now, having been away from it for so long, having walked so many other paths, I'd feared we might be like lovers trying to rekindle a spark when the fire has already burnt out. But as the tears of return pour down my face, chapping my skin in the wind, I finally know this home can't be lost. No matter what happens in life, no matter how far we travel, this strip of earth will always be home. We inhabit this path and it inhabits us. *We're home.*

We head west, relishing the final miles, with an understanding that life isn't easy, but maybe it isn't meant to be easy. Sitting on a headland, looking across the Channel as a squall blurs the horizon, I realize that we don't always have to seek out the easiest path, or take the one that's presented to us; sometimes it's the hardest one that holds the greatest riches.

We stop in a café in Seaton, before the last few miles towards Looe, dragging out the day, making every last step matter, and there's a person who seems to recognize us. I think maybe he's read the book, but as I look again, I know him too and we're standing in a room full of strangers hugging a man we've only met once before, years ago. But it was a moment burnt into our memories. We were in his café when someone finally offered us a place to live after months of homelessness. We'd laughed and danced in the seaweed, and he'd danced with us, having no real idea what was going on.

'You're here! How are you here? I thought you'd gone home to Costa Rica to rear pigs?' Moth's still hugging him.

'I did, I did. But the pigs, oh the pigs. They looked me in the eye, you know, really looked at me. And that was it, I couldn't make bacon. If I couldn't make bacon, I couldn't be a pig farmer. And I missed Cornwall, I love it here, so I had to come back. I think I'm home now.'

'I think we're all home now.'

We pass through Looe at dusk, dodging kids skateboarding in the road, and cars patiently waiting for them to finish. We're about to leave the village when a man steps out in front of us. He has a weather-worn look, the tanned, lined look of a man who spends a long time outside.

'I watched you walking down the hill and I thought, those people have a long way to go.'

'Really? It's the rucksacks, they're a bit of a giveaway.'

'No, not in distance, in life. Sometimes I see things and I see you.'

I watch him looking at Moth and wonder if he's going to

produce a pack of tarot cards or a crystal ball and ask for a fiver.

'But now you're closer, I can see I was wrong. I can see you've already travelled the distance. You've found what you're looking for and you're nearly home.' He turns away before we have time to reply and disappears into the crowd of people. We are home, back in the land of soothsayers.

We pitch the tent on one last headland, for one last night.

'I'm going to miss this.' Moth shuffles around in the darkness, trying to get into his sleeping bag in the confined space.

I'm not sure if I will. It's completely dark, but I can smell his feet by my face even if I can't see them. 'We can always sleep top to tail when we get back, if you really want to.'

'No, you idiot, this. Just being out, every day, just going forwards, following these lines across the land. I feel different, grounded . . .'

He falls asleep mid-sentence, but I know what he means. The freedom of the path has refound us, and we're changed again, in ways we didn't know remained to be changed. I try not to sleep, try to stay awake and soak up one last night, to hold tight to the sound of sea against rock, to the wind shaking the flysheet, and the gulls calling long night calls. Creating an internal runestone, a memory of the paths. But slowly, as a faint green light begins to fill the tent, I finally realize I don't have to. These paths that cross our lands take human energy and imprint it on the earth, connecting us to it, leaving both the land and the human changed by that connection. Thousands of feet over thousands of years have trodden many of the same trails we have, tracing their passage on to the landscape, imprinting their memories into the soil. What remains are not just paths, they're precious landlines that connect us to the earth, to our past and to each other. We've followed them for a thousand miles, seen so much, heard so many stories, until now, at the edge of the land, we've become something other than just walkers. We're at the point where time and place and energy combine, where we become the path, the walker and the story. No need for runestones, it's all held within us; we're already part of our landlines, part of the song of the land.

As the green light becomes morning, I wonder if there's a way we could all share in that sense of connection. If there's a way to find a balance between the loss of our biodiversity, our need to feed ourselves, and the basic human need to be connected to the land, to this earth, to this place we call home. It's not an easy equation to balance. But sea eagles soar over the cliffs of Sheigra, lapwings fly through air thick with insects in Teesdale. Possibly the answer to finding that balance lies somewhere between the monoculture of the maize field we slept in and the wildlife corridor of the canal that stretched behind.

What if we re-imagine this land? Create one where biodiversity and humanity are set free. A land where we can feed ourselves without destroying our environment. What if we join up the islands of stranded biodiversity? Bypass the monocultures. Link our areas of wildlife-dense habitat to other areas, creating corridors of natural abundance. Landlines that join, one to the other, across the country, giving biodiversity free passage through a network of wild arteries that flow into every depleted corner, where wildlife, plants and humans roam free. A return of hedgerows, broad field headlands and mycorrhizal fungi that join a tree in Cornwall to one in Scotland. What if farmers reduce their dependence on chemicals, becoming educators, teaching non-farmers and future generations that food is a precious commodity, that our farmland is priceless, but our biodiversity is too? Maybe by returning our land to a tapestry of colour rather than a monochrome of green, allowing access to the land so we truly understand what it is we're losing, we can all find some harmony. Maybe by doing so we can find a land without borders or boundaries, a land that unites, rather than divides. What if we have a dream and the courage to make it real?

★

The sun rises on one final morning. We pack the tent in the early light and walk more slowly than we have for months, along a path that rises and falls over headlands so familiar our feet follow the path while our thoughts fly on the wind. We drop down into Polperro, then finally to Pencarrow Head and beyond, to the last bench before Polruan. A place where I've watched storms change the seascape and sunsets turn the water to the colours of burnt earth. A place I've run to in times of fear and despair. But always a place where my eyes are drawn to the horizon, to the possibility that hangs there in the play of light between cloud and sea. Sitting here, at the southern edge of the land, I'm overwhelmed by a sense of an island. Of a thousand miles of heath, moor and mountain, stretching all the way back to the north coast, to the beach at Sheigra. The start of a path where we put ourselves 'in the way of hope' and then let fate take its course. We follow the last steps down into Polruan, to a village where all our paths seem to end and to the waiting arms of family, and Monty, who explodes with dog-shaped joy. The word Sheigra seems to have no meaning in any language, but I know what it means. Hope. The Sheigra Trail, the trail of hope.

After

Is a thousand miles far enough to turn darkness into light? Can using a body in the way it was made to be used reverse symptoms that are thought to be irreversible? Will we find the answers under the fluorescent lights of a hospital waiting room?

In the artificial brightness of the corridor, I know the scientific answers to my questions are no. No, it's not possible for the DAT scan results to show more lights on the screen. What we'll see is the same picture of fading lights, or worse, more lights will have gone out; it's just a question of how many. No, you can't simply walk off neurodegenerative symptoms; no matter how far you walk, they will stay with you. Every medical professional in the neurodegenerative field will tell you the same thing: 'The key is in the word – degenerative. The condition can only degenerate.' And yet, despite already knowing the answers, we're still here, sitting on the plastic chairs, in the unnatural atmosphere of yet another hospital. Hoping. When the best we can hope for is that nothing has changed.

But even here, I can't stop thinking about the miles we've walked, the landlines we've followed across the country, the people we've met. People connected, inspired and uplifted by following long paths through the natural world. I'm beginning to see those paths like a network of connection that has the same effect on human life as mycorrhizal fungi does on tree roots – forming connections, passing nutrients, moving energy to those trees that need it most. And wondering how lives could change if we all had access to that. But as a door opens and a consultant walks out, there's an overwhelming sense that the trees are probably more intelligent than us: they don't waste time hoping for the impossible.

★

The consultant moves around the room in a glow of green winter light coming from evergreen trees beyond the window. He's animated, expressive.

'How are you feeling, Moth?'

'Good, really good, better than I have for years.'

'Why do you think that is? Why are you feeling so well?'

Moth sits back in his chair, more relaxed than he's ever been in a consultant's room. 'Because last summer we walked a thousand miles. From the north of Scotland back to Cornwall.'

'Okay. That's a long way. Well, we've got your DAT scan results. Would you like to see them? What do you think you'll see? What would you like to see?'

Moth glances at me, briefly raising an eyebrow. 'What would I *like* to see? I'd like to see the screen light up like a Christmas tree.'

The consultant smiles, turning back to the screen. Then with a flourish, as if he's producing a rabbit from a top hat, he turns the screen towards us. I can't look, I don't want to see what it shows – I don't need to. I know it's going to show a decline. It's going to tell us that despite everything, despite all the miles, all the sweat and pain and tears, this illness will march on regardless. I hold Moth's hand, looking at him, looking at the wall, looking anywhere but at the screen. But then I hear the consultant as he looks at Moth, waiting for a reaction.

'There you have it. There's your Christmas tree.'

The screen is alight. Bright shining lights. Brighter than the moon over Sheigra, or the stars over Barrisdale Bay; brighter than Manchester from the darkness of Bleaklow, or the headlights on the M5 from the windswept ramparts of the fort. The screen is alight in red and orange.

The world has stopped. Every question I'd prepared drains away, no longer relevant. All I can see are the lights. The consultant waits, giving us time to take in the view. But I can't see the screen, all I can see is the prism of light over Loch an Nid as the stag shakes the rain from his coat, the lightning at Byrness as it hits the moors all around us in shattering forks of brilliance.

All I can feel are a thousand miles of hope taking shape on a screen.

'What we're seeing are two sets of results. The old DAT scan, showing an abnormal reading, and this, the new one, showing a normal reading. If you consider the sizeable brain mass shown on your recent MRI scan alongside this normal DAT scan, then what we have is a very different result to the previous one. But with the understanding we have of Parkinsonisms, the one shouldn't follow the other.'

I've walked with wild horses through the dense fog of a mountain top, woken in nights so dark no light can penetrate, but saw more then than I can now. Tears pour down my face, turning the room into a wild landscape of radiance. Right now, I don't need the consultant to look for answers that he doesn't have, but simply let the warmth of the lights soothe away years of fear and sadness. Right now, I'm in the tent above the Falls of Glomach as Moth makes tea on the gas stove and hope rises in the soft night air.

Moth sits on the plastic chair, unmoving, staring at the computer screen in disbelief. The same man who lay face down in the mud of the orchard, so close to that final corner. The same man who walked a thousand miles, climbed bealachs, negotiated boulder fields and slept in a plastic bag under the stars. All current scientific knowledge would say that shouldn't be possible, that the man in the orchard can't be the same man as the one on the bealach, that normal doesn't follow abnormal. But we do know that a number of areas of the brain can grow in response to physical activity, and we do know that neuroplasticity exists, although we know very little about it. We used to think the earth was flat. We used to think no universe existed beyond our own.

One day there'll be answers for questions as yet unasked. Until then, I hold the hand that first held mine when I was a teenage girl in orange trainers, and he was twenty-one, his plaited hair blowing in the wind, his eyes alive with the wild passion of life. As sure of the feeling that passes between us now as we were all those years ago.

. . . choose a place where you won't do very much harm
and stand in it for all you are worth, facing the sunshine.

A Room with a View, E. M. Forster

Acknowledgements

We sit on a rocky outcrop of the coast path, pouring tea from a flask. Giant Atlantic waves crash against the cliffs, driven by winter storms out at sea. Somewhere in the wild air and salt spray I've come to accept that we may never have all the answers, but we can go on without them. I pack the flask away and we walk down from the headland, our feet instinctively following the path, Moth's footsteps straight and even, despite the mud. I think I'm finally coming to understand what belief is. It's about understanding something to be true, without proof of that truth. As yet there is no proven scientific link between an abnormal and a normal scan, but I believe it lies somewhere out there, in a thousand miles of landlines.

It took four months to walk those thousand miles, and as long again to record them on the page. But for those words to become *Landlines* has taken a lot of effort from many people. So a huge thank you to Fenella Bates for her unwavering belief that I can actually write, Olivia Thomas for encouraging other people to think the same, Paula Flanagan, Sophie Shaw, Lucy Beresford-Knox and everyone else at Penguin Michael Joseph who work so hard to make my books happen. To Jennifer Christie of Graham Maw Christie for always being in my corner. To Richenda Todd for her incredible attention to detail, Angela Harding for her beautiful cover artwork and Hannah Bailey for the wonderful maps.

Thanks to Dave and Julie for the warmth of friendship, the paths trodden and the trails yet to be found, and to all the many generous people who offered us kindness, food and shelter along the way.

But above all else, thank you to the Team. To Tom and Rowan for their endless patience, encouragement, love and dog-sitting. And to Moth, for having the courage to find his own truth.

He just wanted a decent book to read ...

Not too much to ask, is it? It was in 1935 when Allen Lane, Managing Director of Bodley Head Publishers, stood on a platform at Exeter railway station looking for something good to read on his journey back to London. His choice was limited to popular magazines and poor-quality paperbacks – the same choice faced every day by the vast majority of readers, few of whom could afford hardbacks. Lane's disappointment and subsequent anger at the range of books generally available led him to found a company – and change the world.

'We believed in the existence in this country of a vast reading public for intelligent books at a low price, and staked everything on it'
Sir Allen Lane, 1902–1970, founder of Penguin Books

The quality paperback had arrived – and not just in bookshops. Lane was adamant that his Penguins should appear in chain stores and tobacconists, and should cost no more than a packet of cigarettes.

Reading habits (and cigarette prices) have changed since 1935, but Penguin still believes in publishing the best books for everybody to enjoy. We still believe that good design costs no more than bad design, and we still believe that quality books published passionately and responsibly make the world a better place.

So wherever you see the little bird – whether it's on a piece of prize-winning literary fiction or a celebrity autobiography, political tour de force or historical masterpiece, a serial-killer thriller, reference book, world classic or a piece of pure escapism – you can bet that it represents the very best that the genre has to offer.

Whatever you like to read – trust Penguin.

read more
www.penguin.co.uk